The
Hot 100
Emerging Growth
Stocks
in America

Gene Walden

CENTUM
PRESS

Research and project development: Larry Nelson

Cover design and production: Dennis Melton

Copy-editing: Edith Walden

Published by Centum Press

Printed in the United States of America

97 98 10 9 8 7 6 5 4 3 2 1

Publisher's Cataloging in Publication
(Prepared by Quality Books, Inc.)

Walden, Gene
      The hot 100 emerging growth stocks in America / Gene Walden.
      p. cm.
      Includes index
      Preassigned LCCN: 96-93111
      ISBN 0-9656550-0-8

      1. Stocks--United States I. Title.
HG4963.W35 1997   332.63'22'0973
                           QBI97-40219

CENTUM
PRESS

P.O. Box 39373
Minneapolis, MN 55439-9781

This book is available at quantity discounts for bulk purchasers.
 For information, call 800-736-2970

TABLE OF CONTENTS

Alphabetical listing of the Hot 100 Stocks

Dedication

To my parents,
James and Edith Walden

Acknowledgements

This book would not have been possible without the considerable efforts of Larry Nelson, who once again served as the chief researcher for this book (as he has for all of my most recent books and newsletters). He helped collect, organize and dissect volumes of research material on each of the *Hot 100* companies, scanning through thousands of pages of information to compile the financial tables included in each profile.

Thanks also to Dennis Melton, who designed the book jacket (flames and all) and helped push the book through the production and printing stage. And thanks to Dennis Kleve, whose ideas and input helped shape the book. And finally, my heartfelt appreciation to the few corporations out there who still answer their telephone with a live human voice.

-- Gene Walden

INTRODUCTION
SMALL STOCKS
FRANK TALK

WARNING: DANGEROUS CURVES AHEAD.

The road to riches in the emerging growth stock market is thickly strewn with the tangled wreckage of market darlings gone awry. Before you decide to sink your next paycheck into the type of exciting young growth stocks that make up *The Hot 100 Emerging Growth Stocks in America,* there are a few points you should keep in mind:

• The stock price of software-maker Sybase Corporation, a long-time favorite on Wall Street, plunged 75 percent over the past two years (from a high of $54 to a low of $13.50).

• Shares of DSC Communications, a high-flying telecommunications concern, fell 80 percent over the same two-year period (from a high of $64 to a low of $12.50).

• Shares of Stratosphere, the widely-touted company that built the spiraling 1,200-foot-high casino tower on the edge of the Las Vegas strip, dropped from $14 to just 75 cents—and ultimately into bankruptcy— in a span of just nine months. (So much for the old adage, "Always bet on the house.")

Make no mistake about it: emerging growth stocks are risky ventures. They are not the kind of investments you gamble your children's lunch money on. For every McDonald's, every Microsoft, every Coca-Cola that hits it big, there are a hundred Stratospheres that rocket to prominence, then tumble into obscurity. Any time you roll the dice on a hot new issue, an up-and-coming software company, a leading edge telecommunications concern, or a trendy new retailer, you run the risk of kissing a sizable chunk of your investment dollars good-bye.

The stocks of the *Hot 100* share that same precarious nature. Most are unproven young companies with under $1 billion in annual revenue. And while some will soar to new highs almost every year, others will fizzle and never recover.

For all of their promise, emerging growth stocks can make for sleepless nights and maddening days. Before you invest your money, you need to be well prepared—financially and psychologically—for the dizzying, exhilarating, and sometimes exasperating roller coaster ride that characterizes the emerging stock market. You could be in for the ride of your life.

NOW FOR THE GOOD NEWS

Now that you've learned the dark side of small stock investing, here are a few cheerier thoughts to keep in mind:

During this century, small stocks as a group have provided the best long-term performance of all conventional investments—better than real estate, better than bonds or Treasury bills, better than blue chip stocks or utilities, better than commodities, and better even than precious metals. Many small stocks have enjoyed phenomenal returns.

In the past three years, for instance, Cisco Systems has climbed 431 percent (from $12.25 to $65), Altera has climbed 464 percent (from $11 to $64), and Dell Computer has climbed 780 percent (from $10 to $88). All three were featured in a book I published in 1993 called *America's New Blue Chips*—as was ADC Telecommunications, Amgen, Linear Technology and dozens of other stocks that have more than doubled since then.

Dreams *can* come true—and fortunes earned—in the emerging growth stock market.

Since 1925, small stocks have provided an average annual return of 12.5 percent, compared with a 10.5 percent return for large stocks. *(See chart below.)*

GROWTH OF SMALL STOCKS VS. LARGE STOCKS 1925–1995

	Avg. Annual Growth %	Current value of $1,000 invested in 1925
Large Stocks	10.5%	$1.14 million
Small Stocks	12.5	4.0 million

The difference has been even more dramatic in recent decades, particularly among stocks with market capitalizations of under $25 million. A $10,000 investment in small stocks at the end of 1951, if held through 1994, would have grown to $29 million, according to a study by James P. O'Shaughnessy, author of *What Works on Wall Street*. That's an annual average return of 20 percent!

Another study by Mark Reinganum of the University of Southern California also showed a dramatic difference in the performance of small stocks versus large stocks during a 17-year period from 1963 through 1980. Reinganum divided all stocks of the New York Stock Exchange into eight categories from smallest to largest—reassembling the list anew each of the 17 years. As the chart on the next page demonstrates, there was a clear and dramatic correlation between the size of the stock and the rate of growth.

SMALL STOCKS VS LARGE STOCKS, 1963–1980*
(Listed from largest to smallest stocks)

	Avg. Annual Return %	1980 value of $10,000 invested in 1963
1.	11.8 (largest)	$ 75,000
2.	12.9	88,200
3.	15.1	126,800
4.	15.2	127,000
5.	16.2	139,500
6.	18.5	201,000
7.	17.9	185,000
8.	23.7% (smallest)	452,000

* Based on a study of the stocks of the New York Stock Exchange by Mark Reinganum of the University of Southern California

As the chart demonstrates, for investors interested in explosive growth, smaller stocks clearly offer more potential. But great performance of small stocks *as a group* doesn't necessarily translate into great performance of small stocks on an individual basis. The challenge is finding the stocks that are most likely to live up to that potential.

WHERE TO FIND EMERGING GROWTH STOCKS

Like many investors, I've searched for years for an easy, obvious approach to uncovering promising emerging growth stocks. But the strategies and screens that are effective in identifying the best big blue chip stocks simply don't apply to emerging growth stocks. For instance, in the book, *The 100 Best Stocks to Own in America (Dearborn Publishing, 4th Edition),* I selected and rated the 100 stocks based on earnings growth, stock growth and consistency over a ten-year period. It's a system that has worked well in rating large, long-established companies, but it wouldn't fly for young, emerging stocks.

The problem is that many of the most dynamic small companies have only been in business a few years. Some are just beginning to turn a profit. And many have only been publicly-traded on the stock exchange for a year or two. A screen based on earnings or stock growth over ten years—or even five years—would exclude many of the best emerging growth stocks.

You could run screens for shorter periods through special computer programs and on-line services, but those screens have their limitations as well. Fast earnings growth for a year or two means very little. Even at three years, many of the companies with the highest growth rates are merely aberrations—average stocks whose earnings may have nose-dived three years ago, and have simply bounced back to normal.

The few really solid emerging growth stocks that do show up on the screens often become so overpriced (after all, thousands of investors use the same screens to uncover the same stocks) that their short-term risk far outweighs their potential for growth.

FOLLOWING THE PROS

Investors could try to use the same selection process that the top mutual fund managers use, but it's no easy task. To identify promising small stocks, fund managers spend hours every day studying charts, paging through trade journals, interviewing CEOs, visiting companies, talking with customers and competitors, and reviewing research reports.

It's a system that works pretty well for investment professionals, but the typical individual investor simply wouldn't have the time or resources to conduct that type of research. But small investors can benefit from the vast efforts of the fund managers. As the saying goes, *if you can't beat 'em, join 'em.*

Mutual funds publish a list of all of their stock holdings in their annual and semi-annual reports, which they will send you free of charge. Those lists can be a great source of ideas for small stock investments. (In fact, they were my source for the stocks in this book.)

There are, of course, some drawbacks in using the mutual fund holdings lists to pick your stocks. For one, mutual funds have dozens—and in some cases, hundreds—of stock holdings. How do you decide which of those stocks to choose for your own portfolio?

In my research, I evaluated the ten largest holdings of several of the top performing funds—assuming that if these were the favorite stocks of the best fund managers, they must be great stocks. Instead, what I discovered was that while some of those top picks beat the market, others were *dismal failures.* Even the world's best stock fund managers, with all of their experience, all of their resources and all of their research, are still remarkably inconsistent in choosing winning stocks for their funds. (But in the best funds, the success of the winners far outweighs the poor performance of the losers—which is one secret of successful investing we will explore later.)

THE BREAKTHROUGH

With yet another failed theory behind me, I took my research one step further. I compiled a list of all the top ten stocks of all the mutual funds in my book, *The 100 Best Mutual Funds to Own in America* (*Dearborn Publishing, 1995, 1997*), then looked for stocks that made it onto more than one fund list. That's when I discovered the breakthrough I was hoping for—a possible correlation between the number of funds that hold a specific stock and the performance of that stock.

The research was limited, and far from conclusive, but the results were very intriguing. After scanning through the top ten holdings of each of the funds, I added up the number of fund lists in which each emerging growth stock was included. For instance, Intel was listed among the top ten holdings of 18 of the *100 Best Mutual Funds*, Microsoft made the top ten list of 12 funds, Cisco Systems and United Healthcare were each included in 11 lists and Oracle Systems was among the top ten holdings of nine of the funds.

How did those five stocks fare? Over the first 12 months, from January 1, 1995 through January 1, 1996, they were up, on average, 64.7 percent. And over the first 18 months, from January 1, 1995, through July 1, 1996, they were up 112.3 percent. By comparison, the Dow Jones Industrial Average (DJIA) was up 33.5 percent for 1995 and 47.5 percent for the 18 months through July 1, 1996. In other words, those five stocks grew at about twice the rate of the Dow. *(See chart next page.)*

PERFORMANCE OF THE MOST COMMON FUND STOCK HOLDINGS

The following chart shows the emerging growth stocks most commonly included among the top 10 holdings of funds in *The 100 Best Mutual Funds to Own in America*, and their 1-year and 18-month returns beginning Jan 1, 1995.

Stock	Held by # Funds	Total return 1st year	18 months
Intel	18	77.8%	130.0%
Microsoft	12	43.6	96.6
Cisco Sys.	11	112.2	222.1
United Healthcare	11	44.8	11.9
Oracle	9	45.3	101.1
Avg. return:		**64.7%**	**112.3%**

Among the top 20 stocks—those that were listed among the top ten holdings of the most *Best 100* funds— the average 12-month return was 50.2 percent (compared with a 33.5 percent return of the DJIA). (See chart below.)

Stock	Held by # Funds	Total 1-year return (1995)
Intel	18	77.8%
Microsoft	12	43.6
Cisco Sys	11	112.2
United Healthcare	11	44.8
Oracle	9	45.3
Micron Technology	7	77.0
Microchip Tech	6	32.7
3Com	6	79.9
Columbia Health	6	39.0
EMC	6	-30.1
Applied Materials	5	86.8
Health Systems	5	5.7
Seagate Tech.	5	97.9
Sybase	5	-30.7
U.S. Healthcare	5	12.7
Cabletron	4	74.2
Maxim Integrated	4	120.0
Tellabs	4	32.7
CUC	4	53.0
CSX	4	31.0
Avg. return:		**50.2%**

As with any investment strategy, this is not a fail-safe system. As the chart above demonstrates, two of the 20 stocks declined in value. EMC and Sybase both dropped about 30 percent. But 18 winners out of 20 stocks is still a great return.

The discerning observer could certainly find some flaws with the system. It is very possible, for instance, that by the time the fund's annual report is printed and mailed out, the fund manager will already have unloaded some of those top holdings. Things change quickly in the small stock market. But remember, this is a starting point, a prospecting technique for finding hot stocks worth considering further—not the final step in your selection process.

Imperfections aside, this technique does have some very appealing advantages:

• It identifies great stocks that don't show up on the other more common stock selection screens. Knowing something that other investors don't know gives you an edge in the market.

• It identifies stocks that are considered to be worthy of a sizable investment by more than one of the nation's most successful stock fund managers. That's a pretty solid endorsement of that company's investment potential.

• It identifies many stocks that are largely undiscovered even on Wall Street. With a few exceptions, you are learning about many of these stocks even before the big investment houses and the large pension funds and institutional investors on Wall Street discover them. It gives you a rare opportunity to beat the big boys to the punch.

SELECTING THE *HOT 100*

In selecting the stocks for this book, my first step was to find the nation's best emerging stock mutual funds, including the top aggressive growth funds, the top small stock funds and the top sector funds. I wanted only funds that had compiled a strong, consistent five-year track record, and that still had the same portfolio manager who established that record. My list included about 85 funds in all.

The next step was to compile a list of all the stocks that made the top ten holdings of each of the 85 funds. (With a few of the very best ranked funds, I used the top 20 holdings in order to get a few more stocks for my prospect list.) I sorted through that list to identify the stocks that made it on multiple fund lists. In all, I found about 130 stocks that were included among the top holdings of more than one fund. Those were the stocks I used as my prospect list for *The Hot 100*.

To pare down the list from 130 stocks to the final 100, I pored through the annual and quarterly reports of each of the 130 stocks, reviewed key financial information (I wanted companies with strong earnings and revenue growth momentum), looked at future earnings projections, read through recent news reports, checked into whether company insiders were buying, selling or holding their shares, and reviewed the buy and sell recommendations of analysts who covered those stocks. After analyzing each stock, I eliminated all the companies for which I had serious reservations.

I also looked at the size of the companies, eliminating the ones I felt were too big for the list, such as Intel, WorldCom, Oracle Systems and Microsoft. Those companies have grown beyond the "emerging growth" stage.

Exactly what is an emerging growth stock? By my definition, it's a fast-growing company that is young or small or both (although it doesn't have to be both). For instance, it could be a small stock that's been in business for years, but has just entered a new phase of rapid growth. Or it could be a fairly young stock that has grown so quickly it has already reached blue chip proportions—such as 3Com or Cisco Systems—but is still growing rapidly and appears to have plenty of room for further growth.

Several companies in the *Hot 100* have annual revenues of over $1 billion, and a few have revenues of under $100 million. Most are in the middle—in the range of $200 million to $700 million a year.

After eliminating the oversized companies, and the companies with marginal financial records, I settled on a final list of 100 stocks that all seemed to have the potential for solid, if not spectacular, future growth. As you'll see in reading through the profiles of *The Hot 100*, the list is brimming with outstanding, exciting, fast-growth companies from a broad range of industries. It's a great starting point for any individual interested in investing in emerging growth stocks.

NOW IT'S YOUR TURN

Think of this book very much as you would a shopping catalog: a guide to 100 stocks you might be interested in buying.

Keep in mind that these are not recommendations, but merely prospects—stocks that have caught the eye (and pocketbook) of some of the nation's top mutual fund managers. For you, it's a *starting point* in your buying decision. But before you invest in any of these stocks, investigate the companies thoroughly just as you would any business you might consider buying.

Read through the profiles in this book, study the financial information, and when you find a stock that piques your interest, call or write the company (the address, phone and fax numbers are listed at the top of each profile), and request the following information:
- the most recent annual report
- a 10-K report and a 10-Q report (These reports offer a lot of good information about the company, its products, its marketing and its key officers.)
- the most recent quarterly reports
- any other information about the company that might be relevant to an interested investor.

Most companies will send the information to you within about a week, although some will take a little longer (and a few will take an extra call or two to nudge them into sending you the information). Be persistent.

Once you receive the information, read through it to see if you like the company, and its products or services. Then look through the financials—both the annual report and the recent quarterly reports—to be sure that the company's growth momentum is continuing. **You want stocks with consistently increasing revenue and earnings per share.** If you have a broker or financial adviser, you might ask the broker if he or she can provide any further information or advice on the stock.

Learn as much as possible about the company and the industry, review its stock price trend, and check out any other information you can dig up on the company.

Once you've done your research, and judged the stock worthy of a gamble, remember the two cardinal rules of small stock investing:
1. Don't invest any money you can't afford to lose.
2. Don't bet the house on one stock. Spread your risks. Diversify.

THE SCATTER SHOT STRATEGY

Once you find some solid stocks worth buying, success in the emerging growth market is largely a numbers game. The more stocks you buy, the better your odds of picking at least a few good winners. And in the emerging growth stock market, a few winners can more than make up for a basketful of losers.

What many investors don't understand about emerging stocks is that you don't have to hit a homerun with every pick to be successful. Bad picks are part of the game, and every investor who has ever been actively involved in the market—including the nation's top fund managers—has picked more than a few losers. You will too. Count on it, but keep this in mind: A bad $10 stock, worst case scenario, can only cost you a maximum of $10. But a good $10 stock could very well grow to $50 or $100 per share and beyond. If just one out of every ten of your stock picks grows 10-fold (which is not uncommon), you're automatically assured of coming out ahead on your overall investment portfolio. And odds are, based on historic averages, that you will do much, much better than that if you pursue a persistent, lifetime investment program.

To further illustrate the point, let's revisit some of the stocks I discussed in the opening pages of this chapter. I mentioned three big losers, *Sybase, DSC Communications* and *Stratosphere*, and three big winners, *Cisco Systems, Altera* and *Dell*. Let's assume that you invested $10,000 in each of those six stocks. On the surface, with half winners and half losers, it might seem that your portfolio would break about even. But as the chart below demonstrates, it would do *considerably* better:

STRENGTH IN NUMBERS
The off-setting effect of good stocks over bad stocks

The chart assumes an initial $10,000 investment in each stock, for a total initial investment of $60,000.

Stock	Initial Shares @	Initial Price/share*	Final Price/share	Total Gain/Loss	Value of original $10,000 after Gain/Loss
Sybase	185	$54	$13.50	-$7,502	$2,498
DSC	156	64	12.50	- 8,050	1,950
Stratosphere	714	14	0.50	- 9,643	357
(Total				- $25,195	$4,805)
Cisco	816	$12.25	$65	$43,040	$53,040
Altera	909	11.00	64	48,176	58,176
Dell	1,000	10.00	88	78,000	88,000

Total value of original $60,000 investment: **$204,021**

The total net gain from the $60,000 initial investment is $144,021. That's a total return of 240 percent over just three years! And all from a portfolio that has as many big losers as it does big winners.

A TIME TO SELL

Unlike many of the big blue chip stocks that you can buy and ride for a lifetime, emerging growth stocks require closer attention, and a greater willingness by investors to prune their portfolios from time to time. That's not to say that patience doesn't have its place in the small stock market—many young growth stocks hang around the same trading range for two or three years, then suddenly double or triple in value in a matter of months.

But with with some stocks there truly does come *a time to sell*. How do you recognize exactly when that is? That's a question investment experts have answered a thousand different ways, none of which are right all the time. However, let me offer a few loose guidelines:

• **Sell when the stock no longer meets your expectations.** Periodically you should review the performance of each stock in your portfolio to make sure they're still meeting your expectations. If you originally bought a stock because of its rapid growth, and now you find that the company has stopped growing, that's *a time to sell*. There's no shame in selling. It's part of the game. Pull the trigger. *Dump the loser*, and put your money into another emerging growth stock with positive momenutum.

• **Sell when insiders are selling.** If you learn that company insiders are unloading big chunks of a stock you own, that's *a time to sell*. Heavy insider selling is almost always a precursor to a disappointing earnings report or some other bit of bad news from the company. If insiders don't want the stock, why should you? *Dump the loser and move on.*

Investment professionals call this hair-trigger approach the "cockroach strategy." If you see one cockroach on your kitchen counter, chances are there are more hiding in the cupboards. Likewise, if a company reports one bit of bad news, chances are there's more bad news hiding in the corporate cupboards that's yet to come out. That's why many of the top emerging growth fund managers have a policy of unloading a stock at the first sign of trouble.

(Some investors believe you should do just the opposite, buying more shares of a stock as its price declines. That's called "buying down a stock." It may be a sound strategy for the larger, more well-established blue chip stocks, but it's a risky move for smaller stocks. It's one thing to try to buy a stock at the low end of its trading range, and yet another to follow it down through a series of new lows. Some investors I know, for instance, bought Stratosphere stock all the way down from its high of $14 to just $1 a share, only to watch the company file Chapter 11 bankruptcy. You want winners. *Dump the losers and move on.*)

• **Sell if the stock keeps dropping.** One way to squeeze a bit better performance out of your portfolio is to try to minimize your losses by setting a sell limit. It's not unusual for an emerging growth stock that falls out of favor to drop 60 to 80 percent. By that point, that stock should be long gone from your portfolio. But when is the logical sell point?

That can vary from stock to stock, but generally speaking, if the market is going down (use NASDAQ as the benchmark for emerging stocks), and your stock is moving down with it, you have little reason for concern. Hold. But if your stock has gradually declined by 25 to 30 percent while the market has held steady or moved up, that's *a time to sell*.

There may be times when you 'll regret having sold a stock that later recovers. But there will also be times when, much to your delight, the stock you've just sold will continue its plunge to new lows. Those are the moments you live for in investing, when you can smugly smile and commend yourself for having had the foresight, the intellect and the intitiative to *dump the loser and move on.*

RANKING THE STOCKS

The stocks in this book are ranked from 1 to 100 based on a wide range of criteria. The first factor I considered in rating the stocks was how many top mutual funds listed the stock as one of its top holdings.

For instance, Cisco Systems is listed among the top 10 holdings of 17 funds, which makes it the number one ranked stock in the book. HBO (a healthcare software company—not the cable movie channel) is held by 16 funds, which puts it at number two, and U.S. Robotics is held by 14 funds, which makes it number three.

Most of the stocks in the *Hot 100* are held by just two or three funds. To break ties, I looked at a combination of factors. How fast are the company's earnings and revenue growing, has the company established a track record of consistent performance, has the stock moved up along with the market over the past two years, and does the stock still seem to have strong growth momentum?

Regardless of my rankings, ultimately it is you who will have to decide which stocks are best for your portfolio. I've tried to give you as much information as possible to assist you with that decision. As I've already stressed, you can't make a prudent decision to buy a stock based strictly on what you read here. But I have tried to provide a fairly comprehensive snapshot of each of the 100 companies, including:

- Detailed company profiles, with a section on late developments
- Financial performance analysis
- Five-year earnings, revenue and stock price histories
- 24-month stock price movement graph
- Address, key officers, phone number, trading symbol and other vital data
- Assets, liabilities, international sales, P/E range and projected earnings
- Up-to-date stock prices through Jan. 1, 1997.

ABBREVIATIONS

As you page through the profiles, you will often see the abbreviations, *P/E* and *NA*. Following is an explanation of those abbreviations:

P/E ratio. *Price-earnings ratio.* Wall Street's most commonly used measure of a stock's relative value to investors, P/E refers to a company's stock price divided by its earnings per share. P/Es are like golf scores—the lower the better. A company with a stock price of $20 and earnings per share of $1 has a P/E of 20 ($20 divided by $1); a company with a stock price of $10 and the same $1 in earnings has a P/E of 10. The higher a stock's P/E, the more expensive the stock is relative to its earnings. But typically, the faster a company is growing, the more Wall Street is willing to pay for the stock, which is why many of the fast-growing companies featured in this book have very high price-earnings ratios. Analysts like to compare a stock's current P/E with its past P/E. If the current P/E is considerably higher than its past P/E, the stock may be overpriced; if it is considerably lower, the stock may be a good value.

NA. *Not applicable*. Sometimes you'll see *NA* in the five-year stock tables of a company that has recently issued stock. The stock tables go back to 1992, but if the company issued stock in 1994, for instance, you'll see *NA* for the years 1992 and 1993. You'll also see *NA* under earnings growth, if the company had a previous loss. For instance, if a company had a loss of $1 per share two years ago, and now earns $1 per share, it's impossible to calculate the earnings growth. You'll also see *NA* under P/E ratio if the company had a loss. As mentioned above, P/E stands for stock price divided by earnings per share, so if the company had no earnings, then neither can it have a price/earnings ratio. Instead you'll see *NA*.

Investing is a long-term process. Success may not come in the first month—or even the first year or two. But for investors with patience, persistence and a spirit of adventure, emerging growth stocks can be an exciting way to achieve exceptional long-term returns. Here's hoping you can cull from this *Hot 100* list some of the great growth stocks of the next century.

1

Cisco Systems, Inc.

170 West Tasman Drive
San Jose, CA 95134
Phone: 408-526-4000; FAX: 408-526-4100

Chairman: John Morgridge
President and CEO: John Chambers

Cisco Systems has become one of the world's fastest growing companies over the past decade by designing products capable of tying together the once-disparate world of computer technology. Cisco's products help computers communicate with each other, and tap into resources such as host computers, databases, software and printers.

Cisco was formed in 1984 by a group of Stanford University scientists who were determined to find a way to link the computer world together. They brought their first product to market in 1986. A decade later, the company's sales had soared to more than $5 billion a year.

Today, Cisco is the leading global supplier of internetworking products for corporate intranets and the global Internet. It's also the *number one* emerging growth stock in America. Over the past four years, its stock price has grown seven-fold, its earnings have grown eight-fold and its revenue has grown 12-fold. And while its $5 billion in revenue is very high by emerging growth stock standards, the company is still growing at a fast pace, and it is still among the leading stock holdings of 17 of the nation's top ranked small and emerging growth stock mutual funds.

The company produces a broad range of networking products, including routers, bridges, terminal servers, local area network (LAN) switches, wide area network (WAN) switches, dial access servers and network management software.

Cisco's primary customer base consists of four types of organizations—large organizations with complex internetworking needs such as corporations, government agencies and universities; service providers such as telecommunications carriers, cable companies and Internet service providers; volume markets such as small businesses, home offices and residential users; and other suppliers who license features of Cisco software for inclusion in their products or services.

The San Jose-based operation has a direct sales force of about 2,500 individuals, plus an international network of about 75 distributors and resellers around the world. Nearly half of the company's total sales are generated outside the U.S. Cisco has about 9,000 employees.

Late developments

Cisco made a series of acquisitions in 1996, including Telebit Corp. for about $200 million, and Netsys Technologies for $79 million.

Performance

Stock growth (past two years through 12/31/96): 262% (from $17.56 to $63.63).
Revenue growth (past two years through 1/31/97): 230% (from $1.64 billion to $5.4 billion).
Earnings per share growth (past two years through 1/31/97): 155% (from $0.60 to $1.53).

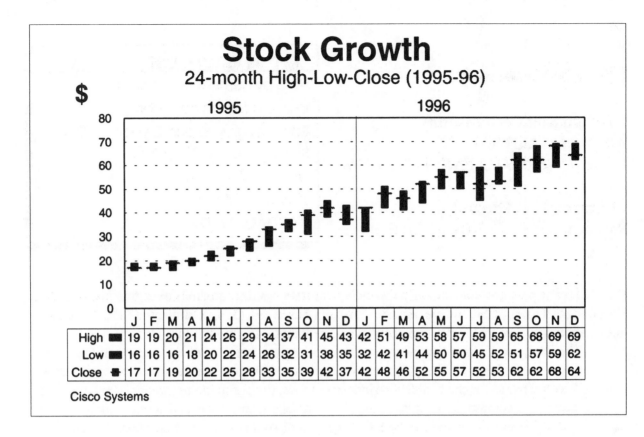

Stock Growth
24-month High-Low-Close (1995-96)

	J	F	M	A	M	J	J	A	S	O	N	D	J	F	M	A	M	J	J	A	S	O	N	D
High	19	19	20	21	24	26	29	34	37	41	45	43	42	51	49	53	58	57	59	59	65	68	69	69
Low	16	16	16	18	20	22	24	26	32	31	38	35	32	42	41	44	50	50	45	52	51	57	59	62
Close	17	17	19	20	22	25	28	33	35	39	42	37	42	48	46	52	55	57	52	53	62	62	68	64

Cisco Systems

Quick Fix

P/E range (past two years):	22 -62
Earnings past four quarters:	$1.53 (through 1/31/97)
Projected 1997 earnings (median):	$2.03
International sales:	42% of total sales
Total current assets:	$2.16 billion (1996); $1.18 billion (1995)
Total current liabilities:	$769.4 million (1996); $388.9 million (1995)
Net Income:	$913.3 million (1996); $456.5 million (1995)

Financial history

Fiscal year ended: July 31
(Revenue in millions)

	1992	1993	1994	1995	1996
Revenue	$339.6	$649	$1,334.4	$2,232.6	$4,096
Earnings per share	0.17	0.34	0.60	0.72	1.37
*Stock price: High	10.09	16.44	20.38	44.69	69.13
Low	4.03	9.53	9.38	16.19	31.94
Close	9.83	16.16	17.56	37.31	63.63

Stock prices (only) reflects calendar year.

13

2

HBO & Company

301 Perimeter Center North
Atlanta, GA 30346
Phone: 770-393-6000; FAX: 770-393-6092

Chairman: H.T. Green
President and CEO: Charles McCall

HBO's recent performance certainly merits two thumbs up, but don't confuse this HBO with the Home Box Office cable movie channel. Atlanta-based HBO & Company (HBOC) develops information software that serves the hospital and healthcare facility market.

The company designs specialized software programs that allow healthcare facilities to track patient care and clinical information as well as financial matters. It also develops strategic management software for the health care industry. In all, the company has about 3,000 customers, most of which are community hospitals. HBOC also sells its products and services internationally through subsidiaries in England, Ireland, Canada, Saudi Arabia, Australia and New Zealand. The company, which was incorporated in 1974, has about 3,400 employees.

In all, about 45 percent of the community hospitals in the U.S. use at least one product from HBOC. The company plans to continue its rapid growth through several strategic steps:

* *Leveraging its existing customer base.* The company hopes to sell additional products to the facilities that already have HBOC products.

* *Expanding into new markets.* The company expects to continue to develop products designed to serve a wider area of the healthcare market. For instance, the company may soon begin marketing products to long-term care facilities.

* *Upgrading existing line.* HBOC plans to continue to develop improved software to upgrade the capabilities of its existing customer base. Its leading products now include HealthQuest and STAR systems, and the QUESETNET national information network.

* *Acquiring related companies.* HBOC has acquired about a dozen smaller companies in recent years, including two acquisitions in late 1996. (See "**Late developments**" below.)

Late developments

HBOC acquired two companies in late 1996, CyCare Systems, a provider of physician practice management software and electronic data services, and Management Software, a provider of homecare information systems. HBOC also announced its intentions to acquire software developer GMIS.

Performance

Stock growth (past two years through 11/1/96): 270 % (from $16.25 to $60.12).
Revenue growth (past two years through 12/31/96): 115% (from $357.4 million to $769.3 million).
Earnings per share growth (past two years through 12/31/96): 142% (from $0.43 to $1.04).

Stock Growth
24-month High-Low-Close (1995-96)

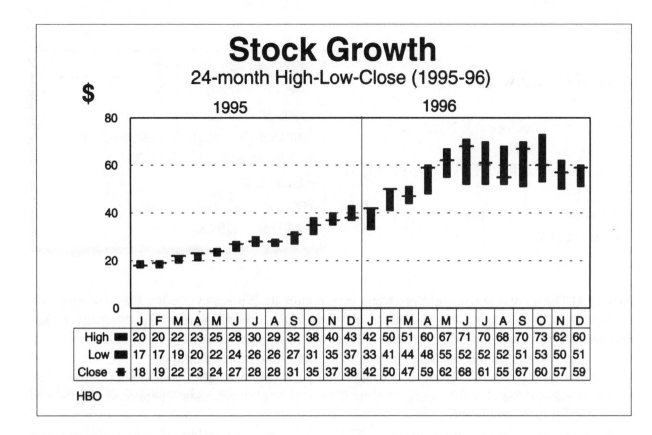

		J	F	M	A	M	J	J	A	S	O	N	D	J	F	M	A	M	J	J	A	S	O	N	D
High		20	20	22	23	25	28	30	29	32	38	40	43	42	50	51	60	67	71	70	68	70	73	62	60
Low		17	17	19	20	22	24	26	26	27	31	35	37	33	41	44	48	55	52	52	52	51	53	50	51
Close		18	19	22	23	24	27	28	28	31	35	37	38	42	50	47	59	62	68	61	55	67	60	57	59

HBO

Quick Fix

P/E range (past two years):	32 - 70
Earnings past four quarters:	$1.04 (through 12/31/96)
Projected 1997 earnings (median):	$1.51
International sales:	1% of total sales
Total assets:	$535.1 million (1995); $264.1 million (1994)
Total current liabilities:	$205.1million (1995); $136.2 million (1994)
Net Income:	$91.8 million (1996); $56.7 million (1995)

Financial history

Fiscal year ended: Dec. 31

(Revenue in millions)

	1992	1993	1994	1995	1996
Revenue	$ 229.0	$267.1	$357.4	$495.6	$769.3
Earnings per share	0.21	0.26	0.43	0.72	1.04
Dividends	0.07	0.07	0.08	0.08	0.08
Stock price: High	6.50	11.56	18.38	43.25	72.50
Low	2.38	4.19	9.38	16.44	32.75
Close	6.44	11.50	17.19	38.31	59.38

3

U.S. Robotics Corp.

8100 North McCormick Blvd.
Skokie, IL 60076
Phone: 847-982-5010; FAX: 847-933-5551

Chairman, President and CEO:
  Casey Cowell

AT A GLANCE

Held by number of funds: 14
Industry: Computer modems
Earnings growth past 2 years: 275%
Stock price 1/1/97: $72.00
P/E ratio: 40
Year ago P/E: 57
NASDAQ: USRX

Run for it! The robots are coming! Your worst sci-fi nightmare is upon us! Or is it? Well, maybe not. In fact, despite its name, U.S. Robotics isn't even in the robot business. The company makes computer modems and networking products. There are no robots—at least not from U.S. Robotics.

The Skokie, Illinois operation breaks its products into three categories:

• *Systems products.* U.S. Robotics makes computer network hubs, modem pools and remote access servers for use in data centers, branch offices and small businesses. These products are sold under the Total Control brand name.

• *Mobile communications products.* The company makes a variety of modems for portable computers sold under the Megahertz, Sportster, Courier and Worldport brand names.

• *Desktop products.* The firm makes high speed dial-up external and internal modems for desktop computers. Its leading entry level brand is the Sportster, which is targeted to home office and professional users. Its Courier desktop modems, called "V.Everything," are marketed to corporate users, and provide universal compatibility at the highest available standard transmission speed.

U.S. Robotics markets its products both in the U.S. and abroad. Internationally, its products are marketed by more than 100 distributors. The firm has sales offices in France, England, Ireland, Germany and Italy. International sales account for about 20 percent of the company's total revenue.

The company has expanded rapidly in recent years through two significant acquisitions. In 1995, it acquired Megahertz Corp., a leading supplier of high speed PC Card data/fax modems and other mobile access products. Also in 1995, the company acquired ISDN Systems Corp. and Palm Computing, Inc.

U.S. Robotics has about 3,400 employees.

Late developments

In early 1997, the company announced plans to begin selling a new personal computer modem with twice the speed of standard modems. The modems provide on-line connections as fast as 56 kilobits per second. About 325 Internet and online service providers are installing the new technology so that they can accommodate consumers with the high speed modems. The firm expects to produce about 1 million of the new modems per month.

Performance

Stock growth (past two years through 12/31/96): 566% (from $10.81 to $72.00).
Revenue growth (past two years through 9/29/96): 296% (from $499.1 million to $1.98 billion).
Earnings per share growth (past two years through 9/30/96): 275% (from $0.47 to $1.79).

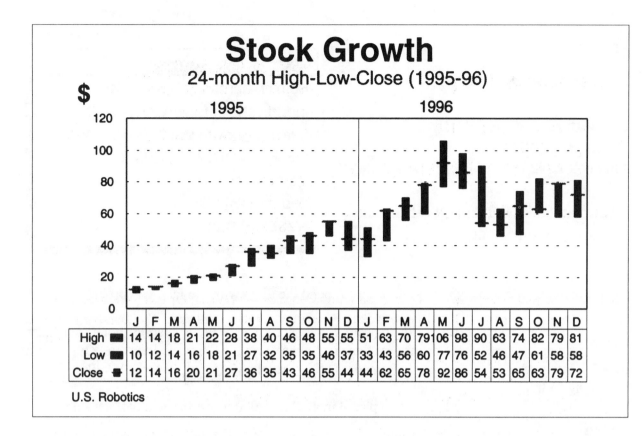

Stock Growth
24-month High-Low-Close (1995-96)

	J	F	M	A	M	J	J	A	S	O	N	D	J	F	M	A	M	J	J	A	S	O	N	D
High	14	14	18	21	22	28	38	40	46	48	55	55	51	63	70	79	106	98	90	63	74	82	79	81
Low	10	12	14	16	18	21	27	32	35	35	46	37	33	43	56	60	77	76	52	46	47	61	58	58
Close	12	14	16	20	21	27	36	35	43	46	55	44	44	62	65	78	92	86	54	53	65	63	79	72

U.S. Robotics

Quick Fix

P/E range (past two years):	13 - 71
Earnings past four quarters:	$1.79 (through 9/30/96)
Projected 1997 earnings (median):	$3.29
International sales:	20% of total sales
Total current assets:	$750.6 million (1996); $534.3 million (1995)
Total current liabilities:	$333.7 million (1996); $166.3 million (1995)
Net Income:	$170 million (1996); $66 million (1995)

Financial history

Fiscal year ended: Sept.30
(Revenue in millions)

	1992	1993	1994	1995	1996
Revenue	$129.7	$242.6	$499.1	$889.3	$1,977.5
Earnings per share	0.19	0.35	0.47	0.77	1.79
*Stock price: High	6.06	8.81	11.50	55.25	105.50
Low	3.34	4.25	6.00	9.81	32.50
Close	5.13	8.66	10.81	43.88	72.00

*Stock prices (only) reflect calendar year.

4

HFS, Inc.

339 Jefferson Road
Parsippany, NJ 07054
Phone: 201-428-9700; FAX: 201-428-6057

Chairman and CEO: Henry Silverman
President: John Snodgrass

This is the kind of company you might want to spend the night with. In fact, you probably already have.

Formerly known as Hospitality Franchise Systems, HFS is the world's largest hotel franchisor. The firm operates nine hotel franchise systems including Days Inn, Howard Johnson, Knights Inn, Park Inn International (U.S.), Super 8, Ramada (U.S.), Travelodge (North America), Village Lodge and Wingate Inn.

In all, HFS oversees a franchise empire of more than 5,000 properties and half a million hotel rooms.

HFS is also a major force in the residential real estate brokerage business. The company acquired Century 21 in 1995 and Electronic Realty Associates (ERA) in 1996. The Century 21 and ERA systems are, respectively, the world's largest and fourth largest franchisors of residential real estate brokerage offices. The systems together include more than 10,000 independently owned offices.

As a franchiser, HFS does not own the thousands of properties with which it is affiliated, but rather it licenses the owners of independent hotels and real estate brokerage offices to use the company's brand names. HFS provides its customers with services designed to increase their revenue and profitability, such as marketing and co-marketing arrangements and global procurement. Hotel owners have access to a national reservation system, national advertising and promotional campaigns and volume purchasing discounts.

Real estate brokerage affiliates can benefit from regional and national advertising, referrals, awards, training and volume purchasing discounts.

Late developments

HFS acquired Avis, the rental car company, in October 1996 for about $800 million. In November 1996, HFS announced plans to acquire PHH Corp. for about $1.7 billion. PHH operates a number of businesses including a mortgage business and a corporate fleet service that spends $20 million a year on rental cars -- which gives it a natural tie-in with Avis.

Performance

Stock growth (past two years through 12/31/96): 351% (from $13.25 to $59.75).
Revenue growth (past two years through 12/31/96):156% (from $312.5 million to $800 million).
Earnings per share growth (past two years through 12/31/96): 140% (from $0.53 to $1.27).

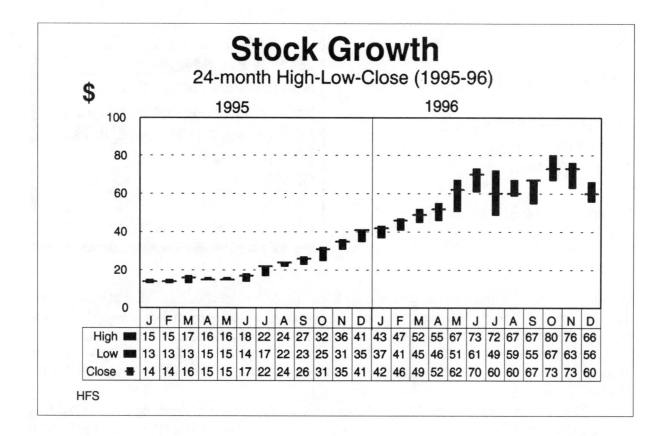

Stock Growth
24-month High-Low-Close (1995-96)

$	J	F	M	A	M	J	J	A	S	O	N	D	J	F	M	A	M	J	J	A	S	O	N	D
High	15	15	17	16	16	18	22	24	27	32	36	41	43	47	52	55	67	73	72	67	67	80	76	66
Low	13	13	13	15	15	14	17	22	23	25	31	35	37	41	45	46	51	61	49	59	55	67	63	56
Close	14	14	16	15	15	17	22	24	26	31	35	41	42	46	49	52	62	70	60	60	67	73	73	60

HFS

Quick Fix

P/E range (past two years):	17 - 65
Earnings past four quarters:	$1.27 (through 1996)
Projected 1997 earnings (median):	$2.19
International sales:	NA
Total assets:	$1.17 billion (1995); $774.1 million (1994)
Total current liabilities	$124.9 million (1995); $70 million (1994)
Net Income:	$170.4 million(1996); $81.4 million (1995)

Financial history

Fiscal year ended: Dec. 31
(Revenue in millions)

	1992	1993	1994	1995	1996
Revenue	$203	$257.1	$312.5	$413	$800
Earnings per share	0.23	0.35	0.53	0.74	1.27
Stock price: High	5.06	13.44	16.75	41.13	79.88
Low	4.50	4.69	10.38	12.50	36.50
Close	4.84	13.28	13.25	40.88	59.75

19

5

Ascend Communications, Inc.

1275 Harbor Bay Parkway
Alameda, CA 94502
Phone: 510-769-6001

President and CEO: Mory Ejabat

AT A GLANCE

Held by number of funds: 12

Industry: computer communications

Earnings growth past 2 years: 889%

Stock price 1/1/97: $62.13

P/E ratio: 89

Year ago P/E: 144

NASDAQ: ASND

Computer communications manufacturer Ascend Communications has been growing at cyber-speed, riding the Internet through six straight years of record sales. The company makes networking access products that enable computer users to call a central computer from home, office or on the road.

Founded in 1989, the Alameda, California, firm saw its sales jump from $39 million in 1994 to $149 million in 1995. Sales doubled again through the first three quarters of 1996, topping the $300 million mark.

The company makes a broad range of high speed digital remote networking products such as routers and switches. The products work with existing networks by adjusting the bandwidth, which controls information traffic. The company sells its products both to Internet service providers such as UUNET and BBN, and telecommunications companies such as AT&T and MCI.

Ascend's leading product is its MAX remote communications devices, which provide Wide Area Network (WAN) access and integrated voice, video and data access. MAX accounts for about 60 percent of total sales. Other leading products are Pipeline telecommuting, remote office access and Internet access devices (20 percent of sales); and Multiband videoconferencing network products (15 percent of sales).

Part of the company's growth has come through its international sales, which accounts for about 30 percent of total sales.

The company, which went public with its initial stock offering in 1994, has about 304 employees.

Late developments

The company recently introduced a new WAN switching system called the MAX TNT designed to provide users with the ability to support 2,000 simultaneous modem users in a single eight foot track. The units start at $18,750. The company also introduced a new product called Ascend Access Control, which the company describes as "the first network-wide security system that includes authentication, authorization and an accounting server.

Performance

Stock growth (past two years through 12/31/96): 1120% (from $5.09 to $62.13).
Revenue growth (past two years through 12/31/96): 491% (from $92.8 million to $549 million).
Earnings per share growth (past two years through 12/31/96): 889% (from $0.09 to $0.89).

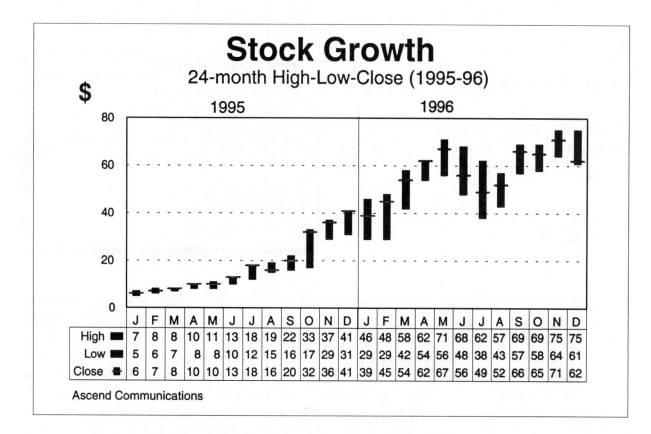

Stock Growth

24-month High-Low-Close (1995-96)

	J	F	M	A	M	J	J	A	S	O	N	D	J	F	M	A	M	J	J	A	S	O	N	D
High ■	7	8	8	10	11	13	18	19	22	33	37	41	46	48	58	62	71	68	62	57	69	69	75	75
Low ■	5	6	7	8	8	10	12	15	16	17	29	31	29	29	42	54	56	48	38	43	57	58	64	61
Close ✦	6	7	8	10	10	13	18	16	20	32	36	41	39	45	54	62	67	56	49	52	66	65	71	62

Ascend Communications

Quick Fix

P/E range (past two years):	18 - 145
Earnings past four quarters:	$0.89 (through 1996)
Projected 1997 earnings (median):	$1.40
International sales:	29 percent of total sales (Asia/Pacific, 16%; Europe, 13%)
Total current assets:	$455 million (1995); $247.7 million (1995)
Total current liabilities:	$54.4 million (1996); $18.6 million (1995)
Net Income:	$113.1 (1996); $30.6 million (1995)

Financial history

Fiscal year ended: Dec. 31

(Revenue in millions)

	1992	1993	1994	1995	1996
Revenue	$7.2	$16.2	$92.8	$149.6	$549.3
Earnings per share	-0.33	0.02	0.09	0.28	0.89
Stock price: High	NA	NA	5.56	40.63	75.25
Low	NA	NA	1.41	4.94	28.75
Close	NA	NA	5.09	40.56	62.13

6

Shiva Corporation

28 Crosby Drive
Bedford, MA 01730
Phone: 617-270-8300; FAX: 617-270-8999

Chairman, President and CEO:
   Frank A. Ingari

Shiva keeps you in the loop. The Bedford, Massachusetts, manufacturer makes software and hardware products that enable personal computer users to tap into distant mainframes and computer networks from just about anywhere. Using Shiva servers, users can connect to computer networks while at home, on the road, at a branch office, or as part of a multi-user worksite.

Founded in 1985, Shiva offers a full line of remote access products, including single-port servers for work groups and multi-port servers for enterprise networks. Not only do the company's NetModern LanRover and Shiva Integrator product families provide telecommuters, mobile professionals and branch offices with dial-in access to Local Area Networks (LANs), it also enables LAN-based users to make dial-out connections from the desktop to the Internet or other on-line services.

Shiva's ShivaPort communications products allow users to connect terminals, printers, modems and other serial devices to Ethernet networks.

The company markets its products in the U.S. and throughout Europe through a wide network of independent distributors, resellers and strategic partners.

In 1995, Shiva acquired Spider Systems Ltd., a British networking product manufacturer, strengthening its foothold in the European market. More than 40 percent of Shiva's revenue comes from European customers.

Originally, Shiva produced communications products primarily for Apple computers, but it has expanded to other manufacturers in recent years. The firm has developed strategic partnerships with leading manufacturers such as Microsoft, Hewlett-Packard and IBM. Shiva holds about a 25 percent share of the remote access hardware and software market, making it the world leader in that market.

Shiva has about 500 employees, and has sold products to about 800 of the Fortune 1000 companies. In all, the company has installed about 70,000 remote access servers.

Late developments
In 1996, Shiva bought AirSoft, a California-based developer of remote-access software.

Performance
Stock growth (past two years through 12/31/96): 75% (from $19.94 to $34.88).
Revenue growth (past two years through 12/31/96): 147% (from $81.0 million to $200 million).
Earnings per share growth (past two years through 12/31/96): 217% (from $0.17 to $0.54).

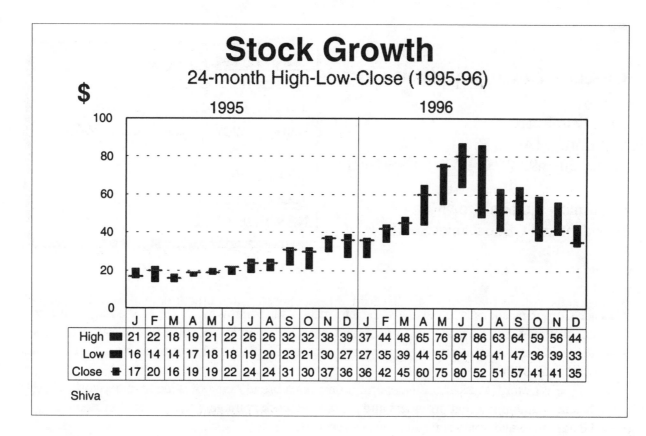

Stock Growth
24-month High-Low-Close (1995-96)

$

	J	F	M	A	M	J	J	A	S	O	N	D	J	F	M	A	M	J	J	A	S	O	N	D
High	21	22	18	19	21	22	26	26	32	32	38	39	37	44	48	65	76	87	86	63	64	59	56	44
Low	16	14	14	17	18	18	19	20	23	21	30	27	27	35	39	44	55	64	48	41	47	36	39	33
Close	17	20	16	19	19	22	24	24	31	30	37	36	36	42	45	60	75	80	52	51	57	41	41	35

Shiva

Quick Fix

P/E range (past two years):	47 - 162
Earnings past four quarters:	$0.54 (through 12/31/96)
Projected 1997 earnings (median):	$1.04
International sales:	47 percent of total sales (primarily Europe)
Total current assets:	$152.1 million (1996); $134.6 million (1995)
Total current liabilities:	$34.2 million (1996); $25.7 million (1995)
Net Income:	$16.8 million (1996); $10.5 million (1995)

Financial history

Fiscal year ended: Dec. 31

(Revenue in millions)

	1992	1993	1994	1995	*1996
Revenue	$52.8	$61.3	$81.0	$117.7	$200.1
Earnings per share	-0.32	0.06	0.17	0.38*	0.54
Stock price: High	NA	NA	21.50	38.75	87.25
Low	NA	NA	13.25	13.50	25.13
Close	NA	NA	19.94	36.38	34.88

1995 earnings per share does not include a $0.48 per share charge for merger expenses.

7

Cascade Communications Corp.

5 Carlisle Road
Westford, MA   01886
Phone: 508-692-2600; FAX: 508-692-9214

Chairman: Victoria Brown
President and CEO: Daniel Smith

Cascade Communications is helping pave the information superhighway. Three of the largest Internet service providers are Cascade customers, and nearly 70 percent of all Internet traffic traverses Cascade switches. The company has grown from sales of less than $1 million in 1992 to more than $300 million in 1996.

The Westford, Massachusetts, operation makes a broad range of wide area network (WAN) switches that enable Internet providers and private network managers to offer cost-effective, high-speed data, video and voice communications services.

Cascade has pioneered the concept of using a single powerful switching platform to simultaneously support the three major broadband packet communications services – frame relay, SMDS (Switched Multi-Megabit Data Service), and ATM (Asynchronous Transfer Mode).

Cascade switches are modular in design, and can be configured with many types of network interface modules to support a wide variety of end user access devices and network connections.

The company is the worldwide market share leader for the overall frame relay equipment market with about a 30 percent share of the $650 million market, which includes carrier switches, Internet services provider switches, enterprise switches and access equipment.

Cascade, which became a publicly-traded company with its initial stock offering in 1994, has about 450 employees.

Late developments

The company recently introduced its new AX 800 and AX 1600 high capacity access switches, giving it a presence in the dial access segment of the Internet and carrier markets. The AX switches integrate analog modem-based applications with high speed digital services. The AX products provide the highest dial-up densities for modem and ISDN access in the industry. The AX 1600 supports up to 672 integrated digital modems or up to 1,344 ISDN connections in a single shelf.

Performance

Stock growth (past two years through 12/31/96): 436% (from $ 10.29 to $55.13).
Revenue growth (past two years through 12/31/96): 582% (from $50 million to $341 million).
Earnings per share growth (past two years through 12/31/96): 564% (from $0.11 to $0.73).

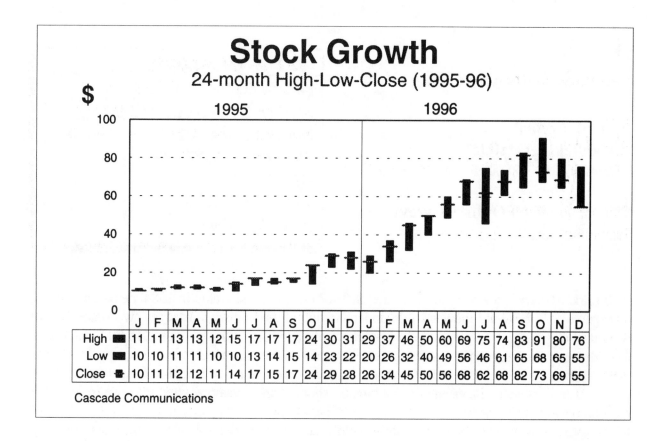

Stock Growth
24-month High-Low-Close (1995-96)

$

	J	F	M	A	M	J	J	A	S	O	N	D	J	F	M	A	M	J	J	A	S	O	N	D
High	11	11	13	13	12	15	17	17	17	24	30	31	29	37	46	50	60	69	75	74	83	91	80	76
Low	10	10	11	11	10	10	13	14	15	14	23	22	20	26	32	40	49	56	46	61	65	68	65	55
Close	10	11	12	12	11	14	17	15	17	24	29	28	26	34	45	50	56	68	62	68	82	73	69	55

Cascade Communications

Quick Fix

P/E range (past two years):	34 - 126
Earnings past four quarters:	$0.73 (through 1996)
Projected 1997 earnings (median):	$1.12
International sales:	16% of total sales (Asia/Pacific, 6%; Europe, 9%; other, 1%)
Total current assets:	$178.4 million (1996); $94.7 million (1995)
Total current liabilities:	$36.6 million (1996); $25.5 million (1995)
Net Income:	$70.8 million (1996); $25.4 million (1995)

Financial history

Fiscal year ended: Dec. 31

(Revenue in millions)

	1992	1993	1994	1995	1996
Revenue	$0.816	$7.0	$50.0	$134.8	$341
Earnings per share	-0.05	-0.04	0.11	0.28	0.73
Stock price: High	NA	NA	10.83	30.83	91.25
Low	NA	NA	3.50	9.54	20.42
Close	NA	NA	10.29	28.42	55.13

8

Corporate Express, Inc.

1 Environmental Way
Broomfield, CO 80021
Phone: 303-373-2800; FAX: 303-438-5181

Chairman and CEO: Jirka Rysavy
President: Bob King

When Jirka Rysavy first moved to the United States from Czechoslovakia in 1984, he had no money, no experience in business and very little understanding of the English language. Two years later, he bought a struggling stationery store in Boulder, Colorado for $100 -- plus the $15,000 in accounts payable the store had run up -- and began to turn the business around.

His first step was to refocus the store's emphasis from retail and small business customers to larger corporate clients. Sales and profits quickly shot up, and Rysavy started to move from a local market to a national market.

Now Corporate Express is the world's largest provider of office products for large corporations. The company operates in more than 500 locations, with 100 distribution centers in the United States, Canada, Australia, New Zealand, Germany, France and the United Kingdom.

Customers who select products from the company's full-color "In-Stock Catalog" may receive next-business-day delivery via the company's fleet of 7,000 delivery vehicles.

Corporate Express offers a broad selection of office supplies, computer products, software and office furniture. The company also offers printing and forms management services. The company markets to its customers and prospects through a direct sales force. Existing customers receive a catalog that includes about 5,000 products.

Much of Corporate Express's growth has been through acquisitions, such as its November 1996, acquisition of Harvard Information Support, based in Paris, France. Harvard is a leading software distributor that sells primarily to the 500 largest corporations in France. The Bloomfield, Colorado operation has 14,000 employees. The company went public with its initial stock offering in September 1994

Late developments

In addition to the acquisition of Harvard Information Support in France, Corporate Express announced the acquisition of 22 other companies in November 1996. New acquisitions included two German companies, a British firm, two Canadian firms, a second French firm and 15 U.S.-based companies. The completed acquisitions have a combined revenue of $270 million. The company also expected to complete the acquisition of United TransNet by the end of 1996.

Performance

Stock growth (past two years through 10/1/96): 180 % (from $13.88 to $38.88).
Revenue growth (past two years through 8/30/96): 296% (from $503.4 million to $1.99 billion).
Earnings per share growth (past two years through 8/30/96): NA (from -$0.11 to $0.13).

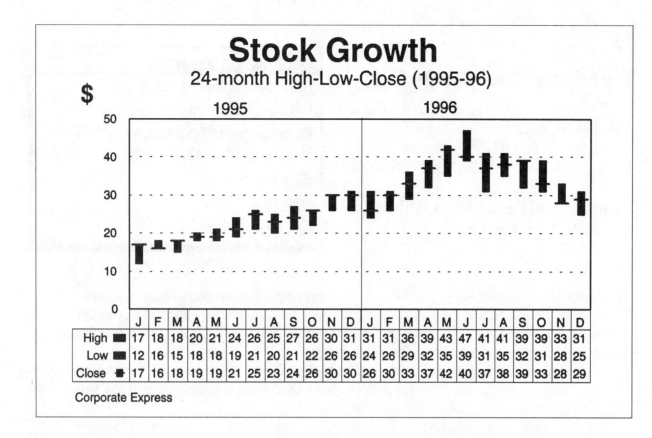

Stock Growth
24-month High-Low-Close (1995-96)

$

	J	F	M	A	M	J	J	A	S	O	N	D	J	F	M	A	M	J	J	A	S	O	N	D
High	17	18	18	20	21	24	26	25	27	26	30	31	31	31	36	39	43	47	41	41	39	39	33	31
Low	12	16	15	18	18	19	21	20	21	22	26	26	24	26	29	32	35	39	31	35	32	31	28	25
Close	17	16	18	19	19	21	25	23	24	26	30	30	26	30	33	37	42	40	37	38	39	33	28	29

Corporate Express

Quick Fix

P/E range (past two years):	88 - 768
Earnings past four quarters:	$0.13 (through 8/30/96)
Projected 1997 earnings (median):	$0.75
International sales:	10.5% of total sales
Total assets:	$910.5 million (1996); $568.2 million (1995)
Total current liabilities:	$242.2 million (1996); $156.1 million (1995)
Net Income:	$2.7 million (1996); $12.7 million (1995)

Financial history

Fiscal year ended: March 31
(Revenue in millions)

	1992	1993	1994	1995	1996
Revenue	$77.7	$103.1	$337.1	$927.9	$1,590.1
Earnings per share	-0.02	-0.21	-0.22	0.24	0.04
*Stock price: High	NA	NA	16.33	30.75	46.75
Low	NA	NA	10.83	11.50	24.13
Close	NA	NA	13.00	30.13	29.44

*Stock prices (only) reflect calendar year.

27

9

Parametric Technology Corp.

128 Technology Drive
Waltham, MA 02154
Phone: 617-398-5000; FAX: 617-398-6000

Chairman and CEO: Steven Walske
President: C.R. Harrison

The days of the T-square are long gone in the engineering and manufacturing world, replaced by CAD (computer-aided design), CAM (computer-aided manufacturing) and CAE (computer-aided engineering). Parametric Technology is a leader in the CAD/CAM/CAE market, offering several leading software programs for manufacturing companies.

Parametric's leading product is its Pro/Engineer software, which features a unique parametric modeling technique that uses a single data structure to capture changes made in any stage of the engineering process, from design through manufacturing.

The Waltham, Massachusetts, operation produces several other design software products, including:

- Pro/Access, which enables companies to use product information from a variety of sources in the engineering process;
- Pro/CDRS (conceptual design and rendering system), which enables product developers to create, evaluate and modify multiple concept models;
- Pro/JR., the entry-level version of Pro/Engineer;
- Pro/Manufacturing, which combines with Pro/Engineer to enable a manufacturer to produce a product from design through manufacturing; and
- Pro/Mechanica, which allows engineers to analyze and optimize a product design throughout the development cycle.

Parametric focuses primarily on the electronics, aerospace, automotive, consumer products and telecommunications industries. The company has about 140 offices in 26 countries worldwide. The company has seen its greatest growth in the international market, where its revenues grew from 38 percent of total sales in 1995 to 56 percent of sales in 1996.

The company, which shipped its first product in 1988, has about 2,500 employees.

Late developments
In late 1996, Matsushita Communications Industrial, of Japan ordered $5.1 million in software from Parametric to automate its complete design-through-manufacturing process.

Performance
Stock growth (past two years through 12/31/96): 198% (from $17.25 to $51.38).
Revenue growth (past two years through 9/30/96): 125% (from $227 million to $600 million).
Earnings per share growth (past two years through 9/30/96): 86% (from $0.56 to $1.04).

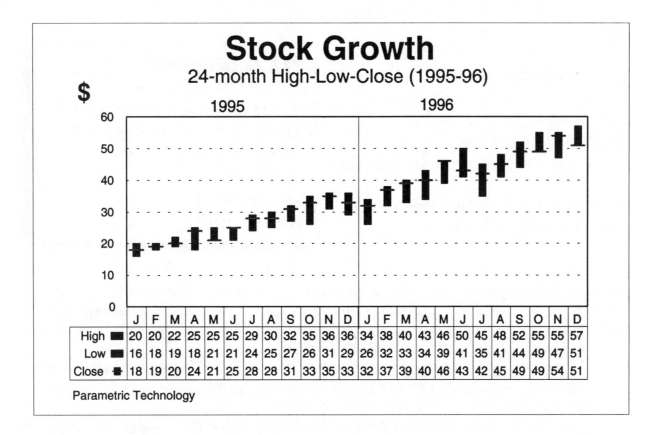

Stock Growth
24-month High-Low-Close (1995-96)

		J	F	M	A	M	J	J	A	S	O	N	D	J	F	M	A	M	J	J	A	S	O	N	D
High	■	20	20	22	25	25	25	29	30	32	35	36	36	34	38	40	43	46	50	45	48	52	55	55	57
Low	■	16	18	19	18	21	21	24	25	27	26	31	29	26	32	33	34	39	41	35	41	44	49	47	51
Close	●	18	19	20	24	21	25	28	28	31	33	35	33	32	37	39	40	46	43	42	45	49	49	54	51

Parametric Technology

Quick Fix

P/E range (past two years):	26 - 52
Earnings past four quarters:	$1.04 (through 9/30/96)
Projected 1997 earnings (median):	$1.64
International sales:	56% of total sales
Total current assets:	$485.4 million (1996); $353.3 million (1995)
Total current liabilities:	$114.7 million (1996); $70.1million (1995)
Net Income:	$138 million (1996); $77.4 million (1995)

Financial history

Fiscal year ended: Sept. 30
(Revenue in millions)

	1992	1993	1994	1995	1996
Revenue	$86.7	$179.3	$267	$394.3	$600
Earnings per share	0.19	0.36	0.54	0.60	1.04
*Stock price: High	14.06	22.38	20.13	36.28	56.75
Low	6.31	11.25	10.75	16.00	25.88
Close	13.25	19.38	17.25	33.25	51.38

Stock prices (only) reflect calendar year.

10
3Com Corp.

5400 Bayfront Plaza
Santa Clara, CA 95052
Phone: 408-764-5000; FAX: 408-764-5001

Chairman, President and CEO:
  Eric Benhamou

Founded in 1979, 3Com has been a pioneer in the computer networking industry. The firm has evolved from a supplier of discrete networking products to a broad-based supplier of local area network (LAN) and network access systems for the large enterprise, small business, home office and network service provider markets.

With annual revenue of about $2.3 billion, 3Com is one of the largest of the *Hot 100* stocks, and it continues to grow at a rapid rate.

Its primary product line includes routers, hubs, remote access servers, switches and adapters for a variety of high speed networks. The firm also offers Integrated Services Digital Network (ISDN) adapters and internetworking products for small businesses and home users. It also makes integrated digital remote access systems used by network service providers and telecommunications carriers.

The company counts among its customers finance, health care, manufacturing, government, educational and service organizations.

The Santa Clara, California, operation is global in scope, generating more than 50 percent of its revenue outside the U.S. It maintains sales offices in 32 countries, with new offices opened in 1996 in Eastern Europe, Latin America and the Asia Pacific region. It has "parts banks" at more than 25 locations, and electronic bulletin boards throughout the world. Including its U.S. operations, 3Com has a total of about 140 offices, and serves more than 32 million computer users.

Most of 3Com's product manufacturing is done at its Santa Clara and Ireland facilities. The company has about 5,200 employees.

Late developments
In late 1996, 3Com introduced a new OfficeConnect Networking Kit designed specifically for small businesses. It allows businesses to connect up to three personal computers into a network. Retail cost is $399.

Performance
Stock growth (past two years through 12/31/96): 184% (from $25.81 to $73.38).
Revenue growth (past two years through 8/30/96): 159% (from $979.6 million to $2.5 billion).
Earnings per share growth (past year through 8/30/96): 41% (from $0.85 to $1.20).

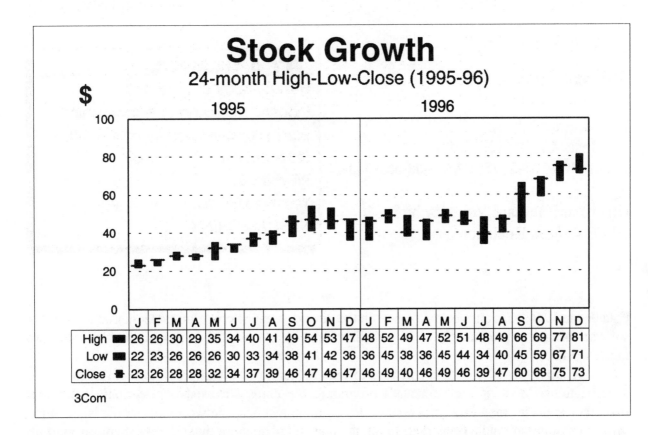

Stock Growth
24-month High-Low-Close (1995-96)

		J	F	M	A	M	J	J	A	S	O	N	D	J	F	M	A	M	J	J	A	S	O	N	D
High	■	26	26	30	29	35	34	40	41	49	54	53	47	48	52	49	47	52	51	48	49	66	69	77	81
Low	■	22	23	26	26	26	30	33	34	38	41	42	36	36	45	38	36	45	44	34	40	45	59	67	71
Close	■	23	26	28	28	32	34	37	39	46	47	46	47	46	49	40	46	49	46	39	47	60	68	75	73

3Com

Quick Fix

P/E range (past two years):	22 - 67
Earnings past four quarters:	$1.20 (through 8/30/96)
Projected 1997 earnings (median):	$2.29
International sales:	53% of total sales (Europe, 33%; other, 20%)
Total current assets:	$1.4 billion (1996); $781.2 million (1995)
Total current liabilities:	$458.7 million (1996); $271.7 million (1995)
Net Income:	$178 million (1996); $144.6 million (1995)

Financial history

Fiscal year ended: May 31
(Revenue in millions)

	1992	1993	1994	1995	1996
Revenue	$423.8	$617.2	$1,011.5	$1,593.5	$2,327.1
Earnings per share	0.07	0.31	-0.08	0.85	1.01
*Stock price: High	7.50	12.13	26.63	53.63	81.38
Low	2.41	4.91	10.06	22.19	33.50
Close	7.41	11.75	25.78	46.63	73.38

Stock prices (only) reflect calendar year.

11
Xilinx, Inc.

2100 Logic Drive
San Jose, CA 95124-3400
Phone: 408-559-7778; FAX: 408-559-7114

Chairman: Bernard Vonderschmitt
CEO: Willem Roelandts

Founded in 1984, Xilinx has been a pioneer in the development of programmable microchips and the software needed to program those chips. Xilinx is the largest supplier of programmable logic chips in the world.

Xilinx sells its chips and software to manufacturers who can program them to their own specifications. Most of the company's programmable chips are used by electronic equipment manufacturers in the data processing, telecommunications, networking, industrial control, instrumentation and military market. In all, the company has more than 15,000 clients around the world.

The San Jose operation has offices throughout North America, Europe and Asia. About 25 percent of the company's revenue comes from customers outside the U.S.

The real competitive edge Xilinx brings to the market is speed. Standard logic chips can require weeks or months of design time before they are ready for the manufacturing stage, but Xilinx's "field programmable gate array" chips enable customers to accelerate the programming and development stage to just a few days, allowing them to bring their products to market much faster. Xilinx chips can also be changed in just a few hours, whereas other chips can require several weeks for the same type of adjustments.

Xilinx does not own or operate its own silicon wafer production facilities. Rather it forms strategic alliances with chip manufacturers who produce chips to Xilinx's specifications at their foundries. That strategy allows Xilinx to focus its resources on research and development, technical support and marketing.

The company has about 1,200 employees.

Late developments
The company recently reached agreement with Seiko Corp. in Japan to build a new wafer fabrication facility. Xilinx will advance $200 million to Seiko to build the plant, and Seiko will reimburse Xilinx in the form of chips, which will begin shipping in 1998.

Performance
Stock growth (past two years through 12/31/96): 86% (from $19.75 to $36.81).
Revenue growth (past two years through 9/30/96): 94% (from $296.6 million to $574.6 million).
Earnings per share growth (past two years through 9/30/96): 144% (from $0.64 to $1.56).

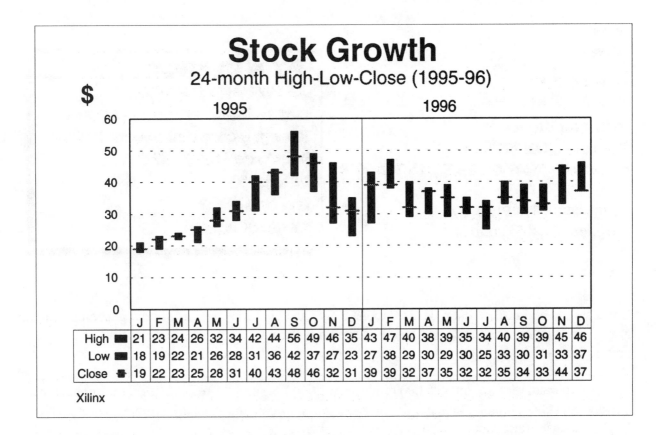

Stock Growth
24-month High-Low-Close (1995-96)

	J	F	M	A	M	J	J	A	S	O	N	D	J	F	M	A	M	J	J	A	S	O	N	D
High	21	23	24	26	32	34	42	44	56	49	46	35	43	47	40	38	39	35	34	40	39	39	45	46
Low	18	19	22	21	26	28	31	36	42	37	27	23	27	38	29	30	29	30	25	33	30	31	33	37
Close	19	22	23	25	28	31	40	43	48	46	32	31	39	39	32	37	35	32	32	35	34	33	44	37

Xilinx

Quick Fix

P/E range (past two years):	14 - 43
Earnings past four quarters:	$1.56 (through 9/30/96)
Projected 1997 earnings (median):	$1.41
International sales:	25% of total sales (Asia/Pacific,12%; Europe, 13%)
Total current assets:	$552.7 million (1996); $231.3 million (1995)
Total current liabilities:	$107 million (1996); $86.7 million (1995)
Net Income:	$101.4 million (1996); $59.3 million (1995)

Financial history

Fiscal year ended: March 31
(Revenue in millions)

	1992	1993	1994	1995	1996
Revenue	$135.8	$178	$256.4	$355.1	$560.8
Earnings per share	0.30	0.38	0.57	0.80	1.29
*Stock price: High	10.33	18.17	20.67	55.50	46.50
Low	4.83	7.83	9.67	18.08	24.50
Close	8.42	15.92	19.75	30.50	36.81

Stock prices (only) reflect calendar year.

12

Omnicare, Inc.

2800 Chemed Center
255 East Fifth Street
Cincinnati, OH 45202
Phone: 513-762-6666; FAX: 513-762-6678

Chairman: Edward Hutton
President: Joel Gemunder

Omnicare serves a market that is destined to get bigger and bigger as the baby boom generation turns grayer and grayer. The Cincinnati-based operation is the nation's leading independent provider of prescription and non-prescription drugs for nursing homes, retirement centers and other long-term care facilities.

Omnicare serves about 225,000 residents in 2,600 long-term care facilities. The company has operations in Ohio, Illinois, Indiana, Kentucky, Kansas, Michigan, Missouri, Ohio, Oklahoma, New York, Massachusetts, Connecticut and West Virginia.

The firm also provides computerized medical recordkeeping, third-party billing for patients in the long-term care facilities, and consultant pharmacist services. It also provides infusion therapy and medical supplies for nursing facilities, and monthly drug patient evaluation and monitoring of the drug administration procedures within each facility.

Omnicare went public with its initial stock offering in 1981. While growth was slow at first, in recent years, the company has expanded rapidly through a series of acquisitions. The company acquired seven pharmacy services and related businesses in 1992, four more in 1993, seven in 1994 and nine in 1995. Omnicare's network of institutional pharmacies serves 14 percent of the long-term care market in the U.S.

By establishing a growing presence in each of the markets it enters, Omnicare is able to achieve the economies of scale and increased operating leverage it needs to remain a low-cost provider, while still offering a broad range of pharmaceutical services.

Late developments

Omnicare acquired Hallmark Medical, an institutional pharmacy in Ridgewood, New Jersey, and Squire Drugs of Folcroft, Pennsylvania, in late 1996. The acquisitions added about $6.8 million in revenue to Omnicare's balance sheet, and about 4,900 long-term care facility residents to its customer base. The firm also acquired Jacobs Health Care Systems of Des Plaines, Illinois, Value Heath of Southington, Connecticut, and the long-term care division of Cornell Medical of Coraopolis, Pennsylvania, in early 1997.

Performance

Stock growth (past two years through 12/31/96): 192% (from $10.99 to $32.13).
Revenue growth (past two years through 12/31/96): 75% (from $307.7 million to $536.6 million).
Earnings per share growth (past two years through 12/31/96): 113% (from $0.30 to $0.64).

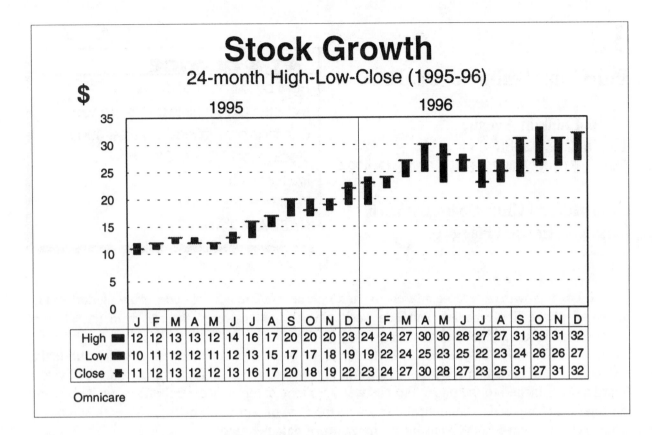

Stock Growth
24-month High-Low-Close (1995-96)

$		1995												1996											
		J	F	M	A	M	J	J	A	S	O	N	D	J	F	M	A	M	J	J	A	S	O	N	D
High		12	12	13	13	12	14	16	17	20	20	20	23	24	24	27	30	30	28	27	27	31	33	31	32
Low		10	11	12	12	11	12	13	15	17	17	18	19	19	22	24	25	23	25	22	23	24	26	26	27
Close		11	12	13	12	12	13	16	17	20	18	19	22	23	24	27	30	28	27	23	25	31	27	31	32

Omnicare

Quick Fix

P/E range (past two years):	22 - 52
Earnings past four quarters:	$0.64 (1996)
Projected 1997 earnings (median):	$0.77
International sales:	None
Total current assets:	$407.8 million (9/30/96); $151.6 million (9/30/95)
Total current liabilities:	$58.2 million (9/30/96); $37.1 million (9/30/95)
Net Income:	$43.5 million (1996); $24.7 million (1995)

Financial history

Fiscal year ended: Dec. 31
(Revenue in millions)

	1992	1993	1994	1995	1996
Revenue	$131.9	$223.1	$307.7	$399.6	$536.6
Earnings per share	0.13	0.26	0.30	0.47	0.64
Stock price: High	7.88	8.03	11.31	22.69	32.50
Low	4.06	3.31	6.72	10.22	18.63
Close	7.72	8.00	10.94	22.38	32.13

13

PairGain Technologies, Inc.

14402 Franklin Avenue
Tustin, CA 92680
Phone: 714-832-9922; FAX: 714-832-9924

Chairman and CEO: Charles Strauch
President: Howard Flagg

The explosive growth of video-conferencing and Internet surfing has created a growing demand for increased phone line capacity. PairGain Technologies has answered the call with its "HiGain" transmission boxes and related products.

The HiGain boxes speed the flow of information over the old copper wiring, which still makes up a large part of the nation's phone line network. The boxes, which house a complex array of circuit boards, are attached to the phone lines between a phone company's central office and its business customers, and are used to dramatically speed up the flow of data over the lines. The HiGain boxes, which sell for about $1,000, transmit 1.5 megabits of data per second.

In addition to its business line boxes, the company has also introduced similar devices to speed up data transmission on residential lines that are now under increasing demand from Internet users.

Founded in 1988, the company launched its first product in 1989. The firm went public in 1993 with its initial stock offering. PairGain has about 400 employees.

The Tustin, California, operation sells its HiGain boxes and related products primarily to local phone companies such as Bell Atlantic, Bell South and NYNEX. PairGain also makes a "Campus" transmission product designed for private networks. Campus systems are used for phone systems at universities, hospitals, utility plants, military bases, industrial parks and corporate complexes. List prices is about $2,500 per unit. Among its Campus customers are University of Illinois, MCI International, Warner Brothers Studios, Indiana Department of Transportation and Unisys Corp.

Most of the firm's sales are in North America, although PairGain has begun to push international sales through offices in the United Kingdom and China.

Late developments

PairGain's Megabit Modem products were recently installed by ATU Telecommunications of Anchorage, Alaska, to provide high speed data transmission for corporate LAN customers and Internet access. PairGain also signed a two-year contract to supply Bell Canada with HiGain systems for its network of copper telephone wire.

Performance

Stock growth (past two years through 12/31/96): 755% (from $ 3.56 to $30.44).
Revenue growth (past two years through 9/30/96): 237% (from $52.5 million to $177 million).
Earnings per share growth (past two years through 9/30/96): 400% (from $0.22 to $1.10).

Stock Growth
24-month High-Low-Close (1995-96)

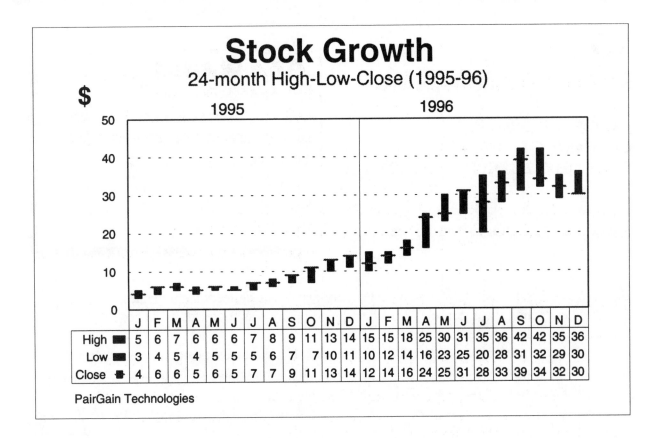

	J	F	M	A	M	J	J	A	S	O	N	D	J	F	M	A	M	J	J	A	S	O	N	D
High	5	6	7	6	6	6	7	8	9	11	13	14	15	15	18	25	30	31	35	36	42	42	35	36
Low	3	4	5	4	5	5	5	6	7	7	10	11	10	12	14	16	23	25	20	28	31	32	29	30
Close	4	6	6	5	6	5	7	7	9	11	13	14	12	14	16	24	25	31	28	33	39	34	32	30

PairGain Technologies

Quick Fix

P/E range (past two years):	30 -100+
Earnings past four quarters:	$1.10 (through 9/30/96)
Projected 1997 earnings (median):	$1.25
International sales:	Less than 5% of total sales
Total current assets:	$132.6 million (1996); $100.1 million (1995)
Total current liabilities:	$29.6 million (1996); $10.5 million (1995)
Net Income:	$1.1 million (1995); $8.6 million (1994)

Financial history

Fiscal year ended: Dec. 31
(Revenue in millions)

	1992	1993	1994	1995	*1996
Revenue	$9.5	$36.3	$59.5	$107.2	$142.3*
Earnings per share	-0.11	0.31	0.28	0.03	0.64*
Stock price: High	NA	11.13	8.13	28.00	41.88
Low	NA	4.63	3.44	6.63	9.75
Close	NA	6.88	7.13	27.38	30.44

1996 revenue and earnings through Sept. 30 (nine months).

14

United Waste Systems, Inc.

4 Greenwich Office Park
Greenwich, CT   06830
Phone: 203-622-3131; FAX: 203-622-6080

Chairman and CEO: Bradley Jacobs
President and COO: Edward Sheehan

United Waste Systems not only collects waste, it collects waste collection companies—and it wastes little time collecting them. Since 1989, when the company was founded, it has acquired over 140 smaller waste collection services.

United's primary strategy has been to establish a dominant position as a waste hauler in selected regional areas by acquiring smaller haulers in that area. United is the number one or number two waste services provider in eight of its 10 markets.

Most of the company's acquisitions are merged into existing regional operations. In all, the Greenwich, Connecticut, company has about 25 landfills, 30 hauling companies and 41 transfer stations. Collection operations account for about 65 percent of the company's revenue, landfill operations account for 30 percent, and waste reuse and reduction programs and other services make up the final 5 percent.

Under United's growth strategy, the company looks for attractive, lightly-populated areas with a fragmented waste services market that are served by few, if any, well-capitalized and entrenched waste companies. The company often enters a market by buying a landfill, and then purchasing surrounding collection services and transfer stations to increase waste volume.

Once the company has acquired several regional operations, it consolidates the operations, cutting out overhead, combining routes, and implementing certain financial controls. The strategy has helped United achieve profit margins that are among the highest in the industry.

The company may also acquire larger regional operations, such as Waste Systems Corp., a regional waste company covering northern Iowa and southern Minnesota that United acquired in 1995. In addition to Minnesota and Iowa, the company offers services in Michigan, Wisconsin, California, Kentucky, Massachusetts, Mississippi, New Hampshire, New York, Pennsylvania and West Virginia.

United went public with its initial stock offering in 1992.

Late developments
United Waste acquired 54 smaller regional waste services through the first nine months of 1996, and was continuing an aggressive acquisition program through the final three months of the year.

Performance
Stock growth (past two years through 11/29/96): 227% (from $10.25 to $33.50).
Revenue growth (past two years through 9/30/96):167% (from $114.7 million to $306 million).
Earnings per share growth (past two years through 9/30/96): 41% (from $0.58 to $0.82).

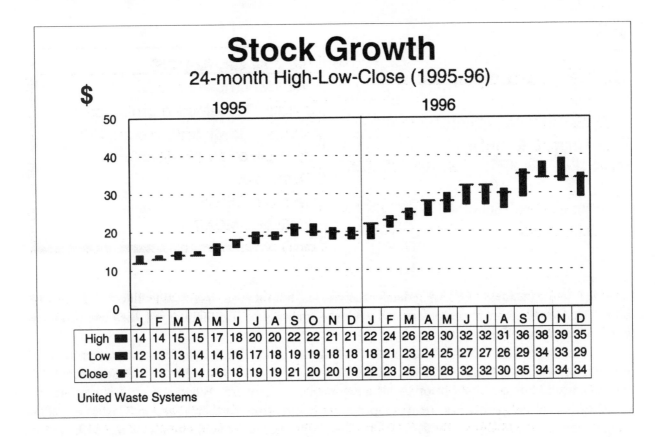

Stock Growth
24-month High-Low-Close (1995-96)

$

	J	F	M	A	M	J	J	A	S	O	N	D	J	F	M	A	M	J	J	A	S	O	N	D
High	14	14	15	15	17	18	20	20	22	22	21	21	22	24	26	28	30	32	32	31	36	38	39	35
Low	12	13	13	14	14	16	17	18	19	19	18	18	18	21	23	24	25	27	27	26	29	34	33	29
Close	12	13	14	14	16	18	19	19	21	20	20	19	22	23	25	28	28	32	32	30	35	34	34	34

United Waste Systems

Quick Fix

P/E range (past two years):	15 - 47
Earnings past four quarters:	$0.82 (through 9/30/96)
Projected 1997 earnings (median):	$1.45
International sales:	None
Total current assets:	$97.7million (1996); $59.4 million (1995)
Total current liabilities:	$74.4 million (1996); $63.4 million (1995)
Net Income:	$23.8 million (9/30/96); $18.4 million (1995)

Financial history

Fiscal year ended: Dec. 31
(Revenue in millions)

	1992	1993	1994	1995	*1996
Revenue	$43.8	$95.7	$128.5	$211.8	$241.9*
Earnings per share	-0.20	0.50	0.62	0.75	0.60*
Stock price: High	6.50	8.50	12.75	21.88	38.75
Low	5.88	4.63	7.38	11.50	17.88
Close	6.13	7.75	12.50	18.63	34.38

1996 revenue and earnings through Sept. 30 (nine months).

15

McAfee Associates, Inc.

2710 Walsh Avenue, Suite 200
Santa Clara, CA 95054
Phone: 408-988-3832; FAX: 408-970-9727

Chairman, President and CEO:
  William Larson

McAfee is in the business of fighting dangerous viruses, but this is no medical technology firm. The viruses McAfee fights are in computers, and while they may not be life-threatening, they can certainly wreak havoc on the lives of their victims.

The Santa Clara, California, company's flagship product is VirsusScan, a virus protection program for Windows, Macintosh, Dos and OS/2 computer operating systems. VirsusScan scans for known and unknown viruses prior to installation of the software. When the scan is completed, VirusScan becomes memory resident and protects systems from further infection. Cost of a 1,000-user VirusScan site license is about $20,000. The single user retail version costs about $49.

Other McAfee virus protection products include:

• **NetShield.** Netshield protects network file servers by blocking viruses from being transferred over networks by scanning files accessed from the server. Cost for a 1,000-node site license is $11,800.

• **Webscan.** Webscan is used to protect Internet services, Web browsers and E-mail from viruses. Cost is $20,500.

• **Bootshield.** Bootshield provides pre-boot protection from boot-sector viruses.

McAfee also makes a line of network management software such as Saber LAN Workstation, which allows network administrators to manage and maintain local area network (LAN) resources; SiteMeter, a monitoring and reporting tool for DOS and Windows that is used primarily by corporate, government and institutional customers to maintain software compliance; SiteInventory, a network management program that tracks the types and amounts of software and hardware used on a network of personal computers; and SiteExpress, a software product that allows network administrators to distribute, install and update software at sites, servers and workstations on LANs and wide area networks. The company, which was founded in 1989 by John McAfee, has about 250 employees.

Late developments

McAfee acquired FSA Corp. in late 1996, and used FSA's core technology for McAfee's new NetCrypto product, which provides transparent encryption and user authentication for desktop computers.

Performance

Stock growth (past two years through 12/31/96): 633 % (from $6.00 to $44.00).
Revenue growth (past two years through 12/31/96): 101% (from $90.1 million to $181 million).
Earnings per share growth (past two years through 12/31/96): 462% (from $0.13 to $0.73).

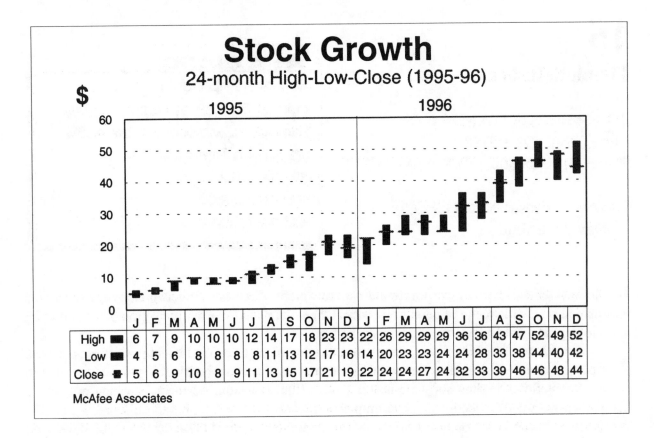

Stock Growth
24-month High-Low-Close (1995-96)

		J	F	M	A	M	J	J	A	S	O	N	D	J	F	M	A	M	J	J	A	S	O	N	D
High		6	7	9	10	10	10	12	14	17	18	23	23	22	26	29	29	29	36	36	43	47	52	49	52
Low		4	5	6	8	8	8	8	11	13	12	17	16	14	20	23	23	24	24	28	33	38	44	40	42
Close		5	6	9	10	8	9	11	13	15	17	21	19	22	24	24	27	24	32	33	39	46	46	48	44

McAfee Associates

Quick Fix

P/E range (past two years):	15 -78
Earnings past four quarters:	$0.73 (through 12/31/96)
Projected 1997 earnings (median):	$1.18
International sales:	29% of total sales
Total assets:	$54.8 million (1995); $73.7 million (1994)
Total current liabilities:	$35.8 million (1995); $28.2 million (1994)
Net Income:	$39 million (1996); $14.9 million (1995)

Financial history

Fiscal year ended: Dec. 31
(Revenue in millions)

	1992	1993	1994	1995	1996
Revenue	$13.7	$31.0	$52.9	$90.1	$181.1
Earnings per share	NA	0.44	0.13	0.68	0.73
Stock price: High	6.89	6.00	6.00	23.50	51.75
Low	3.85	1.33	1.93	4.44	13.75
Close	5.04	2.22	6.00	19.50	44.00

16

PeopleSoft, Inc.

4440 Rosewood Drive
Pleasanton, CA 94588
Phone: 510-225-3000; FAX: 510-225-3100

Chairman, President and CEO:
   David Duffield

AT A GLANCE

Held by number of funds: 6
Industry: Business software
Earnings growth past 2 years: 265%
Stock price 1/1/97: $47.94
P/E ratio: 112
Year ago P/E: 70
NASDAQ: PSFT

PeopleSoft software gives corporate human resources directors fingertip access to detailed information on a wide range of personnel matters, benefits plans, affirmative action plans and work and biographical data on every employee in the firm.

Since it was founded in 1987, PeopleSoft has continued to expand its line of offerings aimed at helping human resources directors run their departments more smoothly.

PeopleSoft's leading software product is its Human Resources module, which provides a comprehensive range of functions such as employee record keeping, health and safety records, skills inventory, affirmative action, position management and recruitment. The firm has also developed several add-on software packages that expand the capability of its human resources program, including:

   • *PeopleSoft Benefits Administration,* which supports daily benefits administration activities, and helps managers control costs and comply with government regulations.

   • *PeopleSoft FSA Administration,* which is geared to companies that have the more flexible "cafeteria" benefits plans.

   • *PeopleSoft Payroll,* which provides in-house payroll administration and production capabilities, including payroll calculations, check printing, tax reporting and deduction, and benefit calculations.

The company also offers comprehensive software for other corporate functions, including a financial management system with separate modules for general ledger, receivables, payables, asset management, billing, budgeting, purchasing, inventory and order management.

The California-based operation has a worldwide marketing distribution network, with offices in Canada, Mexico, the Netherlands, France, Germany, England, Australia, Argentina and Singapore. About 16 percent of its total sales are generated outside the U.S.

PeopleSoft, which had its initial public stock offering in 1992, has 1,400 employees.

Late developments

PeopleSoft reached agreement in early 1997 with Intrepid Systems, Inc., to cooperate in developing human resources and financial management software for the retail industry.

Performance

Stock growth (past two years through 12/31/96): 408% (from $9.44 to $47.94).
Revenue growth (past two years through 9/30/96): 294% (from $94.6 million to $373 million).
Earnings per share growth (past two years through 9/30/96): 265% (from $0.23 to $0.84).

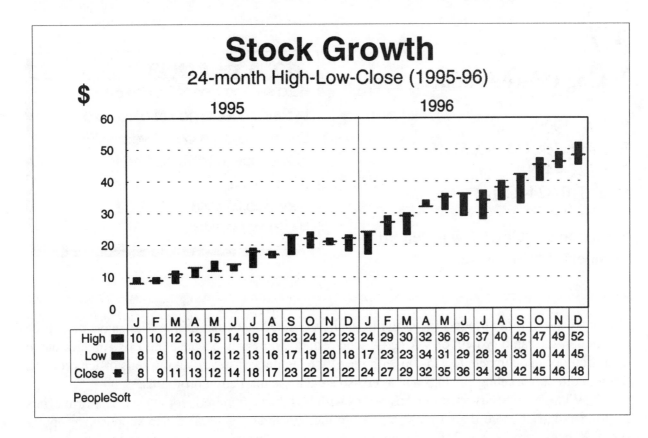

Stock Growth
24-month High-Low-Close (1995-96)

	1995												1996											
	J	F	M	A	M	J	J	A	S	O	N	D	J	F	M	A	M	J	J	A	S	O	N	D
High	10	10	12	13	15	14	19	18	23	24	22	23	24	29	30	32	36	36	37	40	42	47	49	52
Low	8	8	8	10	12	12	13	16	17	19	20	18	17	23	23	34	31	29	28	34	33	40	44	45
Close	8	9	11	13	12	14	18	17	23	22	21	22	24	27	29	32	35	36	34	38	42	45	46	48

PeopleSoft

Quick Fix

P/E range (past two years):	39 - 113
Earnings past four quarters:	$0.84 (through 9/30/96)
Projected 1997 earnings (median):	$1.38
International sales:	16 percent of total sales
Total current assets:	$309.3 million (1996); $175.3 million (1995)
Total current liabilities:	$203.1 million (1996); $96.8 million (1995)
Net Income:	$29.4 million (1995); $14.5 million (1994)

Financial history

Fiscal year ended: Dec. 31
(Revenue in millions)

	1992	1993	1994	1995	*1996
Revenue	$31.6	$58.2	$112.9	$227.6	$296.5*
Earnings per share	0.12	0.17	0.28	0.54	0.64*
Stock price: High	8.00	10.13	19.75	47.00	52.25
Low	5.63	5.88	6.50	15.00	17.13
Close	7.06	7.81	18.88	43.00	47.94

1996 revenue and earnings through Sept. 30 (nine months).

17

Viking Office Products, Inc.

879 W. 190th Street
Los Angeles, CA 90061-1000
213-321-4493
Fax: 310-324-2396

Chairman and CEO: Irwin Helford
President: M. Bruce Nelson

The new wave of office product mega-marts, such as Office Depot and Office Max, have done little to dampen the rapid growth of Viking Office Products, primarily because the Los Angeles-based operation doesn't compete toe-to-toe with the office retailers. Instead, Viking sells office products through direct marketing catalogs and aggressive database marketing programs.

Viking's target customers are businesses with less than a hundred employees. The firm offers a broad range of more than 10,000 office products including general office supplies, computer supplies, paper products, office furniture, selected business machines, janitorial and safety supplies and presentation supplies.

The company markets its products through frequent mailings of full-color catalogs. Viking emphasizes prompt delivery and low prices (its prices normally fall 30 to 50 percent below suggested retail prices).

Regular Viking customers receive a catalog of general office merchandise each month, and may also receive one of the company's thirteen specialty catalogs, which focus on specific areas such as office furniture, computer supplies, custom printed business forms, paper products, shipping and warehouse supplies, and presentation products. The company mailed out a total of 155 million catalogs in 1996 -- more than double the number of catalogs distributed five years earlier. Its active customer base has grown from 745,000 in 1992 to 1.92 million in 1996. Average annual revenue per customer is about $550.

The firm's biggest growth area has been its overseas operations, which now account for nearly 60 percent of total sales. Viking has distribution centers in England, Ireland, France, Germany and Australia.

Viking was founded in 1960, but did not go public (issue stock) until 1990.

Late developments

The company continues to open new distribution centers, adding centers in Minneapolis and Washington D.C. in 1995, and San Francisco in 1996. Viking plans to open its tenth distribution center in 1997.

Performance

Stock growth (past two years through 11/1/96): 88% (from $15.50 to $29.12).
Revenue growth (past two years through 9/30/96): 81% (from $617 million to $1.12 billion).
Earnings per share growth (past two years through 9/30/96): 72% (from $0.43 to $0.74).

Stock Growth
24-month High-Low-Close (1995-96)

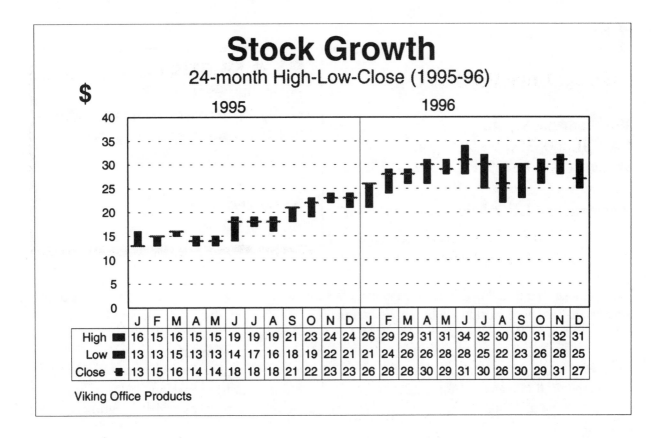

		J	F	M	A	M	J	J	A	S	O	N	D	J	F	M	A	M	J	J	A	S	O	N	D
High		16	15	16	15	15	19	19	19	21	23	24	24	26	29	29	31	31	34	32	30	30	31	32	31
Low		13	13	15	13	13	14	17	16	18	19	22	21	21	24	26	26	28	28	25	22	23	26	28	25
Close		13	15	16	14	14	18	18	18	21	22	23	23	26	28	28	30	29	31	30	26	30	29	31	27

Viking Office Products

Quick Fix

P/E range (past two years):	23 - 49
Earnings past four quarters:	$0.74 (through 9/30/96)
Projected 1997 earnings (median):	$0.90
International sales:	59% ($626.3 million)
Total assets:	$399.6 million (1996); $308.3 million (1995)
Total current liabilities:	$122 million (1996); $99.4 million (1995)
Net Income:	$60.5 million (1996); $46.1million (1995)

Financial history

Fiscal year ended: June 30
(Revenue in millions)

	1992	1993	1994	1995	1996
Revenue	$320.1	$449.7	$565.1	$811.9	$1,055.8
Earnings per share	0.17	0.21	0.38	0.54	0.70
Stock price: High	7.25	12.31	16.25	24.31	34.00
Low	3.69	5.38	10.50	12.50	20.88
Close	6.56	12.25	15.31	23.25	26.69

Stock prices (only) reflect calendar year.

18
Tellabs, Inc.

4951 Indiana Avenue
Lisle, IL 60532
Phone: 708-969-8800; FAX: 708-512-8202

President and CEO: Michael Birck

Tellabs makes the data flow. The company manufactures voice and data transport and network access systems that are used worldwide by phone companies, cellular and other wireless service providers, cable operators, government agencies, utilities and businesses.

The Chicago-area operation makes digital cross-connection systems, managed digital networks and network access products. Its digital cross-connection systems are used by telecommunication managers for centralized and remote testing of transmission facilities, grooming of voice, data, and video signals, automated installation of new services and restoration of failed facilities.

Tellab's managed digital networks are used by telecommunications services to provide businesses with high speed data access, frame relay and voice telephony. The company's Martis DXX system acts as the transport infrastructure for mobile networks such as digital and analog cellular, paging, trunked mobile radio and mobile data.

The company's network access systems products are used in a variety of areas, including echo cancellation (removing feedback from one's own voice that occurs on many long distance connections and many wireless connections) and voice compression, which doubles the capacity of digital transmission facilities used for voice and data services.

Tellabs markets its products through its own direct sales force, and through selected distributors. Bell operating companies account for about 28 percent of the company's total revenue. The firm sells to customers worldwide. International sales account for about 37 percent of the company total revenue.

Tellabs was founded in 1975. It went public with its initial stock offering in 1980.

Late developments
Tellabs signed a contract in February, 1997, for $5 million to supply its Martis DXX managed access and transport network platform for Centertel's mobile network in Poland. Centertel is a joint venture between the Polish national phone operator and France Telecom.

Performance
Stock growth (past two years through 12/31/96): 170% (from $13.94 to $37.63).
Revenue growth (past two years through 9/30/96): 72% (from $452.8 million to $777.4 million).
Earnings per share growth (past two years through 12/31/96): 60% (from $0.40 to $0.64).

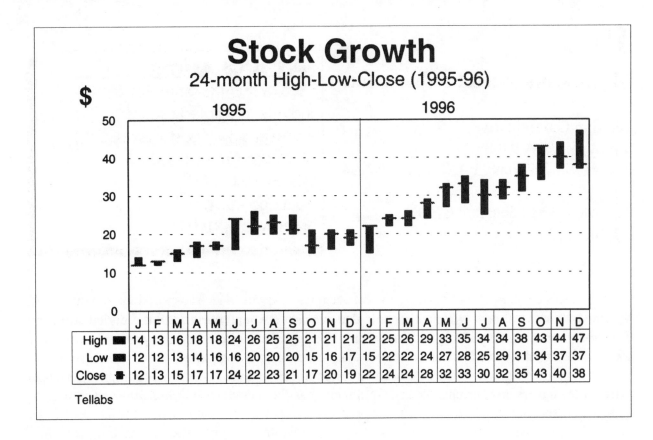

Stock Growth
24-month High-Low-Close (1995-96)

$	J	F	M	A	M	J	J	A	S	O	N	D	J	F	M	A	M	J	J	A	S	O	N	D
High	14	13	16	18	18	24	26	25	25	21	21	21	22	25	26	29	33	35	34	34	38	43	44	47
Low	12	12	13	14	16	16	20	20	20	15	16	17	15	22	22	24	27	28	25	29	31	34	37	37
Close	12	13	15	17	17	24	22	23	21	17	20	19	22	24	24	28	32	33	30	32	35	43	40	38

Tellabs

Quick Fix

P/E range (past two years):	19 - 73
Earnings past four quarters:	$0.64 (through 12/31/96)
Projected 1997 earnings (median):	$2.25
International sales:	37% of total sales (Canada, 4% ; other, 33%)
Total current assets:	$348 million (1996); $366.4 million (1995)
Total current liabilities:	$120.1 million (1996); $98.6 million (1995)
Net Income:	$118 million (1996); $115.6 million (1995)

Financial history

Fiscal year ended: Dec. 31
(Revenue in millions)

	1992	1993	1994	1995	1996
Revenue	$258.6	$320.5	$494.2	$635.2	$869
Earnings per share	0.10	0.17	0.40	0.63	0.64
Stock price: High	2.20	6.79	14.00	26.38	46.75
Low	1.32	1.58	5.47	11.75	15.25
Close	2.07	5.91	13.94	18.50	37.63

19

Maxim Integrated Products, Inc.

120 San Gabriel Drive
Sunnyvale, CA 94086
Phone: 408-737-7600; FAX: 403-737-7194

Chairman, President and CEO:
  John Gifford

Maxim Integrated Products makes circuits that connect the real world with the digital world by detecting, measuring, amplifying and converting measures such as temperature, pressure, speed and sound into digital signals that can be stored and processed on a computer.

Maxim's integrated circuits are used on microprocessor-based electronics equipment such as personal computers and peripherals, test equipment, handheld devices, wireless phones and pagers, and video displays.

In addition to its linear and mixed-signal integrated circuits, Maxim manufactures data converters, interface circuits, microprocessor supervisors, operational amplifiers, power supplies, multiplexers, switches, battery chargers, battery management circuits, fiber optic transceivers and voltage references.

In all, the Sunnyvale, California, operation markets more than 1,000 products to about 35,000 customers in four primary industries: communications companies use Maxim products for phones, broadband networks, fiber optics, pagers and video communications; industrial control companies use them to control temperature, flow, pressure, velocity and position; instrumentation firms use them in testers, analyzers, data recorders and measuring instruments; and data processing companies use them for workstations, personal computers, printers, point-of-sale terminals, bar-code readers, minicomputers, mainframes, disk drives and tape drives.

The firm markets its products in the U.S. through a direct sales organization with 12 regional offices. Internationally, the firm has sale offices in 10 foreign cities. About 56 percent of the company's net revenue is generated outside the U.S.

Founded in 1983, Maxim has about 2,000 employees.

Late developments

Maxim is building a new 115,000-square-foot test and assembly plant in the Philippines that should be operational by late 1997. The firm has also acquired nine acres next to its Sunnyvale headquarters, which will be used to expand its wafer fabrication capacity.

Performance

Stock growth (past two years through 12/31/96): 147% (from $17.50 to $43.25).
Revenue growth (past two years through 9/30/96):147% (from $172.8 million to $426 million).
Earnings per share growth (past two years through 9/30/96): 335% (from $0.43 to $1.87).

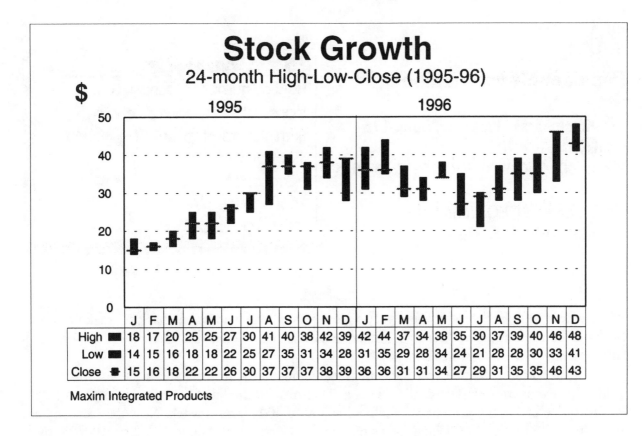

Stock Growth
24-month High-Low-Close (1995-96)

Maxim Integrated Products

	J	F	M	A	M	J	J	A	S	O	N	D	J	F	M	A	M	J	J	A	S	O	N	D
High	18	17	20	25	25	27	30	41	40	38	42	39	42	44	37	34	38	35	30	37	39	40	46	48
Low	14	15	16	18	18	22	25	27	35	31	34	28	31	35	29	28	34	24	21	28	28	30	33	41
Close	15	16	18	22	22	26	30	37	37	37	38	39	36	36	31	31	34	27	29	31	35	35	46	43

Quick Fix

P/E range (past two years):	12 - 72
Earnings past four quarters:	$1.87 (through 9/30/96)
Projected 1997 earnings (median):	$1.93
International sales:	56% of net revenues
Total current assets:	$264.5 million (1996); $161.8 million (1995)
Total current liabilities:	$88.4 million (1996); $65.8 million (1995)
Net Income:	$123.3 million (1996); $38.9 million (1995)

Financial history

Fiscal year ended: June 30
(Revenue in millions)

	1992	1993	1994	1995	1996
Revenue	$86.9	$110.2	$153.9	$250.8	$421.6
Earnings per share	0.24	0.29	0.38	0.59	1.74
*Stock price: High	7.44	12.25	17.08	41.88	48.25
Low	4.81	6.13	10.88	14.13	20.63
Close	7.38	11.97	17.50	38.50	43.25

Stock prices (only) reflect calendar year.

20

Papa John's International, Inc.

11492 Bluegrass Parkway, Suite 175
Louisville, KY 40299
Phone: 502-266-5200; FAX: 502-266-2925

Chairman and CEO: John Schnatter
President: Blaine E. Hurst

When he was 23, John Schnatter was a very serious young man who had a knack for making people laugh—at him, not with him. "Vendors, bankers and even some friends just laughed when I told them I'd be opening five or six stores a month."

That was in 1984, the year Schnatter cleared out a broom closet and installed a pizza oven in his father's tavern in Jeffersonville, Indiana. That marked the humble beginning of Papa John's Pizza. By the end of the year, he was delivering 300 to 400 pizzas a week. Now the company has expanded to more than 1,000 Papa John's outlets in 24 states, and it opens another 20 to 25 stores per month. The last laugh is Schnatter's.

Most of the company's restaurants are operated by independent franchise owners. Papa John's charges a fee of $20,000 for new franchises, plus a royalty fee of 4 percent of sales once the business opens.

Papa John's is the fastest growing pizza delivery and carryout company in the nation. The company's focus has been on simplicity. Its menus are limited to a few core products—pizza, breadsticks, cheesesticks and soft drinks—available for delivery or carryout.

Papa John's restaurants, which range in size from about 1,200 to 1,500 square feet, typically stay open long from about 11 a.m. to 12:30 a.m. on weekdays, and until 1:30 a.m. on weekends.

The company is preparing for explosive continued expansion. It is opening a new distribution center in Arizona and Iowa, which gives the company production and distribution capacity to service about 2,400 restaurants.

Papa John's, which went public with its initial public stock offering 1993, has about 7,000 employees.

Late developments

The company acquired Nortex Pizza, which operates 18 Papa John's restaurants in the Dallas, Texas, area in late 1996.

Performance

Stock growth (past two years through 12/31/96): 164% (from $12.78 to $33.75).
Revenue growth (past two years through 9/30/96):141% (from $141 million to $338 million).
Earnings per share growth (past two years through 9/30/96): 136% (from $0.25 to $0.59).

50

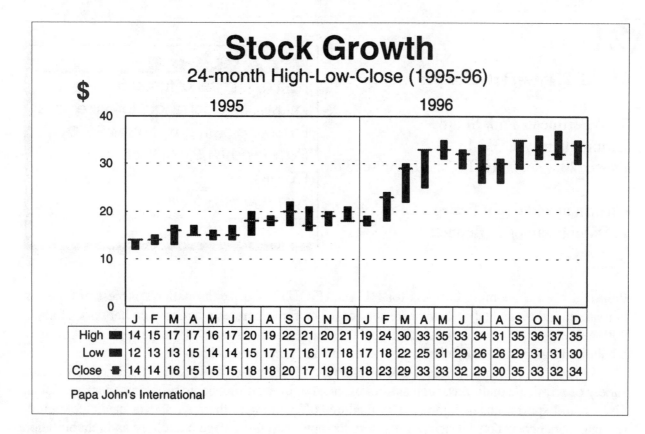

Stock Growth
24-month High-Low-Close (1995-96)

	1995												1996											
	J	F	M	A	M	J	J	A	S	O	N	D	J	F	M	A	M	J	J	A	S	O	N	D
High	14	15	17	17	16	17	20	19	22	21	20	21	19	24	30	33	35	33	34	31	35	36	37	35
Low	12	13	13	15	14	14	15	17	17	16	17	18	17	18	22	25	31	29	26	26	29	31	31	30
Close	14	14	16	15	15	15	18	18	20	17	19	18	18	23	29	33	33	32	29	30	35	33	32	34

Papa John's International

Quick Fix

P/E range (past two years):	27 - 50
Earnings past four quarters:	$0.59 (through 9/30/96)
Projected 1997 earnings (median):	$0.87
International sales:	NA
Total current assets:	$51.6 million (1996); $38.3 million (1995)
Total current liabilities:	$16.1 million (1996); $16.9 million (1995)
Net Income:	$11.2 million (1995); $7.2 million (1994)

Financial history

Fiscal year ended: Dec. 31
(Revenue in millions)

	1992	1993	1994	1995	*1996
Revenue	$49.6	$89.2	$161.5	$253.4	$257.1*
Earnings per share	0.13	0.20	0.31	0.45	0.45*
Stock price: High	NA	13.33	14.78	22.22	37.33
Low	NA	7.56	9.33	12.22	16.81
Close	NA	12.11	12.78	18.31	33.75

1996 revenue and earnings through Sept.30 (nine months).

21

HEALTHSOUTH Corp.

Two Perimeter Park South
Birmingham, AL 35243
Phone: 205-976-7116; FAX: 205-969-6837

Chairman and CEO: Richard Scrushy
President: James P. Bennett

Pain has been a booming business for HEALTHSOUTH Corp., the nation's largest provider of outpatient and rehabilitative healthcare services. The firm operates a nationwide network of about 900 centers in 45 states. HEALTHSOUTH delivers its services at outpatient and inpatient rehabilitation facilities, outpatient surgery centers and other medical centers.

The Birmingham, Alabama, operation's rehabilitation facilities provide treatment for a wide variety of physical conditions, such as strokes, head injuries, orthopaedic problems, neuromuscular disease and sports-related injuries. The facilities offer physical therapy, sports medicine, neuro-rehabilitation, occupational therapy, respiratory therapy, speech-language pathology and rehabilitation nursing.

HEALTHSOUTH has concentrated on delivering its core medical services at a much lower cost than traditional inpatient health centers, in part, by relying heavily on outpatient treatment. The company operates the largest network of free-standing outpatient surgery centers in the U.S.

Founded in 1984, HEALTHSOUTH has grown quickly through a series of acquisitions. The company's management plans to continue to expand both through additional acquisitions and through construction of new facilities.

Part of the company's success has been attributed to its integrated service model. When possible, the company provides all of its core services — outpatient and inpatient rehabilitation, ambulatory surgery and outpatient diagnostics — in each of its market areas.

Typically, the company establishes an outpatient center in a new market, either by acquiring an existing practice or through new construction, and then establishes specialized satellite clinics that rely on the staff of the main facility for management and administrative services. The company has more than 30,000 full- and part-time employees.

Late developments

HEALTHSOUTH made two major acquisitions in 1996. It acquired Surgical Care Affiliates, which operated 67 surgical centers, and Advantage Health Corp., which operated 150 health care facilities.

Performance

Stock growth (past two years through 10/1/96): 362 % (from $8.31 to $38.38).
Revenue growth (past two years through 9/30/96): 109% (from $1.1 billion to $2.2 billion).
Earnings per share growth (past two years through 9/30/96): 120% (from $0.59 to $1.30).

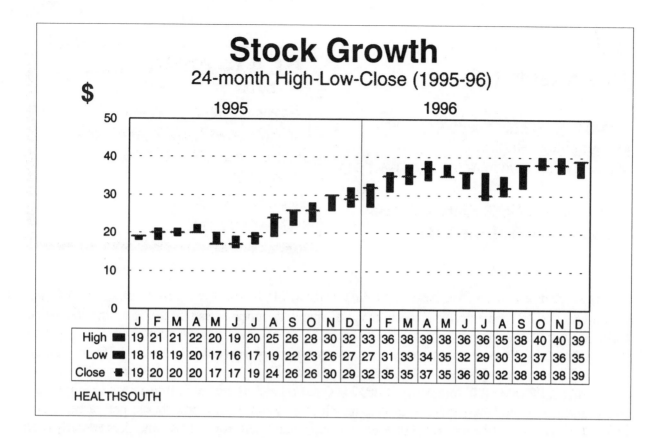

Stock Growth
24-month High-Low-Close (1995-96)

		J	F	M	A	M	J	J	A	S	O	N	D	J	F	M	A	M	J	J	A	S	O	N	D
High	■	19	21	21	22	20	19	20	25	26	28	30	32	33	36	38	39	38	36	36	35	38	40	40	39
Low	■	18	18	19	20	17	16	17	19	22	23	26	27	27	31	33	34	35	32	29	30	32	37	36	35
Close	✦	19	20	20	20	17	17	19	24	26	26	30	29	32	35	35	37	35	36	30	32	38	38	38	39

HEALTHSOUTH

Quick Fix

P/E range (past two years):	19 - 46
Earnings past four quarters:	$1.30 (through 9/30/96)
Projected 1997 earnings (median):	$1.82
International sales:	none
Total assets:	$3.1 billion (1996); $2.5 billion (1995)
Total current liabilities:	$315 million (1996); $236 million (1995)
Net Income:	$79.0 million (1995); $50.5 million (1994)

Financial history

Fiscal year ended: Dec. 31
(Revenue in millions)

	1992	1993	1994	1995	*1996
Revenue	$750.1	$979.3	$1,649.2	$2,003.1	$1,794*
Earnings per share	-0.06	0.22	0.59	0.94	1.30*
Stock price: High	18.63	13.19	19.69	32.38	39.75
Low	7.63	6.06	11.69	16.38	27.00
Close	13.19	12.63	18.50	29.13	38.63

1996 revenue and earnings through Sept.30 (nine months).

22

PETsMART, Inc.

10000 North 31st Avenue, C-100
Phoenix, AZ 85051
Phone: 602-944-7070; FAX: 602-395-6502

Chairman: Samuel Parker
President and CEO: Mark Hansen

PETsMART is yet another in the growing breed of specialty superstores that are storming the nation like a pack of Dalmatians.

The 26,000-square-foot stores offer everything a pet owner could want – from pooper-scoopers to grooming services – all at discount prices.

In all, PETsMART stores carry abut 12,000 pet-related items, including a broad range of pet foods and treats, collars, kennels, leashes, health aids, shampoos, medications, pet carriers, dog houses, cat furniture and equestrian supplies. The stores also sell tropical fish and domestically bred birds.

PETsMART operates more than 300 stores in 35 states. The Phoenix-based retailer's biggest concentration is in the West, including 42 stores in California, 13 in Arizona, 12 in Colorado, 30 in Texas and 11 in Washington. The company also has 22 stores in Illinois, 21 in Ohio, and 27 in Florida. PETsMART added about 50 new stores in 1996.

The company has built its business through three key strategies:

- *Low prices.* The company sells its products for about 10 to 30 percent below those offered by supermarkets and other pet food and pet supply outlets.
- *Knowledgeable staff.* PETsMART emphasizes training and personnel development to maintain a well-qualified, motivated sales staff.
- *Innovative programs and services.* The stores offer on-site professional grooming services, conduct periodic vaccination clinics and obedience classes, and sponsor in-store pet adoption programs.

PETsMART has about 12,000 employees. The company opened its first stores in 1987, and went public with its initial stock offering in 1993.

Late developments

PETsMART is moving into the European market with the acquisition in late 1996 of Pet City Holdings of the United Kingdom in a stock swap deal valued at about $214 million. Pet City had sales of more than $60 million in fiscal 1996, but lost about 4.5 cents per share.

Performance

Stock growth (past two years through 10/31/96): 119% (from $12.31 to $27.00).
Revenue growth (past two years through 10/31/96): 65% (from $818 million to $1.26 billion).
Earnings per share growth (past two years through 10/31/96): NA (from -$0.11 to $0.28).

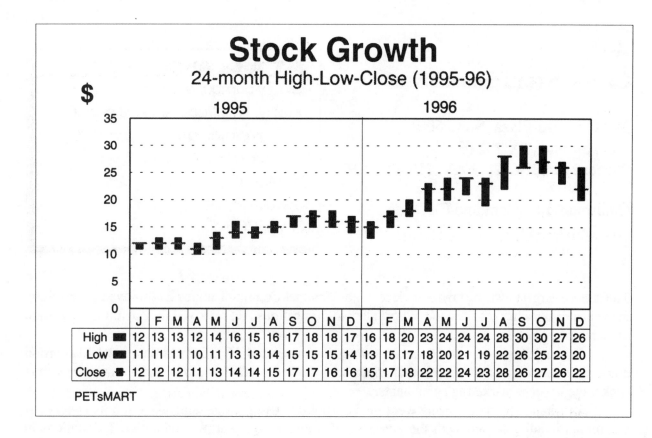

Stock Growth
24-month High-Low-Close (1995-96)

	J	F	M	A	M	J	J	A	S	O	N	D	J	F	M	A	M	J	J	A	S	O	N	D
High	12	13	13	12	14	16	15	16	17	18	18	17	16	18	20	23	24	24	24	28	30	30	27	26
Low	11	11	11	10	11	13	13	14	15	15	15	14	13	15	17	18	20	21	19	22	26	25	23	20
Close	12	12	12	11	13	14	14	15	17	17	16	16	15	17	18	22	22	24	23	28	26	27	26	22

PETsMART

Quick Fix

P/E range (past two years):	100+
Earnings past four quarters:	$0.19 (through 9/30/96)
Projected 1997 earnings (median):	$0.43
International sales:	None
Total current assets:	$336.1 million (1996); $262.8 million (1995)
Total current liabilities:	$197.6 million (1996); $135.2 million (1995)
Net Income:	$15 million {1996 (9 months)}; -$2.8 million (1995)

Financial history

Fiscal year ended: Jan. 31
(Revenue in millions)

	1992	1993	1994	1995	1996*
Revenue	$273.5	$484.1	$817.5	$1,030.7	$972*
Earnings per share	-0.01	-0.12	-0.11	-0.04	0.14*
**Stock price: High	NA	12.00	12.92	18.06	29.88
Low	NA	7.83	7.17	10.42	12.63
Close	NA	9.08	11.50	15.50	21.88

*1996 revenue and earnings through nine months (Oct. 31, 1996).
**Stock price (only) reflects calendar year.*

23

Clear Channel Communications

200 Concord Plaza, Suite 600
San Antonio, TX 78216
Phone: 210-822-2828; FAX: 210-822-2299

Chairman, President and CEO:
L. Lowry Mays

The nation's largest owner of radio stations, Clear Channel Communications has enjoyed clear sailing in the acquisitions market since the 1996 Telecommunications Act removed the cap on radio station ownership restrictions.

When 1996 began, the company owned and operated 36 radio stations and 10 television stations. It also operated seven other radio stations and six TV stations under time sales, time brokerage or local marketing agreements.

But in 1996, the company went on a corporate buying binge unparalleled in its history. It acquired 14 radio stations with the purchase of Radio Equity Partners, plus two TV stations in Providence, 16 radio stations from U.S. Radio, a radio station in Richmond, Virginia, two radio stations in Tulsa, three stations in Grand Rapids, Michigan, and two television stations in Harrisburg, Pennsylvania.

Clear Channel also bought controlling interest in the Heftel Broadcasting Corp., which operates 16 Spanish language radio stations in the U.S.

The San Antonio-based operation also recently entered the international market by acquiring a 50 percent share of the Australian Radio Network, which serves eight markets in Australia, and a one-third interest in Radio New Zealand, which owns 41 radio stations throughout New Zealand.

Most of the company's U.S. stations are located in the Southwest, the Midwest and the East. Its largest concentration is in its home state of Texas where it owns about 20 radio stations in San Antonio, Austin, Houston and El Paso.

The company was founded in 1972, and went public with its initial stock offering in 1984. The company has about 1,800 employees.

Late developments

Clear Channel completed the remainder of its acquisition of Radio Equity Partners (and its 14 radio stations) in late 1996, when the Federal Communications Commission granted a waiver on its "one-station-to-a-market" rule, allowing the company to own multiple stations in Providence and Memphis.

Performance

Stock growth (past two years through 12/31/96): 184% (from $12.69 to $36.13).
Revenue growth (past two years through 12/31/96): 91% (from $200.7 million to $383 million).
Earnings per share growth (past two years through 12/31/96): 59% (from $0.32 to $0.51).

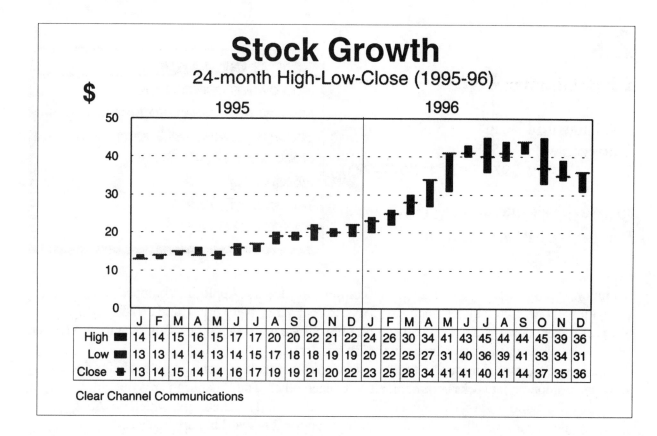

Stock Growth
24-month High-Low-Close (1995-96)

	J	F	M	A	M	J	J	A	S	O	N	D	J	F	M	A	M	J	J	A	S	O	N	D
High	14	14	15	16	15	17	17	20	20	22	21	22	24	26	30	34	41	43	45	44	44	45	39	36
Low	13	13	14	14	13	14	15	17	18	18	19	19	20	22	25	27	31	40	36	39	41	33	34	31
Close	13	14	15	14	14	16	17	19	19	21	20	22	23	25	28	34	41	41	40	41	44	37	35	36

Clear Channel Communications

Quick Fix

P/E range (past two years):	27 - 90
Earnings past four quarters:	$0.51 (through 1996)
Projected 1997 earnings (median):	$0.83
International sales:	Less than 10%
Total current assets:	$96.6 million (1996); $70.5 million (1995)
Total current liabilities:	$733.8 million (1996); $399.3 million (1995)
Net Income:	$37.7 million (1996); $32.0 million (1995)

Financial history

Fiscal year ended: Dec. 31
(Revenue in millions)

	1992	1993	1994	1995	1996
Revenue	$94.5	$135.7	$200.7	$283.4	$383.1
Earnings per share	0.07	0.15	0.32	0.46	0.51
Stock price: High	3.62	9.23	13.00	22.13	45.25
Low	1.73	3.24	7.85	12.53	20.38
Close	3.26	9.20	12.69	22.06	36.13

24

Fore Systems, Inc.

174 Thorn Hill Road
Warrendale, PA 15086
Phone: 412-772-6600; FAX: 412-772-6500

Chairman and CEO: Eric C. Cooper
President: Onat Menzilcioglu

Communications – its been a problem for computers since the Apple first bumped up against the IBM-PC. New technologies such as LANs (Local Area Networks) and WANs (Wide Area Networks) were developed to help computers communicate with each other. But even the LANs and WANs have encountered some incompatibility problems.

Fore Systems has made a fast fortune developing networking technology that helps computers and even computer networks communicate with each other. The Pittsburgh area operation designs its products around the Asynchronous Transfer Mode (ATM) technology, which provides greater speed, capacity and overall performance than conventional networking applications.

Fore's ability to effectively link the computer family together has made it one of the nation's fastest growing companies. Founded in 1990 by four Carnegie Mellon researchers, Fore's revenues have grown from $2 million to $235 million in the past five years.

Fore's line of ATM networking products are capable of integrating video, audio and data communications. ATM technology divides data into small, fixed-sized cells rather than the larger variable-size "packets" used in conventional network technologies. Text images, data files, digitized images and continuous streams of video and audio are all converted into cells for transmission and reassembled at their destinations by ATM adapter cards.

Each ATM switch is capable of maintaining thousands of connections between pairs of senders and receivers, enabling many users to transmit data in the network simultaneously.

Fore System's leading products include ForeRunner ATM switches and adapter cards, PowerHub LAN switches, CellPath WAN multiplexing products, ForeThought internetworking software and ForeView network management software.

Late developments

In late 1996, Fore reached an agreement to license its ForeThought software to Microsoft Corp. for integration into future versions of Microsoft's Windows. The company also reached agreements to provide ATM networks for Westinghouse Communications, the World Health Organization in Geneva and the French National Library.

Performance

Stock growth (past two years through 10/1/96): 272% (from $11.13 to $41.38).
Revenue growth (past two years through 9/30/96): 470% (from $56.3 million to $321 million).
Earnings per share growth (past two years through 9/30/96): 118% (from $0.11 to $0.24).

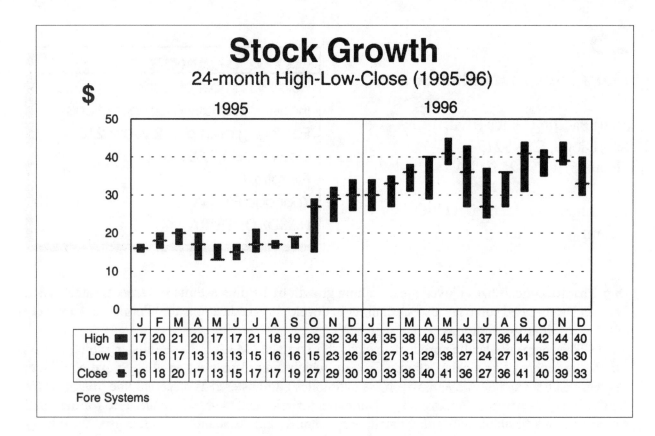

Stock Growth
24-month High-Low-Close (1995-96)

$

	J	F	M	A	M	J	J	A	S	O	N	D	J	F	M	A	M	J	J	A	S	O	N	D
High ■	17	20	21	20	17	17	21	18	19	29	32	34	34	35	38	40	45	43	37	36	44	42	44	40
Low ■	15	16	17	13	13	13	15	16	16	15	23	26	26	27	31	29	38	27	24	27	31	35	38	30
Close ✦	16	18	20	17	13	15	17	17	19	27	29	30	30	33	36	40	41	36	27	36	41	40	39	33

Fore Systems

Quick Fix

P/E range (past two years):	100+
Earnings past four quarters:	$0.24 (through 9/30/96)
Projected 1997 earnings (median):	$0.56
International sales:	39% of sales (Asia/Pacific, 20%; Europe, 20%; other, 6%)
Total assets:	$424 million (1996); $132 million (1995)
Total current liabilities:	$88.4 million (1996); $33.8 million (1995)
Net Income:	$9.7 million (1996); $12.9 million (1995)

Financial history

Fiscal year ended: March 31
(Revenue in millions)

	1992	1993	1994	1995	1996
Revenue	$2.0	$ 12.5	$39.3	$106.2	$235.2
Earnings per share	NA	NA	0.06	0.18	0.36**
*Stock price: High	NA	NA	17.88	33.88	44.75
Low	NA	NA	5.00	12.75	23.38
Close	NA	NA	16.88	29.75	32.88

Stock price (only) reflects calendar year
**1996 earnings per share excludes expenses of $0.25 in merger-related costs. Including those costs, earnings would have been $0.11 per share.*

25

Dura Pharmaceuticals, Inc.

5880 Pacific Center Blvd.
San Diego, CA 92121
Phone: 619-457-2553; FAX: 619-457-2555

Chairman, President and CEO:
  Cam L. Garner

Dura Pharmaceuticals has enjoyed breath-taking growth by helping asthma sufferers breathe easier. The San Diego-based company also specializes in developing medications for allergies and a variety of other respiratory conditions.

The company's leading products include the Tornalate Metered Dose Inhaler, which is used for the treatment of bronchial asthma; Crolom, which is used to treat an allergic eye condition; Capastat Sulfate and Seromycin, which are antibiotics administered as a second line treatment for "multiple drug resistant tuberculosis; Uni-Dur extended release tablets, which are used for the relief and prevention of asthma and some bronchitis symptoms; and Furadantin, which is used for urinary tract infections.

Other leading medications include the D.A. Chewable, Dura-Vent and Dura-Gest products used for treatment of allergies, sinusitis, colds and other respiratory problems; and Rondec oral drops, syrup and tablets, which are used for treatment of coughs and other cold symptoms.

Dura's largest project under development is the Spiros dry powder pulmonary drug delivery system, which aerosolizes pharmaceuticals in dry powder for propellant-free delivery to the lungs and nasal passages. The product is being developed through a separate corporation recently formed by Dura. The Spiros Development Corp. has been set up through a $41 million financing plan including $13 million from Dura and $28 million in private placement funding.

Dura anticipates substantial future returns from the Spiros system by using a three-tiered marketing strategy. First it will develop the system for use with several of its current respiratory drugs; next, it will license the system for use with new respiratory products being developed by other companies, and finally it will begin using the Spiros system for the delivery of non-respiratory drugs such as proteins and peptides.

Late developments

Dura has acquired the exclusive U.S. marketing rights from Eli Lilly for the antibiotics Keftab and Ceclor CD. Cost was about $100 million. The company expects the two drugs to generate annual sales of about $100 million by the year 2000. Dura also acquired the Entex product line from Procter & Gamble. The Entex line includes four prescription drugs for coughs, colds and sinusitis.

Performance

Stock growth (past two years through 12/31/96): 516% (from $7.25 to $47.75).
Revenue growth (past two years through 12/31/96): 343% (from $23.5 million to $104 million).
Earnings per share growth (past two years through 12/31/96): 210% (from $0.19 to $0.59).

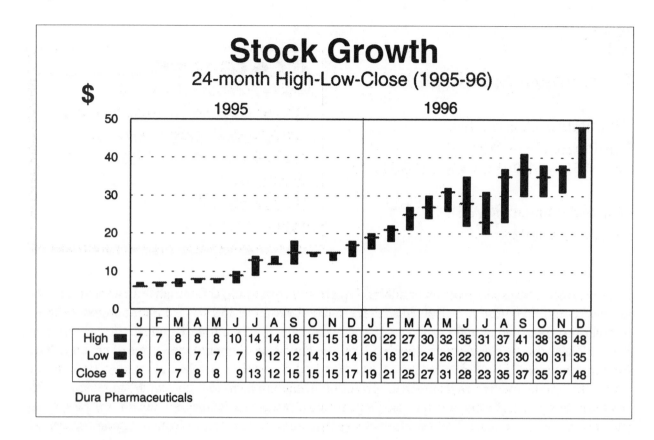

Stock Growth
24-month High-Low-Close (1995-96)

	J	F	M	A	M	J	J	A	S	O	N	D	J	F	M	A	M	J	J	A	S	O	N	D
High	7	7	8	8	8	10	14	14	18	15	15	18	20	22	27	30	32	35	31	37	41	38	38	48
Low	6	6	6	7	7	7	9	12	12	14	13	14	16	18	21	24	26	22	20	23	30	30	31	35
Close	6	7	7	8	8	9	13	12	15	15	15	17	19	21	25	27	31	28	23	35	37	35	37	48

Dura Pharmaceuticals

Quick Fix

P/E range (past two years):	32 - 75
Earnings past four quarters:	$0.59 (through 1996)
Projected 1997 earnings (median):	$0.87
International sales:	None
Total current assets:	$111.4 million (1996); $78.4 million (1995)
Total current liabilities:	$44.9 million (1996); $18.7 million (1995)
Net Income:	$24.3 million (1996); -$35.8 million (1995)

Financial history

Fiscal year ended: Dec. 31
(Revenue in millions)

	1992	1993	1994	1995	1996
Revenue	$9.6	$15.8	$23.5	$43.5	$104.1
Earnings per share	- 0.93	-1.09	0.19	0.55*	0.59
Stock price: High	6.63	3.88	7.25	17.75	47.88
Low	2.38	2.00	3.13	5.75	16.38
Close	3.63	3.63	7.25	17.38	47.75

1995 earnings per share does not include a charge for acquisition expenses of $3.60 per share.

26

CUC International, Inc.

707 Summer Street
Stamford, CT 06901
Phone: 203-324-9261; FAX: 203-348-4528

Chairman and CEO: Walter A. Forbes

Cost-conscious consumers have been flocking by the millions to CUC International, a membership-based discount operation that deals in a broad range of products and services from automobiles to airline tickets. Founded in 1973 as Comp-U-Card America, the Stamford, Connecticut, operation is finally catching fire with consumers. Nearly 50 million consumers are enrolled in one of several CUC discount programs.

The company derives its revenues primarily from membership fees, which range from $6 to $250 per year (depending on the specific program). CUC markets its memberships through special promotions arranged with fund raisers, financial institutions, retailers, credit card companies, oil companies, credit unions, on-line networks, associations and other organizations that receive a commission of about 20 percent of the initial and renewal membership fees.

CUC also sells memberships through direct marketing and, to a growing extent, through an aggressive sales program on the Internet.

One of the company's leading programs is Shoppers Advantage, a discount shopping program that steers members to the lowest priced products available. Consumers may choose from about 250,000 brand name products. CUC shopping consultants check their database to find the lowest price available through their network of manufacturers, distributors and retailers, then place the order for members. The low-priced supplier fills the order, delivering the product directly to the member. CUC simply acts as a conduit between its members and the vendors. As a result, CUC does not have to maintain an inventory of products.

Other leading programs offered by CUC include Travelers Advantage, a discount travel service that provides discounts on airline tickets, hotel rooms, rental cars, cruises and travel packages; AutoVantage, which offers the lowest possible prices on automobiles, tires and other parts; and Premier Dining, which offers two-for-one deals at about 19,000 restaurants. Other CUC programs include PrivacyGuard, Buyers Advantage, HealthSaver and Credit Card Guardian.

Late developments

CUC recently reached an agreement with Microsoft Corp. to make CUC's Entertainment Publications division the sales arm for local advertisements for Microsoft's Cityscape city entertainment guides.

Performance

Stock growth (past two years through 12/31/96): 63% (from $14.75 to $24.00).
Revenue growth (past two years through 10/31/96): 81% (from $1.1 billion to $2 billion).
Earnings per share growth (past two years through 10/31/96): NA (from $0.41 to $0.35).

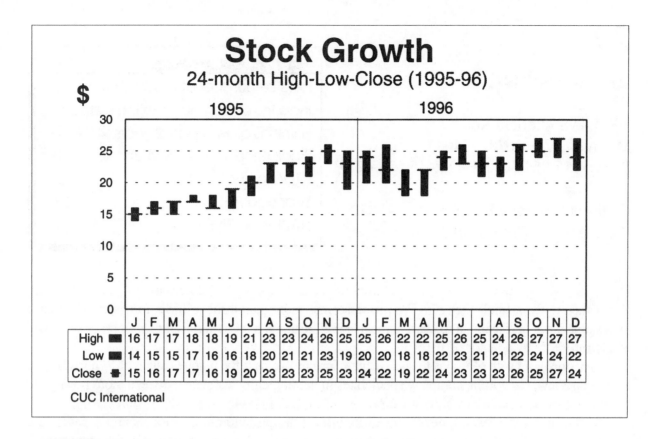

Stock Growth
24-month High-Low-Close (1995-96)

	1995												1996											
	J	F	M	A	M	J	J	A	S	O	N	D	J	F	M	A	M	J	J	A	S	O	N	D
High	16	17	17	18	18	19	21	23	23	24	26	25	25	26	22	22	25	26	25	24	26	27	27	27
Low	14	15	15	17	16	16	18	20	21	21	23	19	20	20	18	18	22	23	21	21	22	24	24	22
Close	15	16	17	17	16	19	20	23	23	23	25	23	24	22	19	22	24	23	23	23	26	25	27	24

CUC International

Quick Fix

P/E range (past two years):	25 - 66
Earnings past four quarters:	$0.66 (through 10/31/96)
Projected 1997 earnings (median):	$0.70
International sales:	1% of total sales
Total assets:	$977.5 million (7/31/96); $937.8 million (1/31/96)
Total current liabilities:	$152.5 million (7/31/96); $218.6 million (1/31/96)
Net Income:	$1.63 billion (1996); $1.24 billion (1995)

Financial history

Fiscal year ended: Jan. 31
(Revenue in millions)

	1992	1993	1994	1995	1996	1997*
Revenue	$644.2	$742.3	$984.8	$1,183	$1,705	$1,673*
Earnings per share	0.11	0.25	0.34	0.44	0.56	0.20*
**Stock price: High	8.59	17.67	15.94	40.63	27.13	NA
Low	5.11	7.37	11.00	4.94	18.15	NA
Close	8.59	16.00	14.75	22.50	24.00	NA

1997 revenue and earnings figures through nine months (10/31/96).
** Stock prices (only) reflect calendar year.*

27

Synopsys, Inc.

700 E. Middlefield Road
Mountain View, CA   94043
Phone: 415-962-5000; FAX: 415-694-4249

Chairman: Harvey Jones
President and CEO: Aart J. de Geus

Here's the problem: Intel's Pentium Pro processor has more than three million transistors integrated on a single piece of silicon—a modern miracle in itself. But the next generation of processor will need to multiply that by a factor of 10!

Coming up with solutions to such mega-micro problems is the unique calling of Synopsys. The Mountain View, California, company specializes in helping chip designers squeeze more power and more components into a tiny silicon wafer.

Synopsys is a leading developer of high-level design automation models and software for designers of integrated circuits and electronic systems. The firm pioneered the commercial development of logic synthesis and test synthesis technology.

The company's software is used to create integrated circuits and other complex electrical systems. It also makes software to test integrated circuit designs prior to actual production. The company also has a library of more than 13,000 different component models which chip makers can use to dramatically reduce design time.

One of the company's leading products is the Behavioral Compiler, a high-level synthesis tool that enables chip designers to test and create chip designs much more quickly than was previously possible.

Synopsys provides software and assistance to many of the world's largest computer manufacturers, such as Hewlett-Packard, Fujitsu, Cirrus Logic and Motorola. Synopsys recently signed a six year agreement with IBM to work together to develop new processes for designing integrated circuits.

Synopsys was founded in 1986 by Aart de Geus, who still serves as company president and CEO. The company went public in 1992 with its initial stock offering.

Late developments

The company introduced a broad variety of new products in late 1996, including its first version of the Windows '95 and Windows NT-based synthesis tool, FPGA Express. Other new products included the Arkos system simulation accelerator, and the Cyclone cycle-based simulator.

Performance

Stock growth (past two years through 12/31/96): 111% (from $21.88 to $46.25).
Revenue growth (past two years through 9/30/96): 77% (from $199.2 million to $353.5 million).
Earnings per share growth (past two years through 9/30/96): 46% (from $0.37 to $0.54).

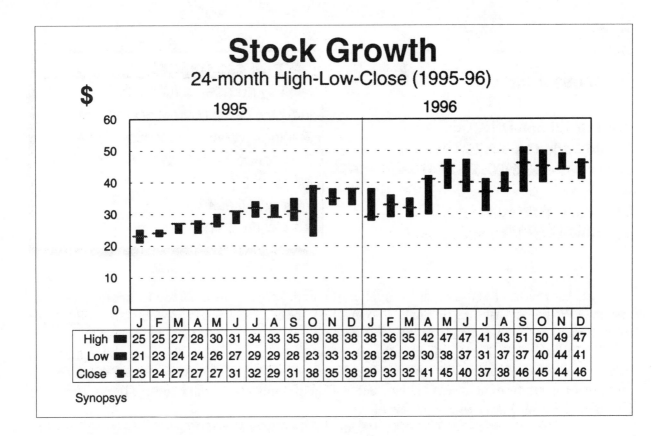

Stock Growth
24-month High-Low-Close (1995-96)

$				1995											1996									
	J	F	M	A	M	J	J	A	S	O	N	D	J	F	M	A	M	J	J	A	S	O	N	D
High	25	25	27	28	30	31	34	33	35	39	38	38	38	36	35	42	47	47	41	43	51	50	49	47
Low	21	23	24	24	26	27	29	29	28	23	33	33	28	29	29	30	38	37	31	37	37	40	44	41
Close	23	24	27	27	27	31	32	29	31	38	35	38	29	33	32	41	45	40	37	38	46	45	44	46

Synopsys

Quick Fix

P/E range (past two years):	29 - 90
Earnings past four quarters:	$0.54 (through 9/30/96)
Projected 1997 earnings (median):	$1.54
International sales:	37 percent of total sales (Asia/Pacific, 23%; Europe, 14%)
Total current assets:	$304 million (1996); $244 million (1995)
Total current liabilities:	$150 million (1996); $110 million (1995)
Net Income:	$24 million (1996); $30 million (1995)

Financial history

Fiscal year ended: Sept. 30
(Revenue in millions)

	1992	1993	1994	1995	1996
Revenue	$91.7	$142.7	$199.2	$265.5	$353.5
Earnings per share	0.13	0.41	0.36	0.75	0.54
*Stock price: High	17.75	26.38	24.38	38.50	50.50
Low	11.13	12.88	16.50	21.38	27.50
Close	17.31	22.63	21.88	38.00	46.25

Stock prices (only) reflect calendar year.

28

Informix Corp.

4100 Bohannon Drive
Menlo Park, CA 94025
Phone: 415-926-6300; FAX: 415-926-6564

Chairman, President and CEO:
  Phillip E. White

Informix characterizes its business as "a supplier of parallel processing database technology for open systems." What does that mean in English? Translation: the company makes products that help people use and manage the information in their computers.

For instance, Informix sells a new product called a "data warehouse" that organizes and stores data from a variety of sources. The product is used primarily by retail chains to evaluate the inventory and sales figures from hundreds or thousands of their stores across the country. It even provides information on who buys what and how often.

Another new product Informix is developing (along with MobileWare Corp.) is a device that will allow users to tap into their computer databases wirelessly from remote locations.

The firm is also developing "smart cards" that can be inserted into computers to perform a variety of functions.

Informix breaks its product line into four segments:

● *Database engines*, such as the Informix-Online, which provides on-line transaction processing;

● *Database tools,* such as the Informix-New Era, which is used to create multi-tier client/server database applications, and Informix-MetaCube, an on-line analytical processing engine that automatically consolidates data and provides a multi-dimensional view of data;

● *Connectivity products,* such as the Informix-Gateway that enables applications built with Informix application development tools to access and modify information in other systems;

●*Object-relational products,* such as the Illustra Server, a database management system used to store, manage and analyze complex data such as audio, video and image files.

The Menlo Park, California, operation was incorporated in 1980.

Late developments

Informix acquired Illustra Information Technologies for about $350 million in 1996. The company reported that its tools sector sales are slowing down, but other business sectors such as its database products have more than made up for the decline in tools sales.

Performance

Stock growth (past two years through 12/31/96): 27% (from $16.06 to $20.38).
Revenue growth (past two years through 12/31/96):100% (from $469 million to $939 million).
Earnings per share growth (past two years through 12/31/96): 29% (from $0.49 to $0.63).

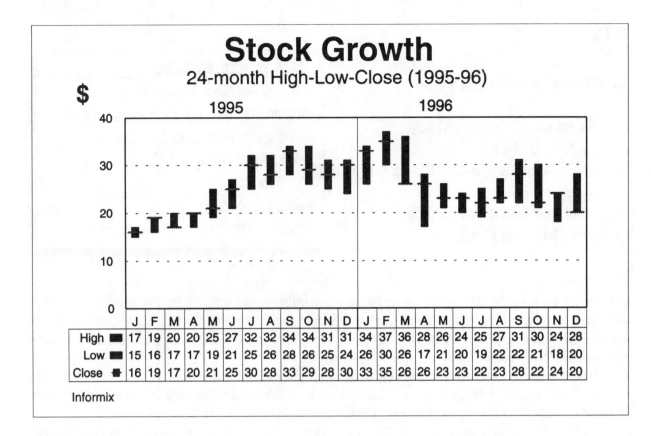

Stock Growth
24-month High-Low-Close (1995-96)

		1995												1996											
		J	F	M	A	M	J	J	A	S	O	N	D	J	F	M	A	M	J	J	A	S	O	N	D
High		17	19	20	20	25	27	32	32	34	34	31	31	34	37	36	28	26	24	25	27	31	30	24	28
Low		15	16	17	17	19	21	25	26	28	26	25	24	26	30	26	17	21	20	19	22	22	21	18	20
Close		16	19	17	20	21	25	30	28	33	29	28	30	33	35	26	26	23	23	22	23	28	22	24	20

Informix

Quick Fix

P/E range (past two years):	19 - 58
Earnings past four quarters:	$0.63 (through 12/31/96)
Projected 1997 earnings (median):	$1.03
International sales:	Europe, 31%; Asia/Pacific, 10%; other, 4%.
Total assets:	$674.4 million (1995); $444.4 million (1994)
Total current liabilities:	$225.6 million (1995); $153.5 million (1994)
Net Income:	$105.3 million (1995); $66.2 million (1994)

Financial history

Fiscal year ended: Dec. 31
(Revenue in millions)

	1992	1993	1994	1995	1996
Revenue	$283.6	$352.9	$468.7	$709.0	$939.3
Earnings per share	0.38	0.42	0.49	0.76	0.63
Stock price: High	9.44	13.63	16.06	34.38	36.75
Low	1.66	6.69	7.13	14.56	16.88
Close	9.06	10.63	16.06	30.00	20.38

29

America Online, Inc.

8619 Westwood Center Drive
Vienna, VA 22182
Phone: 703-448-8700; FAX: 703-883-1532

Chairman and CEO: Stephen Case
President: Michael Connors

America Online is the world's largest computer on-line information service, but, depending on which stock market analyst you're listening to, it is also either (A) the wave of the future still in its infancy, or (B) a mature company that stands to lose market share in the future as more Internet services compete for online customers.

Future projections aside, however, there is no questioning the company's success to date in the online information frontier. With a subscriber base of more than 6 million members, AOL is far ahead of its closest competitors, Prodigy, CompuServe and Microsoft Network.

For a monthly fee ranging from $9.95 to $19.95, AOL members receive access to a variety of information and services, including breaking news, business and financial news, stock quotes, investment research, sports news, e-mail, Internet access, electronic magazines and newspapers, travel features and weather reports, online classes and conferences, an online encyclopedia and a variety of children's games and information features.

The Virginia-based operation has begun to expand its service beyond the U.S., offering online access to customers in Canada, Europe and Japan.

AOL was launched in 1989 as an outgrowth of a much smaller service called Q-Link that was started in 1985. Once AOL was launched, the company began marketing heavily to computer users throughout the U.S. It continues its aggressive marketing campaign with national television ads and mass mailings to computer owners.

The company went public with its initial stock offering in 1992. AOL has about 6,000 employees.

Late developments

AOL launched its new AOL Computing Superstore in late 1996 that offers members various personalized shopping services, including hardware, software and accessories. The company also began offering an unlimited AOL usage package to subscribers for $19.95 per month. The new program caused severe overloading of the system, making it difficult for members to access the service during prime hours. To solve the problem, the company initiated a major capacity upgrading project in early 1997 at a cost of several hundred million dollars.

Performance

Stock growth (past two years through 12/31/96): 143% (from $13.63 to $33.13).
Revenue growth (past two years through 12/31/96): 584% (from $205.4 million to $1.4 billion).
Earnings per share growth (past two years through 12/31/96): NA (from - $0.55 to -$5.21).

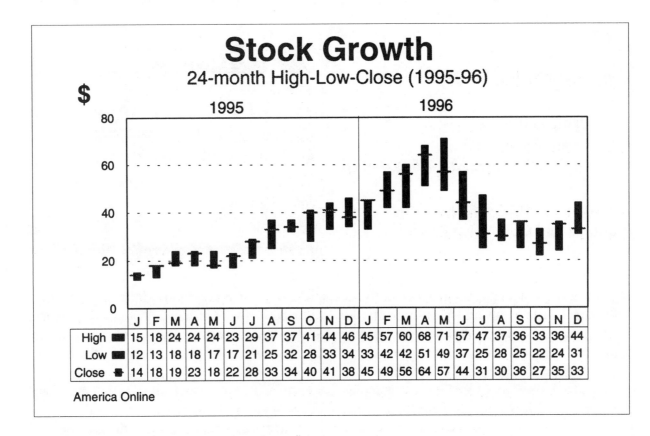

Stock Growth
24-month High-Low-Close (1995-96)

		J	F	M	A	M	J	J	A	S	O	N	D	J	F	M	A	M	J	J	A	S	O	N	D
High	■	15	18	24	24	24	23	29	37	37	41	44	46	45	57	60	68	71	57	47	37	36	33	36	44
Low	■	12	13	18	18	17	17	21	25	32	28	33	34	33	42	42	51	49	37	25	28	25	22	24	31
Close	●	14	18	19	23	18	22	28	33	34	40	41	38	45	49	56	64	57	44	31	30	36	27	35	33

America Online

Quick Fix

P/E range (past two years):	81 - 257
Earnings past four quarters:	-$5.21 (through 12/31/96)
Projected 1997 earnings (median):	$0.96
International sales:	AOL has just entered the international market
Total current assets:	$254.7 million (1996); $133.6 million (1995)
Total current liabilities:	$307.4 million (1996); $133.4 million (1995)
Net Income:	$29.8 million (1996); (-$35.7) million (1995)

Financial history

Fiscal year ended: June 30
(Revenue in millions)

	1992	1993	1994	1995	1996
Revenue	$38.7	$52.0	$115.7	$394.3	$1,093.8
Earnings per share	0.08	0.02	0.03	-0.52	0.23
*Stock price: High	3.66	8.75	14.63	46.25	71.00
Low	1.34	2.22	5.97	12.31	22.38
Close	3.66	7.31	14.00	37.50	33.13

Stock prices (only) reflect calendar year.

69

30

Electronics for Imaging, Inc.

2855 Campus Drive
San Mateo, CA 94403
Phone: 415-286-8600: FAX: 415-286-8686

Chairman: Efraim Arazi
President and CEO: Dan Avida

AT A GLANCE

Held by number of funds: 4
Industry: Computer color imaging
Earnings growth past 2 years: 164%
Stock price 1/1/97: $82.25
P/E ratio: 36
Year ago P/E: 31
NASDAQ: EFII

The world is becoming a much more colorful place thanks to some new innovations by Electronics for Imaging. The company makes computer hardware and software products that enable personal computer users to print high quality color copies quickly and inexpensively. Its systems link personal computers with color laser printers and copy machines, eliminating the need to use the costlier commercial printers for small color print runs.

The firm's *Fiery* Color Servers incorporate hardware and software technologies that transform digital color copiers from all leading copier manufacturers into fast, high-quality networked color printers. The servers are fully scalable to handle printing needs at both the low and the high ends of the color printing market.

Electronics for Imaging (EFI) has mapped out a three-part strategic plan to further penetrate the color printing market:

• *Proliferate and expand the Fiery Color Server product line.* The company continues to introduce new products intended to broaden its revenue base, such as its family of Fiery XJ color servers which can drive a wide range of output devices from basic desktop color laser printers to high speed color copiers and printers capable of printing 40 or more pages per minute.

• *Develop additional relationships with key industry participants.* The company is establishing strategic relationships with major copy machine manufacturers who can incorporate EFI's Fiery Color Server technology into their products. The company already has relationships with Canon, Xerox, Kodak, Minolta, Ricoh and Oce.

• *Leverage its color expertise.* Through continued research and development, EFI hopes to expand the scope and sophistication of its products and gain access to new markets.

The San Mateo, California, operation markets its products worldwide, with 43 percent of its total revenue generated outside the U.S.—primarily in Europe and Japan. Founded in 1989, EFI has about 330 employees.

Late developments

In 1996, the company completed production of a Fiery Color Server to drive the Xerox 40-page-per-minute color copier, and IBM selected the Fiery controller for its desktop color laser printer.

Performance

Stock growth (past two years through 12/31/96): 498% (from $13.75 to $82.25).
Revenue growth (past two years through 12/31/96): 129% (from $130 million to $298 million).
Earnings per share growth (past two years through 12/31/96): 164% (from $0.86 to $2.27).

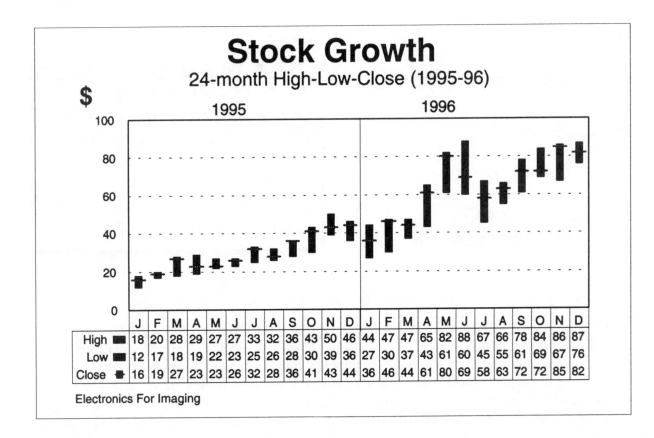

Stock Growth
24-month High-Low-Close (1995-96)

	1995												1996											
	J	F	M	A	M	J	J	A	S	O	N	D	J	F	M	A	M	J	J	A	S	O	N	D
High	18	20	28	29	27	27	33	32	36	43	50	46	44	47	47	65	82	88	67	66	78	84	86	87
Low	12	17	18	19	22	23	25	26	28	30	39	36	27	30	37	43	61	60	45	55	61	69	67	76
Close	16	19	27	23	23	26	32	28	36	41	43	44	36	46	44	61	80	69	58	63	72	72	85	82

Electronics For Imaging

Quick Fix

P/E range (past two years):	9 - 40
Earnings past four quarters:	$2.27 (through 12/31/96)
Projected 1997 earnings (median):	$2.96
International sales:	48% of total sales
Total current assets:	$250.3 million (1996); $187.6 million (1995)
Total current liabilities:	$51.5 million (1996); $30.5 million (1995)
Net Income:	$62.2 million (1996); $37.5 million (1995)

Financial history

Fiscal year ended: Dec. 31
(Revenue in millions)

	1992	1993	1994	1995	1996
Revenue	$53.7	$89.5	$130.4	$190.4	$298
Earnings per share	0.37	0.52	0.86	1.41	2.27
Stock price: High	11.88	11.25	14.75	50.13	88.25
Low	6.88	7.00	6.63	12.00	26.75
Close	9.88	8.25	13.75	43.75	82.25

31

Cambridge Technology Partners

304 Vassar Street
Cambridge, MA 02139
Phone: 617-374-9800; FAX: 617-374-8300

Chairman: Warren Musser
President and CEO: James Sims

In this age of rapidly evolving office technology, corporations sometimes need a guide to usher them through the maze of chips, bytes and baud rates. Cambridge Technology Partners (CTP) specializes in helping companies set up new office computer systems designed to bring them up to speed.

CTP consultants meet with company managers to map out their needs, and then develop software applications (either custom software or third party package software) specifically designed to meet those needs. CTP consultants also train their corporate clients to effectively operate their new systems. CTP collects fees of up to $3 million for the custom software and systems they design and develop for their clients.

A key emphasis for CTP is its policy of fixed prices and fixed timetables. The cost and timetable are determined before CTP enters the design and development stage. Typically, the company tries to complete all of its projects within nine months.

The Cambridge, Massachusetts, company operates sales offices in Atlanta, Dallas, Detroit, Seattle, Chicago, Los Angeles, Miami, New York, San Francisco and Lansing, Michigan. It also has sales offices in Germany, Ireland, Norway, England, the Netherlands and Sweden. About 22 percent of CTP's total revenue is generated in Europe.

CTP's "Business Renewal" proprietary methodology is used to evaluate strategic business changes encompassing all dimensions of the client's operations, including process, organizational structure, technology and personnel.

The firm markets its expertise to companies in a wide variety of industries, as well as to governmental organizations that require extensive information processing.

CTP, which went public with its initial stock offering in 1993, has about 1,100 employees.

Late developments

The company recently acquired Ramos & Associates, a strategic information solutions consulting firm based in San Ramon, California. CTP also recently opened a new office in Brazil, giving the firm a foothold in the Latin American market.

Performance

Stock growth (past two years through 12/31/96): 351% (from $7.44 to $33.56).
Revenue growth (past two years through 9/30/96): 164% (from $68.2 million to $180 million).
Earnings per share growth (past two years through 9/30/96): 127% (from $0.15 to $0.34).

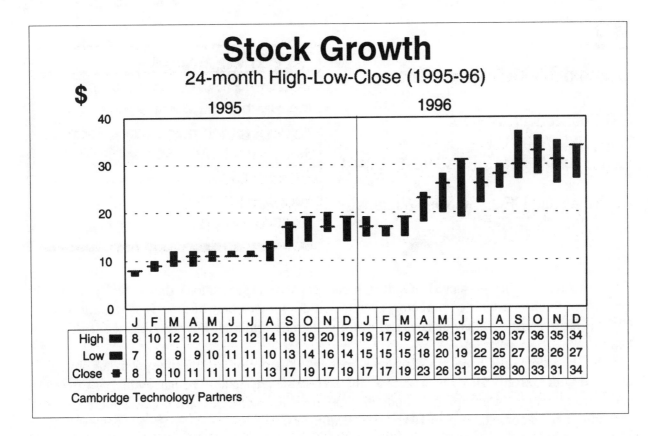

Stock Growth
24-month High-Low-Close (1995-96)

Cambridge Technology Partners

		J	F	M	A	M	J	J	A	S	O	N	D	J	F	M	A	M	J	J	A	S	O	N	D
High		8	10	12	12	12	12	12	14	18	19	20	19	19	17	19	24	28	31	29	30	37	36	35	34
Low		7	8	9	9	10	11	11	10	13	14	16	14	15	15	15	18	20	19	22	25	27	28	26	27
Close		8	9	10	11	11	11	11	13	17	19	17	19	17	17	19	23	26	31	26	28	30	33	31	34

Quick Fix

P/E range (past two years):	28 - 99
Earnings past four quarters:	$0.38 (through 12/31/96)
Projected 1997 earnings (median):	$0.57
International sales:	22% of total sales (Europe)
Total current assets:	$90.8 million (9/30/96); $54.2 million (1995)
Total current liabilities:	$38 million (9/30/96); $20.8 million (1995)
Net Income:	$20.1 million (1996); $12.7 million (1995)

Financial history

Fiscal year ended: Dec. 31
(Revenue in millions)

	1992	1993	1994	1995	1996
Revenue	$32.1	$50.0	$83.5	$132.4	$211
Earnings per share	0.05	0.11	0.16	0.25	0.38
Stock price: High	NA	5.92	7.92	20.33	37.25
Low	NA	3.08	4.67	7.08	14.63
Close	NA	5.25	7.42	19.17	33.56

32

Oxford Health Plans, Inc.

800 Connecticut Avenue
Norwalk, CT 06854
Phone: 203-852-1442; FAX: 203-851-2464

Chairman and CEO: Stephen Wiggins

Here's a unique concept—an HMO (health maintenance organization) that actually allows its customers to choose their own doctor, even if that doctor isn't part of their HMO. Little wonder Oxford Health Plans is making money hand over fist. Perhaps other HMOs could learn a lesson from Oxford.

The company's Freedom Plan gives members the option at any time of using physicians affiliated with Oxford's HMO plan or choosing an outside physician. The plan, which is offered by about 22,000 employer groups, has about 700,000 members. Most of Oxford's customers are small to medium-sized companies with 10 to 1,500 employees.

The Norwalk, Connecticut, HMO has operations in its home state as well as in New York, New Hampshire, New Jersey and Pennsylvania. The company has been expanding steadily through strategic acquisitions.

In addition to its Freedom Plan, Oxford offers a "Liberty Plan" that costs 12 percent less, but gives members fewer options in selecting medical care providers.

For members eligible for Medicare or Medicaid, the company has an "Oxford Medicare Advantage" plan and a "Medicaid Healthy Start" plan that addresses their medical needs.

The company also offers a self-funded health plan to employers who prefer to pay for claims only as they are incurred. Oxford provides the claims processing and health care cost containment services for companies enrolled in the plan.

The firm also has a dental plan that includes a network of more than 1,200 private dentists.

Oxford was founded in 1984 by Stephen F. Wiggins, who continues to serve as chairman and CEO. The company has about 4,000 employees.

Late developments

In February, 1997, Oxford reached a ground-breaking and controversial agreement with clinicians at the Columbia Presbyterian Medical Center that gives specially-trained nurses autonomy in managing the basic health needs of patients. Under the plan patients will have the option of seeing a "nurse practitioner" or a physician, depending on their personal preference. The plan has not gone over well with physicians, who worry that the change could affect their earning power.

Performance

Stock growth (past two years through 12/31/96): 196% (from $19.81 to $58.56).

Revenue growth (past two years through 9/30/96): 352% (from $604.8 million to $2.7 billion).

Earnings per share growth (past two years through 9/30/96): 206% (from $0.35 to $1.07).

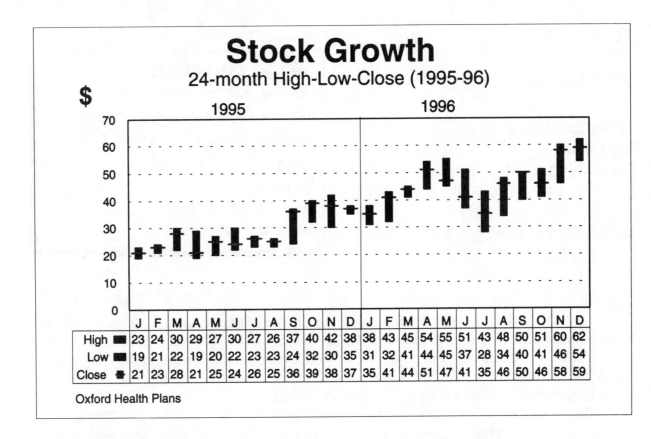

Stock Growth
24-month High-Low-Close (1995-96)

	J	F	M	A	M	J	J	A	S	O	N	D	J	F	M	A	M	J	J	A	S	O	N	D
High	23	24	30	29	27	30	27	26	37	40	42	38	38	43	45	54	55	51	43	48	50	51	60	62
Low	19	21	22	19	20	22	23	23	24	32	30	35	31	32	41	44	45	37	28	34	40	41	46	54
Close	21	23	28	21	25	24	26	25	36	39	38	37	35	41	44	51	47	41	35	46	50	46	58	59

Oxford Health Plans

Quick Fix

P/E range (past two years):	27 - 60
Earnings past four quarters:	$1.07 (through 9/30/96)
Projected 1997 earnings (median):	$1.73
International sales:	None
Total current assets:	$852.2 million (1996); $492.2 million (1995)
Total current liabilities:	$493.0 million (1996); $388.7 million (1995)
Net Income:	$52.4 million (1995); $28.2 million (1994)

Financial history

Fiscal year ended: Dec. 31
(Revenue in millions)

	1992	1993	1994	1995	*1996
Revenue	$151.3	$307.6	$752.8	$1,746.0	$2,194.7*
Earnings per share	0.13	0.18	0.40	0.71	0.86*
Stock price: High	7.09	14.00	20.88	41.88	62.25
Low	2.16	3.91	9.88	19.25	27.69
Close	7.06	13.25	19.81	36.94	58.56

1996 revenue and earnings through Sept. 30 (nine months).

33

PhyCor, Inc.

30 Burton Hills Boulevard
Suite 400
Nashville, TN 37215
Phone: 615-665-9066; FAX: 615-665-9088

Chairman, President, and CEO:
  Joseph Hutts

Physicians who want to get away from the day-to-day hassle of running their businesses, and back to the business of helping their patients use PhyCor to manage their practices. PhyCor has grown quickly to become the nation's largest physician practice management company. The company operates 42 clinics with about 2,800 physicians in 24 states, and manages independent practice associations with more than 8,000 physicians in 15 markets.

PhyCor, which is considered a physician practice management organization (PPM), typically acquires the assets of group practices that have large market share in their community. The company relieves its physicians of handling the business aspects of their practices, freeing them to focus on patient care. PhyCor provides a range of services including strategic planning, billing, regulatory compliance, marketing and day-to-day management.

To increase clinic revenue, PhyCor works with the affiliated physician groups to recruit additional physicians and merge them into the group. The Nashville, Tennessee, operation also negotiates contracts with managed care organizations on behalf of its physicians. To control expenses, PhyCor uses national purchasing contracts for key items, reviews staffing levels and assists physicians in developing more cost-effective clinical practice patterns.

For physicians not interested in joining a PPM, PhyCor offers a less-binding arrangement in which the physicians hold onto their assets, but use PhyCor to provide professional management for their practices.

Most of the company's business is concentrated in the East, Midwest and South, although it has operations in some western states, including Texas, California, Colorado, Utah, Arizona and Oklahoma.

PhyCor was founded in 1988.

Late developments
The company recently acquired certain assets of the Hattiesburg (Mississippi) Clinic, and entered into a long-term service agreement with the 100-physician group associated with the clinic.

Performance
Stock growth (past two years through 12/31/96): 139% (from $11.88 to $28.38).
Revenue growth (past two years through 9/30/96): 221% (from $209.4 million to $671 million).
Earnings per share growth (past two years through 9/30/96): 69% (from $0.32 to $0.54).

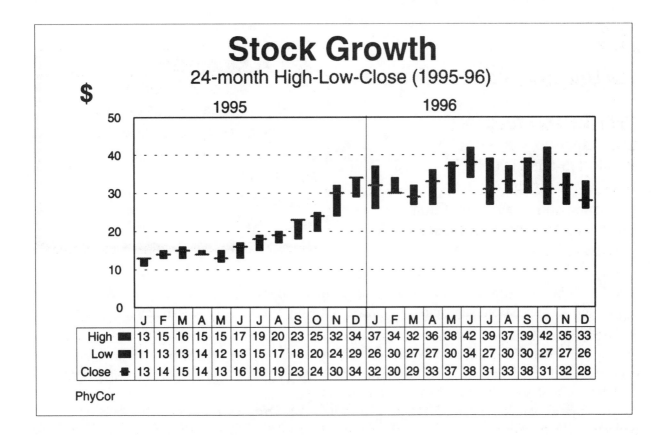

Stock Growth
24-month High-Low-Close (1995-96)

	J	F	M	A	M	J	J	A	S	O	N	D	J	F	M	A	M	J	J	A	S	O	N	D
High	13	15	16	15	15	17	19	20	23	25	32	34	37	34	32	36	38	42	39	37	39	42	35	33
Low	11	13	13	14	12	13	15	17	18	20	24	29	26	30	27	27	30	34	27	30	30	27	27	26
Close	13	14	15	14	13	16	18	19	23	24	30	34	32	30	29	33	37	38	31	33	38	31	32	28

PhyCor

Quick Fix

P/E range (past two years):	27 - 83
Earnings past four quarters:	$0.60 (through 12/31/96)
Projected 1997 earnings (median):	$0.80
International sales:	None
Total current assets:	$294.7 million (6/30/96); $191.4 million (6/30/95)
Total current liabilities:	$135.8 million (6/30/96); $75.4 million (6/30/95)
Net Income:	$36.4 million (1996); $21.9 million (1995)

Financial history

Fiscal year ended: Dec. 31

(Revenue in millions)

	1992	1993	1994	1995	1996
Revenue	$135.9	$167.4	$242.5	$441.6	$766.3
Earnings per share	-0.57	0.28	0.32	0.41	0.60
Stock price: High	5.26	9.11	12.44	34.00	41.75
Low	2.22	4.00	7.48	10.89	25.63
Close	4.59	8.52	11.89	33.71	28.38

34

AirTouch Communications, Inc.

One California Street
San Francisco, CA 94111
Phone: 415-658-2000; FAX: 415-989-7606

Chairman and CEO: Sam Ginn

The future of telecommunications is being decided now on the cellular battle grounds around the world, and AirTouch Communications has made some formidable advances in key markets on three continents.

The San Francisco-based operation has ownership interests and operating influence in national cellular systems in Germany, Japan, Portugal, Poland, Sweden, Belgium, Italy, Spain, India and South Korea.

In the U.S., AirTouch controls or shares control over cellular systems in ten of the 30 largest cellular markets, including Los Angeles, San Francisco, San Diego, Detroit, Dallas, Kansas City, Sacramento and Atlanta.

In all, the company has about 3 million cellular customers worldwide, and controls the market in areas with a total population of about 200 million.

AirTouch is also a leader in the paging market, with about 2.3 million customers in 170 markets in 29 states. The firm offers numeric display, alphanumeric, tone-only and tone and voice paging. AirTouch also has a share of the paging market in Spain, Portugal, Thailand and France.

Formerly known as PacTel, the company was originally formed as part of the breakup of AT&T in 1984. AirTouch went public with its initial stock offering in 1994. The company has about 7,000 employees.

AirTouch is exploring the possibility of expanding into related markets, such as the construction and operation of wireless networks, international long distance service for cellular subscribers, and international wireline long distance services to complement its wireless operation.

Late developments

Continuing its push into the international market, AirTouch recently signed a 10-year license agreement to operate one of two mobile telephone systems in Romania. AirTouch also teamed with several regional Bell companies to form a partnership known as PrimeCo Personal Communications that will offer cellular-like phone service in 16 U.S. cities using a more powerful digital technology that offers better sound quality than traditional cellular service—at rates of 20 to 25 percent below cellular service.

Performance

Stock growth (past two years through 12/31/96): -15% (from $29.13 to $25.25).

Revenue growth (past two years through 9/30/96): 69% (from $1.16 billion to $1.96 billion).

Earnings per share growth (past two years through 9/30/96): 52% (from $0.23 to $0.35).

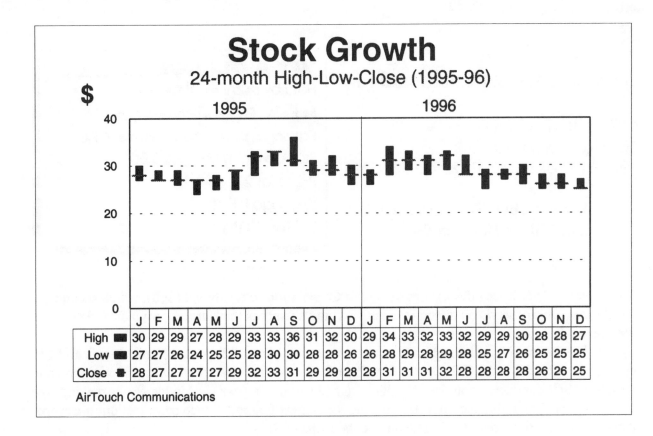

Stock Growth
24-month High-Low-Close (1995-96)

		J	F	M	A	M	J	J	A	S	O	N	D	J	F	M	A	M	J	J	A	S	O	N	D
High	■	30	29	29	27	28	29	33	33	36	31	32	30	29	34	33	32	33	32	29	29	30	28	28	27
Low	■	27	27	26	24	25	25	28	30	30	28	28	26	26	28	29	28	29	28	25	27	26	25	25	25
Close	▪	28	27	27	27	27	29	32	33	31	29	29	28	28	31	31	31	32	28	28	28	28	26	26	25

AirTouch Communications

Quick Fix

P/E range (past two years):	82 - 153
Earnings past four quarters:	$0.35 (through 9/30/96)
Projected 1997 earnings (median):	$0.55
International sales:	Approximately 25% of total sales
Total current assets:	$412.8 million (1996); $597.5 million (1995)
Total current liabilities:	$510 million (1996); $404.7 million (1995)
Net Income:	$131.9 million (1995); $98.1 million (1994)

Financial history

Fiscal year ended: Dec. 31
(Revenue in millions)

	1992	1993	1994	1995	*1996
Revenue	$880.2	$1,057.7	$1,247	$1,618.6	$1,530.9*
Earnings per share	- 0.02	0.09	0.20	0.27	0.33*
Stock price: High	NA	NA	30.63	35.63	33.63
Low	NA	NA	19.88	23.88	24.88
Close	NA	NA	29.13	28.13	25.25

1996 revenue and earnings through Sept. 30 (nine months).

35

Service Corp. International

1929 Allen Parkway
Houston, TX 77019
Phone: 713-522-5141; FAX: 713-525-5285

Chairman and CEO: Robert L. Waltrip
President: William Heiligbrodt

Sooner or later, you'll need the services of Service Corporation International (SCI), which specializes in a different kind of services—funeral services. SCI touts itself as the "largest provider of death care services in the world."

The Houston-based company operates about 2,800 funeral homes, 318 cemeteries and 139 crematoria. Most are in the U.S., but the firm also has "death care" operations in France, England and Australia. SCI conducts about half a million funeral services a year worldwide. After making two major acquisitions in France, SCI has become the largest funeral service organization in Europe. About one-third of its revenue is generated outside the U.S.

If the business of death care strikes you as a bit somber, a look at the company's financials might brighten your outlook. SCI's stock has doubled in the past two years (through 1996), and its earnings have been growing at 15 to 20 percent per year. And while the business lacks for repeat customers, it is guaranteed to see a steady stream of new customers rolling through the doors.

SCI has achieved most of its growth through acquisitions, although it also builds some new funeral homes and cemeteries. In addition to providing funeral and burial services, the company sells caskets, coffins, burial vaults, cremation receptacles and burial garments. SCI also owns 60 flower shops that specialize in funeral floral arrangements.

As the world's largest death care provider, SCI conducts an amazingly high percentage of the total funerals in its key markets. It performs about 29 percent of all funerals in France, 24 percent in Australia, 14 percent in the United Kingdom and 9 percent in North America.

Founded in 1962, the company went public in 1969 with its initial stock offering. The founder, Robert L. Waltrip, still serves as board chairman and CEO. SCI has about 20,000 employees.

Late developments

In early 1997, SCI dropped its $2.9 billion hostile bid to buy the Loewen Group, the Canadian-based company that is SCI's biggest rival in the death services industry.

Performance

Stock growth (past two years through 12/31/96): 102% (from $13.88 to $28.00).
Revenue growth (past two years through 9/30/96): 113% (from $1.04 billion to $2.23 billion).
Earnings per share growth (past two years through 9/30/96): 40% (from $0.75 to $1.05).

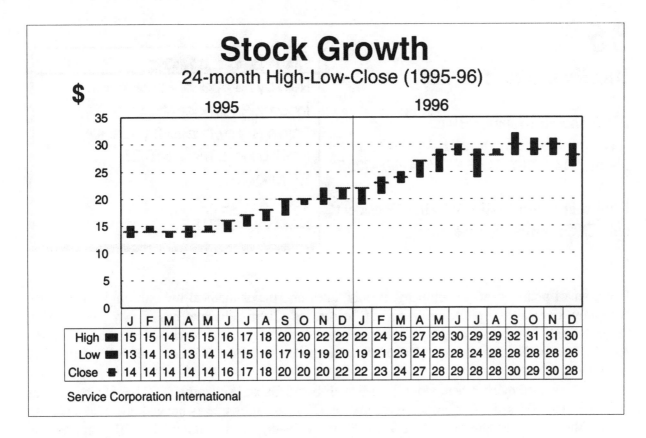

Stock Growth
24-month High-Low-Close (1995-96)

		J	F	M	A	M	J	J	A	S	O	N	D	J	F	M	A	M	J	J	A	S	O	N	D
High	■	15	15	14	15	15	16	17	18	20	20	22	22	22	24	25	27	29	30	29	29	32	31	31	30
Low	■	13	14	13	13	14	14	15	16	17	19	19	20	19	21	23	24	25	28	24	28	28	28	28	26
Close	■	14	14	14	14	14	16	17	18	20	20	20	22	22	23	24	27	28	29	28	28	30	29	30	28

Service Corporation International

Quick Fix

P/E range (past two years):	13 - 30
Earnings past four quarters:	$1.05 (through 9/30/96)
Projected 1997 earnings (median):	$1.28
International sales:	35% of total revenue
Total current assets:	$732 million (1996); $448 million (1995)
Total current liabilities:	$456 million (1996); $245.1 million (1995)
Net Income:	$183.6 million (1995); $131 million (1994)

Financial history

Fiscal year ended: Dec. 31
(Revenue in millions)

	1992	1993	1994	1995	*1996
Revenue	$772.5	$899.2	$1,117.2	$1,652.1	$1,684.7*
Earnings per share	0.56	0.62	0.75	0.90	0.80*
Stock price: High	9.38	13.19	14.00	22.00	31.50
Low	7.83	8.94	11.25	11.38	19.44
Close	9.13	13.13	13.88	22.00	28.00

1996 revenue and earnings through Sept. 30 (nine months).

36

BioChem Pharma, Inc.

275 Armand-Frappier Blvd.
Laval, Quebec, Canada   H7V 4A7
Phone: 514-978-7771; FAX: 514-978-7755

Chairman: Jean-Louis Fontaine   President
and CEO: Francesco Bellini

For a small pharmaceutical company, it only takes one major medical breakthrough to push the company over the top. After years of losses, BioChem Pharma has finally achieved its breakthrough—in a very big way. Within a year after its approval by the U.S. Food and Drug Administration, BioChem's new 3TC medication has captured the number one share of the U.S. market for HIV drugs.

Developed by BioChem along with British-based Glaxo Wellcome, 3TC has achieved some incredible results. Used in conjunction with other AIDS medications, tests have shown that 3TC cuts in half the rate of progression of HIV to AIDS or death, and it reduces the HIV viral load to undetectable levels for 48 weeks for 20 out of 22 patients. The drug has a unique combination of high potency, low side-effects and low cost.

The result has been a boon to the bottom line of the Quebec-based operation. And that growth should continue well into the next decade. Analysts project that 3TC could generate annual sales of well over $1 billion by the year 2000. By comparison, BioChem had total revenue of only $139 million in 1995.

The company is also testing other uses for 3TC (also known as "Lamivudine"), including the treatment of chronic hepatitis B infection.

BioChem is also making advances in other areas. It has developed a wide range of diagnostic products and automated laboratory analyzers for the detection of a variety of infectious diseases, and for use in immunology, endocrinology and hematology. It has also developed a line of vaccines for such ailments as influenza, diphtheria, tetanus and tuberculosis.

The firm focuses its therapeutics research on four main areas, antiviral, pain control, anti-thrombosis and anti-cancer.

BioChem, which was founded in 1987, has about 900 employees. Its stock is traded in the U.S. on the NASDAQ over-the-counter exchange.

Late developments

The company received approval in 1996 for the use of 3TC in Europe, which should be a further boost to profits.

Performance

Stock growth (past two years through 12/31/96): 302% (from $12.50 to $50.25).
Revenue growth (past two years through 9/30/96): 140% (from $91.8 million to $220.5 million).
Earnings per share growth (past two years through 9/30/96): NA (from -$0.30 to $0.33).

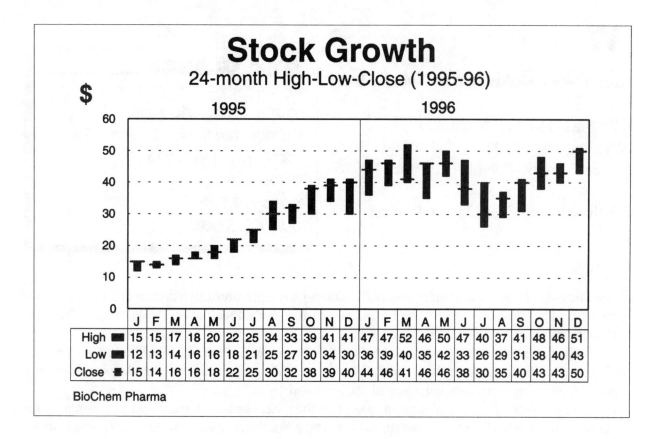

Stock Growth
24-month High-Low-Close (1995-96)

		1995											1996											
	J	F	M	A	M	J	J	A	S	O	N	D	J	F	M	A	M	J	J	A	S	O	N	D
High	15	15	17	18	20	22	25	34	33	39	41	41	47	47	52	46	50	47	40	37	41	48	46	51
Low	12	13	14	16	16	18	21	25	27	30	34	30	36	39	40	35	42	33	26	29	31	38	40	43
Close	15	14	16	16	18	22	25	30	32	38	39	40	44	46	41	46	46	38	30	35	40	43	43	50

BioChem Pharma

Quick Fix

P/E range (past two years):	NA
Earnings past four quarters:	$0.33 (through 9/30/96)
Projected 1997 earnings (median):	$1.15
International sales:	77% of total non-U.S. sales (Canada, 9%; Europe, 68%)
Total current assets:	$318.3 million (1996); $129.0 million (1995)
Total current liabilities:	$65.1 million (1996); $52.1 million (1995)
Net Income:	$2.7 million (1995); -$5.3 million (1994)

Financial history

Fiscal year ended: Dec. 31

(Revenue in millions)

	1992	1993	1994	1995	*1996
Revenue	$27.2	$31.3	$81.4	$139.2	$126.5*
Earnings per share	-0.24	- 0.16	- 0.24	- 0.04	0.19*
Stock price: High	29.88	17.00	13.63	41.13	52.38
Low	10.63	8.50	8.13	12.25	26.00
Close	15.25	10.38	12.50	40.13	50.25

1996 revenue and earnings through Sept. 30 (nine months).

37

Lone Star Steakhouse & Saloon, Inc.

224 East Douglas, Suite 700
Wichita, KS 67202
Phone: 316-264-8899; FAX: 316-264-2926

Chairman: and CEO: Jamie Coulter

Lone Star Steakhouse & Saloon is stampeding through the premium steakhouse market from three directions. The company runs a trio of restaurant chains that all feature fat steaks and full bars, but still cater to distinctly different markets.

Along with the its namesake, Lone Star Steakhouse & Saloon, the Wichita-based operation also owns Del Frisco's Double Eagle Steak House restaurants and Sullivan's Steakhouse restaurants. All of its restaurants are company-owned and operated.

The company's namesake chain, the Lone Star Steakhouse, is the bread and butter of the business, with nearly 200 restaurants spread across the South and Midwest. Ironically, there are no Lone Stars in the Lone Star state of Texas—but there are about a dozen restaurants down under in Australia..

Lone Star restaurants feature a rustic, Western decor, reminiscent of an old Texas roadhouse. The dining areas are large and open, with seating for about 220 people. The menu includes steaks, ribs, chicken, fish and desserts. All dinners are served with salad, bread and butter and a choice of baked potato, baked sweat potato, steak fries or Texas rice. Lunchtime diners can also order burgers, soups, salads or chicken sandwiches. The average dinner price for Lone Star customers is about $19.

The company's other two steakhouse chains target the higher end of the carnivore market. Del Frisco's, which the company acquired in 1995, features an elegant early twentieth century motif, with dark wood, fabric walls, fireplaces and soft background music. The average dinner tab is about $60. Through 1996, there were only three Del Frisco's restaurants, but the company plans to expand aggressively in the next three years.

Sullivan's Steakhouse features a nostalgic 1940s theme, with art deco decor, wood paneling, warm lighting, white table clothes and music from the big band era. Average dinner tab is $35 to $40. Lone Star opened the first Sullivan's Restaurant in Austin, Texas, in 1996.

Lone Star, which initially issued stock in 1992, has about 15,000 employees.

Late developments

The company plans to open 100 Sullivan restaurants and 30 Del Frisco restaurants by year 2000.

Performance

Stock growth (past two years through 12/31/96): 34% (from $20.00 to $26.75).
Revenue growth (past two years through 12/31/96):128% (from $216 million to $491.7 million).
Earnings per share growth (past two years through 12/31/96): 70% (from $0.87 to $1.48).

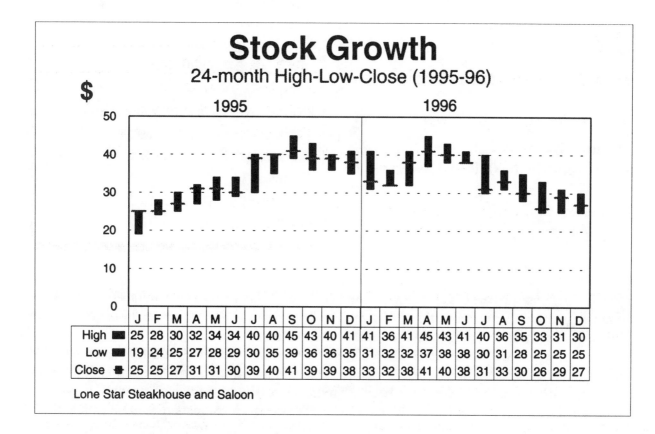

Stock Growth
24-month High-Low-Close (1995-96)

$

		J	F	M	A	M	J	J	A	S	O	N	D	J	F	M	A	M	J	J	A	S	O	N	D
High	■	25	28	30	32	34	34	40	40	45	43	40	41	41	36	41	45	43	41	40	36	35	33	31	30
Low	■	19	24	25	27	28	29	30	35	39	36	36	35	31	32	32	37	38	38	30	31	28	25	25	25
Close	✦	25	25	27	31	31	30	39	40	41	39	39	38	33	32	38	41	40	38	31	33	30	26	29	27

Lone Star Steakhouse and Saloon

Quick Fix

P/E range (past two years):	15 - 35
Earnings past four quarters:	$1.48 (1996)
Projected 1997 earnings (median):	$2.07
International sales:	Less than 10%.
Total current assets:	$181.8 million (9/03/96); $126.6 million (9/05/95)
Total current liabilities:	$35.4 million (9/03/96); $25.4 million (9/05/95)
Net Income:	$59.5 million (1996) $46.9 million (1995)

Financial history

Fiscal year ended: Dec. 31
(Revenue in millions)

	1992	1993	1994	1995	1996
Revenue	$40.6	$112.3	$215.8	$340.8	$491.8
Earnings per share	0.16	0.49	0.87	1.27	1.48
Stock price: High	19.13	30.25	29.25	45.00	45.00
Low	4.13	15.88	16.50	18.50	24.63
Close	18.81	27.50	20.00	38.38	26.75

38

Steris Corporation

5960 Heisley Road
Mentor, OH 44060
Phone: 216-354-2600; FAX: 216-354-7887

Chairman, President and CEO:
    Bill R. Sanford

AT A GLANCE

Held by number of funds: 3

Industry: Medical sterilization devices

Earnings growth past 2 years: 174%

Stock price 1/1/97: $43.50

P/E ratio: 37

Year ago P/E: 61

NASDAQ: STRL

Steris is the mouse that ate the elephant. The medical sterilization systems manufacturer acquired a company in 1996 that was five times its size. The acquisition of Amsco International boosted its annual revenue from $91 million to a projected $600 million.

The Amsco acquisition seems like a natural for Steris, which is the industry leader in on-site low temperature sterilization systems. Amsco is a leader in infection control, contamination control and surgical products. While Steris has been the more successful of the two companies, growing at a rate of about 50 percent per year, Amsco has a broader international marketing base which Steris can now use for its products. Amsco had about 900 service representatives worldwide compared to about 125 for Steris. Amsco also adds another 300 products to the Steris line.

The Cleveland-based company estimates savings of at least $20 million during 1996 and 1997 by closing duplicate facilities and consolidating various management operations.

Steris has captured a dominant position in the surgical equipment sterilization market by developing a line of sterilization systems that use low-temperature chemicals rather than heat to destroy microbes. The compact Steris sterilization equipment is easier to use and more convenient for surgeons than the conventional heat-based systems.

The company's Steris System 1 enables healthcare professionals to economically sterilize immersible surgical and diagnostic devices in less than 30 minutes. The company recently introduced two new infectious waste containment and disposal systems. The EcoCycle 10 destroys and decontaminates potentially infectious solid waste, and the Safe Cycle 40 collects and disposes of blood and other fluid wastes generated in surgical and diagnostic procedures.

Founded in 1987, Steris had about 560 employees prior to the Amsco acquisition. The combined company now has well over 1,600 employees.

Late developments

In late 1996, the company purchased the infection control and contamination control business of Calgon Vestal Laboratories from Bristol-Myers Squibb. Calgon Vestal is involved in instrument cleaning and decontamination, antimicrobial and routine hand washing cleansers, disinfectants and surgical scrubs.

Performance

Stock growth (past two years through 12/31/96): 132% (from $18.75 $43.50).
Revenue growth (past two years through 12/31/96): 650% (from $59 million to $433 million).
Earnings per share growth (past two years through 12/31/96): 174% (from $0.43 to $1.18).

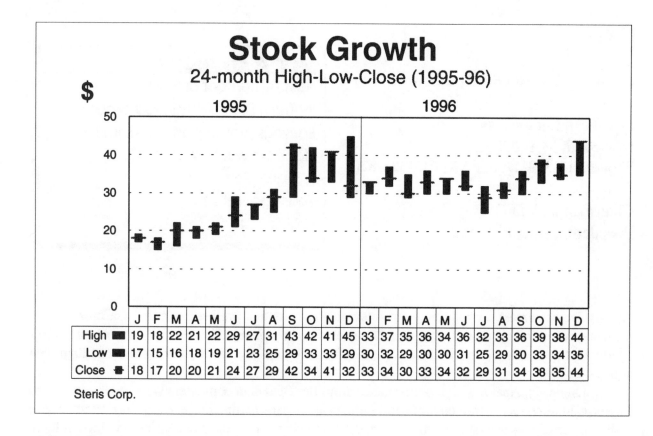

Stock Growth
24-month High-Low-Close (1995-96)

		J	F	M	A	M	J	J	A	S	O	N	D	J	F	M	A	M	J	J	A	S	O	N	D
High	■	19	18	22	21	22	29	27	31	43	42	41	45	33	37	35	36	34	36	32	33	36	39	38	44
Low	■	17	15	16	18	19	21	23	25	29	33	33	29	30	32	29	30	30	31	25	29	30	33	34	35
Close	✚	18	17	20	20	21	24	27	29	42	34	41	32	33	34	30	33	34	32	29	31	34	38	35	44

Steris Corp.

Quick Fix

P/E range (past two years):	23 - 69
Earnings past four quarters:	$1.18 (through 12/31/96)
Projected 1997 earnings (median):	$1.55
International sales:	7% of total sales
Total current assets:	$292.8 million (1996); $39.0 million (1995)
Total current liabilities:	$150.9 million (1996); $9.5 million (1995)
Net Income:	$12.8 million (1996); $8.7 million (1995)

Financial history

Fiscal year ended: March 31
(Revenue in millions)

	1992	1993	1994	1995	1996	**1997
Revenue	$12.9	$26.7	$45.8	$64.3	$302.9	$417.4**
Earnings per share	0	0.02	0.09	0.28	0.86	0.98**
*Stock price: High	9	10.63	5.56	40.63	44	NA
Low	3.63	6.38	1.41	4.94	25	NA
Close	8.81	9.38	5.09	40.56	44	NA

*Stock prices (only) reflect calendar year.
**Revenue and earnings through 12/31/96 (nine months). Revenue and earnings have been restated to include the Amsco merger.

39

Analog Devices, Inc.

One Technology Way
Norwood, MA 02062
Phone: 617-329-4700; FAX: 617-326-8703

Chairman and CEO: Ray Stata
President: Jerald Fishman

AT A GLANCE

Held by number of funds: 3
Industry: Digital integrated circuits
Earnings growth past 2 years: 115%
Stock price 1/1/97: $25.41
P/E ratio: 26
Year ago P/E: 22
NYSE: ADI

Analog Devices makes a wide range of integrated circuits that are used to turn measures such as pressure, temperature, speed and sound into electronic signals. The Boston area manufacturer produces linear, mixed-signal and digital integrated circuits used in a growing array of high tech applications.

Originally, Analog's high performance amplifiers and data converters were sold primarily to traditional industrial, instrumentation and military-aerospace manufacturers. But its customer base is shifting rapidly. Its high-speed converters and amplifiers are being used increasingly in high volume communications, computer, automotive and consumer applications.

For instance, its integrated circuit accelerometers are used as crash sensors in automobile airbag systems. And its mixed-signal devices are used in digital cellular telephones, which are now in widespread used in Western Europe.

Analog has also begun manufacturing chip sets and integrated circuits for use in computer multimedia applications for enhanced audio and fax-modem functions. And in the consumer electronics industry, Analog's integrated circuits are used for compact disc players, digital VCRs, camcorders and digital audio tape equipment.

The company sells its products worldwide through a direct sales force, third-party industrial distributors and independent sales representatives. The company has direct sales offices in 17 countries and the U.S. About 66 percent of its sales are generated outside of North America.

Founded in 1965, Analog Devices has about 6,000 employees. The firm has manufacturing facilities in Massachusetts, California, North Carolina, Ireland, the Philippines and Taiwan.

Late developments

Thanks to strong growth in sales of its Standard Linear Integrated Circuits (SLIC) to the proprietary high-speed and communications product market—where demand has been running well ahead of the firm's ability to supply—Analog Devices has become the largest supplier of SLIC products to North American customers. That's up from fifth in 1994.

Performance

Stock growth (past two years through 12/31/96): 117% (from $15.63 to 33.88).
Revenue growth (past two years through 7/30/96): 54% (from $773 million to $1.19 billion).
Earnings per share growth (past two years through 10/31/96): 115% (from $0.48 to $1.03).

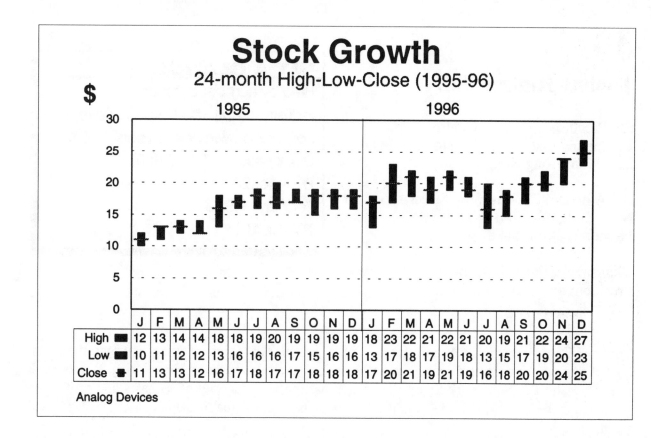

Stock Growth
24-month High-Low-Close (1995-96)

	J	F	M	A	M	J	J	A	S	O	N	D	J	F	M	A	M	J	J	A	S	O	N	D
High ■	12	13	14	14	18	18	19	20	19	19	19	19	18	23	22	21	22	21	20	19	21	22	24	27
Low ■	10	11	12	12	13	16	16	16	17	15	16	16	13	17	18	17	19	18	13	15	17	19	20	23
Close ●	11	13	13	12	16	17	18	17	17	18	18	18	17	20	21	19	21	19	16	18	20	20	24	25

Analog Devices

Quick Fix

P/E range (past two years):	12 - 26
Earnings past four quarters:	$1.03 (through 10/31/96)
Projected 1997 earnings (median):	$1.25
International sales:	46% of total sales (Asia/Pacific, 18%; Europe, 28%)
Total current assets:	$820 million (1996); $526 million (1995)
Total current liabilities:	$270 million (1996); $254 million (1995)
Net Income:	$171.9 million (1996); $119.3 million (1995)

Financial history

Fiscal year ended: Oct. 31
(Revenue in millions)

	1992	1993	1994	1995	*1996
Revenue	$567.3	$666.3	$773.5	$941.5	$1,193.8
Earnings per share	0.10	0.29	0.48	0.75	1.03
*Stock price: High	5.42	9.34	12.25	19.75	26.63
Low	288	5.04	7.79	10.00	12.75
Close	5.42	8.21	11.71	17.69	25.41

*Stock prices (only) reflect calendar year.

40

Tommy Hilfiger, Inc.

6/F Precious Industrial Centre
18 Cheung Yue Street, Cheung Sha Wan
Kowloon, Hong Kong

(USA office) 25 West 39th Street
New York, NY 10018
Phone: 212-840-8888

Chairman: Silas K.F. Chou
President and CEO: Joel Horowitz

Tommy Hilfiger—a name as American as . . . uh . . . sushi. That's right, Tommy Hilfiger, the recent rage of men's and boys' casual apparel, is not American at all. It's based in Hong Kong. But its stock does trade on the New York Stock Exchange, and the vast majority of its sales and profits are generated in the U.S. Outside the U.S., the firm sells its clothing line in Canada, Mexico, Japan and South America.

Founded in 1992, the firm is named for its chief designer, Thomas J. Hilfiger, who still serves on the board of directors, and holds the title of "honorary chairman of the board."

The company markets its clothing through about 2,000 specialty retail shops and major department stores such as Dillard, Federated, Daytons, May, Macy's, Bloomingdale's and Belk Stores. Hilfiger has recently been setting up in-store Tommy Hilfiger shops within large department stores. The company has opened shops in about 1,000 department stores.

Hilfiger also operates about 50 free-standing outlet and specialty stores, including a new flagship store opened in 1996 on Rodeo Drive in Beverly Hills.

Traditionally, Tommy Hilfiger has featured strictly men's and boys' apparel, but it is now moving into women's apparel, as well as shoes, tote bags and other accessories. Its leading lines include Core, which are "seasonless" apparel sold year-round, Core Plus seasonal basic apparel, and "Fashion" seasonal apparel.

While the company's executive headquarters and principal buying offices are in Hong Kong, its sales and marketing department is in New York. Its sales force, which has regional offices in Los Angeles, Chicago, Philadelphia, San Francisco and Cincinnati, sells only Tommy Hilfiger products.

Late developments

Hilfiger recently introduced a new men's fragrance called "tommy," which it is marketing internationally. Company officials hope to use *tommy* to pave the way for an international roll-out of its entire apparel line. The firm also introduced a line of "tommy girl" women's fragrances.

Performance

Stock growth (past two years through 12/31/96): 113% (from $22.56 to $48.00).
Revenue growth (past two years through 9/30/96): 104% (from $274 million to $560 million).
Earnings per share growth (past two years through 9/30/96): 116% (from $0.89 to $1.92).

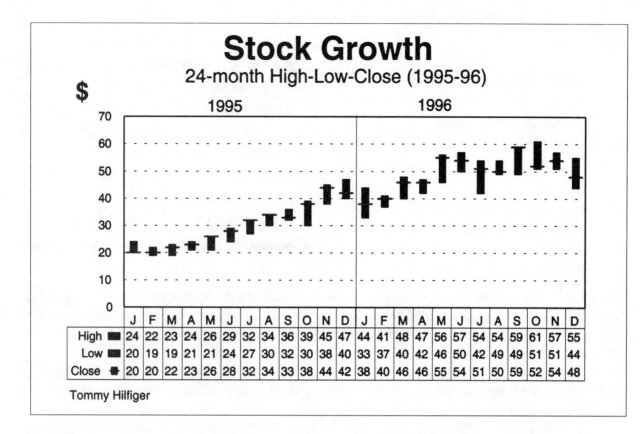

Stock Growth
24-month High-Low-Close (1995-96)

		J	F	M	A	M	J	J	A	S	O	N	D	J	F	M	A	M	J	J	A	S	O	N	D
High		24	22	23	24	26	29	32	34	36	39	45	47	44	41	48	47	56	57	54	54	59	61	57	55
Low		20	19	19	21	21	24	27	30	32	30	38	40	33	37	40	42	46	50	42	49	49	51	51	44
Close		20	20	22	23	26	28	32	34	33	38	44	42	38	40	46	46	55	54	51	50	59	52	54	48

Tommy Hilfiger

Quick Fix

P/E range (past two years):	11 - 28
Earnings past four quarters:	$1.92 (through 9/30/96)
Projected 1997 earnings (median):	$2.15
International sales:	About 80% U.S.; 20% foreign
Total current assets:	$295.7 million (1996); $291.1 million (1995)
Total current liabilities:	$54.6 million (1996); $52.6 million (1995)
Net Income:	$61.5 million (1996); $40.7 million (1995)

Financial history

Fiscal year ended: March 30
(Revenue in millions)

	1993	1994	1995	1996	*1997
Revenue	$138.6	$227.2	$321.0	$478.1	$303*
Earnings per share	0.55	0.77	1.12	1.65	0.97*
Stock price: High	17.00	22.75	47.38	61.13	NA
Low	9.50	14.75	18.50	32.63	NA
Close	15.63	22.56	42.38	48	NA

* 1997 revenue and earnings through Sept.30 (six months).

41

Paychex, Inc.

911 Panorama Trail South
Rochester, NY 14625
Phone: 716-385-6666; FAX: 716-383-3428

Chairman, President and CEO:
   B. Thomas Golisano

Paychex does just as its name suggests. It doles out the pay checks for millions of employees at more than 230,000 small and medium-sized businesses nationwide. In all, Paychex prints out more than 100 million payroll checks a year. The Rochester-based company is the nation's second leading payroll processing service.

In addition to issuing paychecks. the company has expanded to other areas, including employee handbook services, benefits cafeteria plans, payroll tax preparation, insurance services and 401(k) recordkeeping.

For many of its corporate customers, Paychex produces employee checks, management reports and accounting records, and handles the payroll tax returns for federal, state and local jurisdictions. The company prepares nearly six million W-2 forms each year.

The firm's "Taxpay" automatic tax payment and filing service is used by more than 130,000 corporate clients, and its direct deposit option, in which employee wages can be automatically deposited in the employee's checking or savings accounts, is used by more than 50,000 companies. The Paychex check signing and inserting service is used by about 22,000 businesses. And its 401(k) service, in which Paychex handles the recordkeeping for employees enrolled in their company retirement plan, is used by 1,300 businesses.

Paychex also sells a software package call "Paylink" that enables corporate clients to use their personal computers and modems to transmit their own payroll data into the local Paychex processing center. That feature is used by about 14,000 customers.

Founded in 1971, Paychex has offices in 98 locations. The company has about 4,000 employees. Paychex has 754 branch operating centers and 23 sales offices nationwide.

Late developments

Paychex has been making a strong marketing push recently to sell its Taxpay automatic tax payment and filing services to corporations who are affected by the Internal Revenue Service's new electronic filing requirement. The rule, which took effect Jan. 1, 1997, requires certain companies to deposit all of their payroll tax payments electronically.

Performance

Stock growth (past two years through 12/31/96): 186% (from $18.00 to $51.44).
Revenue growth (past two years through 8/30/96): 78% (from $223.6 million to $415.2 million).
Earnings per share growth (past two years through 8/30/96): 80% (from $0.46 to $0.83).

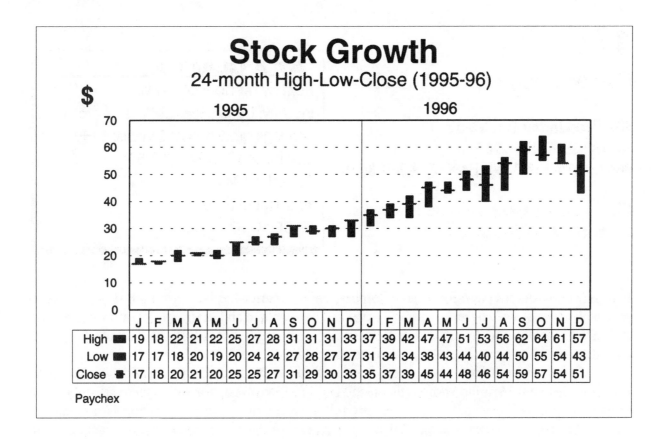

Stock Growth
24-month High-Low-Close (1995-96)

	J	F	M	A	M	J	J	A	S	O	N	D	J	F	M	A	M	J	J	A	S	O	N	D
High	19	18	22	21	22	25	27	28	31	31	31	33	37	39	42	47	47	51	53	56	62	64	61	57
Low	17	17	18	20	19	20	24	24	27	28	27	27	31	34	34	38	43	44	40	44	50	55	54	43
Close	17	18	20	21	20	25	25	27	31	29	30	33	35	37	39	45	44	48	46	54	59	57	54	51

Paychex

Quick Fix

P/E range (past two years):	22 - 72
Earnings past four quarters:	$0.83 (through 8/30/96)
Projected 1997 earnings (median):	$0.97
International sales:	None
Total current assets:	$193.7 million (8/31/96); $124.2 million (1995)
Total current liabilities:	$42.3 million (8/31/96); $26.7 million (1995)
Net Income:	$52.3 million (1996); $39.0 million (1995)

Financial history

Fiscal year ended: May 31
(Revenue in millions)

	1992	1993	1994	1995	1996
Revenue	$161.3	$190.0	$224.1	$267.2	$325.3
Earnings per share	0.21	0.30	0.42	0.58	0.77
Dividends	0.05	0.07	0.10	0.15	0.22
*Stock price: High	11.85	16.78	18.11	33.25	63.63
Low	6.42	10.00	12.67	17.17	26.50
Close	10.42	15.56	15.56	33.25	51.44

Stock prices (only) reflect calendar year.

42

Corrections Corp. of America

102 Woodmont Boulevard
Nashville, TN 37205
Phone: 615-292-3100; FAX: 615-269-8635

Chairman and CEO: Doctor R. Crants
President: David L. Meyers

AT A GLANCE

Held by number of funds: 3

Industry: correction facilities operator

Earnings growth past 2 years: 175%

Stock price 1/1/97: $30.50

P/E ratio: 104

Year ago P/E: 128

NYSE: CXC

Who says crime doesn't pay? Corrections Corporation of America has been growing at more than 30 percent per year by building and managing privatized correctional and detention facilities in the U.S., the United Kingdom and Australia. In all, the company manages 47 facilities with 28,600 beds. It is the nation's leading private sector corrections contractor.

And, for Corrections, crime should continue to pay bigger and bigger dividends. Consider: each year, there are 34 million crimes that result in 12 million arrests for which there are only half a million jail cells—and most of those are already full. Incarceration costs are growing faster than any other part of the government's budget. Private sector operators have proven to be more cost-effective than government-operated facilities.

That's why an increasing number of states and municipalities are turning to private contractors such as Corrections to build and manage jails and prisons. So far, about 20 states and the federal government have used private corrections companies. In all, private sector operators manage only about 4 percent of the jail and prison beds in the U.S. That leaves a lot of room for growth in this burgeoning industry.

Corrections Corp. provides a variety of services, including design, construction and management of new correctional and detention facilities and the redesign and renovation of older facilities. The firm also provides health care, institutional food services, transportation, recreational programs, education, job training, chemical dependency counseling and work programs.

In addition to its U.S. facilities, Corrections Corp. manages one facility in the United Kingdom and two in Australia.

The Nashville-based operation was founded in 1983, and went public with its initial stock offering in 1985. The company has about 5,400 employees.

Late developments

In late 1996, the company received contracts to build and manage two new correctional facilities. It will build a 960-bed, medium-security prison in Sayre, Oklahoma, and a 500-cell, medium-security prison in Wilkinson County, Mississippi. Both should be completed in 1998.

Performance

Stock growth (past two years through 12/31/96): 662% (from $4.00 to $30.50).
Revenue growth (past two years through 9/30/96): 91% (from $136.7 million to $261.1 million).
Earnings per share growth (past two years through 9/30/96): 175% (from $0.12 to $0.33).

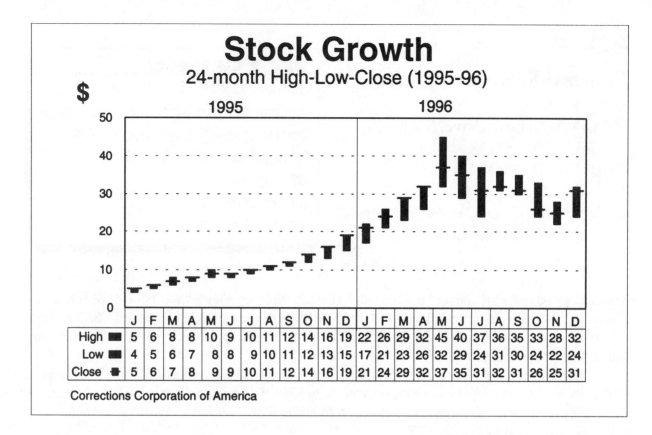

Stock Growth
24-month High-Low-Close (1995-96)

	1995												1996											
	J	F	M	A	M	J	J	A	S	O	N	D	J	F	M	A	M	J	J	A	S	O	N	D
High	5	6	8	8	10	9	10	11	12	14	16	19	22	26	29	32	45	40	37	36	35	33	28	32
Low	4	5	6	7	8	8	9	10	11	12	13	15	17	21	23	26	32	29	24	31	30	24	22	24
Close	5	6	7	8	9	9	10	11	12	14	16	19	21	24	29	32	37	35	31	32	31	26	25	31

Corrections Corporation of America

Quick Fix

P/E range (past two years):	21 - 187
Earnings past four quarters:	$0.33 (through 9/30/96)
Projected 1997 earnings (median):	$0.63
International sales:	Less than 10%
Total current assets:	$187.8 million (1996); $51.4 million (1995)
Total current liabilities:	$46.4 million (1996); $28.8 million (1995)
Net Income:	$14.3 million (1995); $7.9 million (1994)

Financial history

Fiscal year ended: Dec. 31
(Revenue in millions)

	1992	1993	1994	1995	*1996
Revenue	$95.5	$132.5	$152.4	$207.2	$205.9*
Earnings per share	0.06	0.10	0.13	0.19	0.26*
Stock price: High	2.00	2.56	4.44	19.44	45.00
Low	1.19	1.56	2.22	3.97	17.25
Close	1.72	2.25	4.03	18.56	30.50

1996 revenue and earnings through Sept. 30 (nine months).

43

Concord EFS, Inc.

2525 Horizon Lake Drive, Suite 120
Memphis, TN   38133
Phone: 901-371-8000

Chairman and CEO: Dan M. Palmer
President: Edward A. Labry III

The banking business has changed dramatically in the past decade as a growing number of consumers turned to automated teller machines (ATMs) to do most of their banking. Concord EFS has taken advantage of that revolution in the banking business by becoming a major player in the electronic transaction processing business.

The Memphis-based operation provides electronic transaction processing, authorization and settlement services and ATM processing to retailers, grocery stores, financial institutions and trucking companies nationwide. The related electronic terminal equipment used in transaction processing is sold and maintained by Concord EFS.

Founded in 1970, Concord operates a number of subsidiaries that provide a range of financial transaction processing and related services.

Its EFS National Bank subsidiary sells credit, debit and electronic benefits transfer card authorization, data capture and settlement services to retailers and grocery stores. It also sells cash card and cash forwarding services to trucking companies.

Its Concord Computing subsidiary is involved primarily in check authorization and point-of-sale terminal driving, servicing and maintenance for grocery store chains. It also owns and operates ATMs at truck stops and grocery stores nationwide.

Concord's Network EFT subsidiary sells electronic funds transfer services to financial institutions in Illinois through networks of terminals in grocery stores, where customers may make deposits, withdrawals and other electronic banking transactions.

The company's Concord Equipment Sales subsidiary manages some of the company's point-of-sale terminal products and communications equipment used by its clients.

About 80 percent of the company's revenue is generated by its bank card services, while its check authorization services and trucking company processing and banking services account for the other 20 percent. The firm has about 500 employees.

Late developments

The NASDAQ Stock Exchange added Concord EFS to its 100 Index effective Dec. 23, 1996.

Performance

Stock growth (past two years through 12/31/96): 280% (from $7.44 to $28.25).
Revenue growth (past two years through 9/30/96): 77% (from $88.5 million to $156.8 million).
Earnings per share growth (past two years through 9/30/96): 95% (from $0.21 to $0.41).

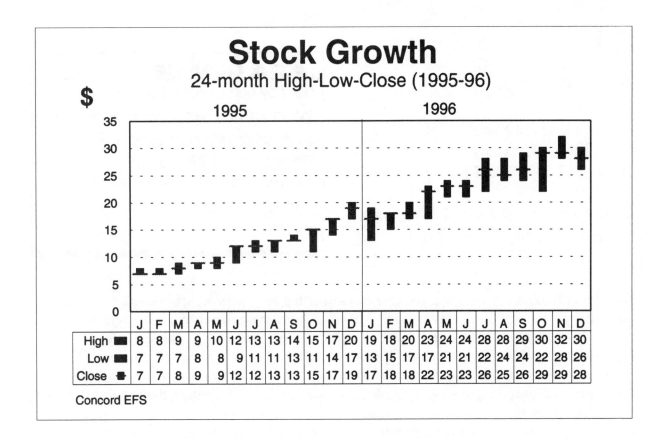

Stock Growth
24-month High-Low-Close (1995-96)

	J	F	M	A	M	J	J	A	S	O	N	D	J	F	M	A	M	J	J	A	S	O	N	D
High	8	8	9	9	10	12	13	13	14	15	17	20	19	18	20	23	24	24	28	28	29	30	32	30
Low	7	7	7	8	8	9	11	11	13	11	14	17	13	15	17	17	21	21	22	24	24	22	28	26
Close	7	7	8	9	9	12	12	13	13	15	17	19	17	18	18	22	23	23	26	25	26	29	29	28

Concord EFS

Quick Fix

P/E range (past two years):	21 - 69
Earnings past four quarters:	$0.41 (through 9/30/96)
Projected 1997 earnings (median):	$0.65
International sales:	None
Total current assets:	$140.8 million (1996); $132.1 million (1995)
Total current liabilities:	$62.0 million (1996); $63.9 million (1995)
Net Income:	$18.3 million (1995); $12.7 million (1994)

Financial history

Fiscal year ended: Dec. 31
(Revenue in millions)

	1992	1993	1994	1995	*1996
Revenue	$65.6	$75.4	$96.2	$127.8	$118.8*
Earnings per share	0.16	0.18	0.23	0.32	0.41*
Stock price: High	5.98	6.67	7.56	20.00	31.50
Low	3.46	3.51	3.94	6.52	12.56
Close	5.83	4.37	7.44	18.78	28.25

1996 revenue and earnings through Sept. 30 (nine months).

44

Andrew Corp.

10500 W. 153rd Street
Orland Park, IL 60462
Phone: 708-349-3300; FAX: 708-349-5943

Chairman, President and CEO:
  Floyd English

Founded in 1937, Andrew Corp. is one of the oldest of the *Hot 100* stocks, but it has found new life the past few years thanks to the explosive growth of the telecommunications industry.

For many years, the Chicago-based manufacturer plodded through painfully slow growth as a manufacturer of standard telephone system products for common carriers. But as that market weakened, Andrew looked into the future of the telecommunications industry, and reshaped its image and its product line during the 1980s to take advantage of some of the more dynamic growth areas within the industry.

Andrew now focuses on three primary segments of the telecommunications market:

• *Commercial.* The firm supplies coaxial cable and antenna system equipment to telecommunications companies and agencies. Its products are used by long distance companies, and cellular phone and land mobile radio companies.

• *Government.* Andrew supplies specialized antenna systems, electronic radar systems, communication reconnaissance systems, coaxial cable, standard antennas and fully integrated systems to various U.S. government agencies and friendly foreign governments.

• *Networking.* The company provides products such as computer cables, local area network gateways, terminal emulators, file transfer software, bridges, routers and adapter cards through resellers to data processing organizations that support the interconnectivity needs of computer networks.

Andrew is well entrenched abroad, with sales in more than 100 companies, and manufacturing plants in Canada, Australia and the United Kingdom. Foreign sales account for about 55 percent of the company's total revenue. In all, the firm has about 6,000 corporate clients, and about 3,400 employees.

Late developments

Andrew has begun marketing several new products, including its Portable Edge amplifier for in-vehicle cellular phones, which boosts the transmit and receive signals; and its new Global Position System antenna for land navigation, which is expected to sell well to automobile manufacturers, trucking companies and public transportation firms.

Performance

Stock growth (past two years through 12/31/96): 128% (from $23.25 to $53.06).
Revenue growth (past two years through 9/30/96): 42% (from $558.4 million to $793.6 million).
Earnings per share growth (past two years through 9/30/96): 95% (from $0.76 to $1.48).

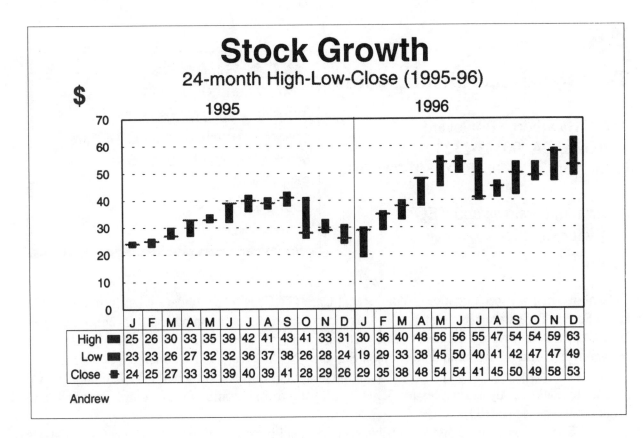

Stock Growth
24-month High-Low-Close (1995-96)

		J	F	M	A	M	J	J	A	S	O	N	D	J	F	M	A	M	J	J	A	S	O	N	D
High	■	25	26	30	33	35	39	42	41	43	41	33	31	30	36	40	48	56	56	55	47	54	54	59	63
Low	■	23	23	26	27	32	32	36	37	38	26	28	24	19	29	33	38	45	50	40	41	42	47	47	49
Close	✦	24	25	27	33	33	39	40	39	41	28	29	26	29	35	38	48	54	54	41	45	50	49	58	53

Andrew

Quick Fix

P/E range (past two years):	20 -37
Earnings past four quarters:	$1.48 (through 9/30/96)
Projected 1997 earnings (median):	$1.82
International sales:	55% of total sales
Total current assets:	$356 million (1996); $294 million (1995)
Total current liabilities:	$162 million (1996); $140.4 million (1995)
Net Income:	$67.8 million (1995); $44.4 million (1994)

Financial history

Fiscal year ended: Sept. 30
(Revenue in millions)

	1992	1993	1994	1995	1996
Revenue	$442	$430.8	$558.4	$652.2	$793.6
Earnings per share	0.39	0.48	0.76	1.15	1.48
*Stock price: High	7.22	12.89	23.89	43.00	63.25
Low	3.30	5.78	10.67	22.67	18.88
Close	7.22	11.41	23.22	25.50	53.06

Stock prices (only) reflect calendar year.

45

Total Renal Care Holdings, Inc.

21250 Hawthorne Boulevard
Torrance, CA 90503-21250
Phone: 310-792-2600; FAX: 301-792-8928

Chairman, President and CEO:
   Victor Chaltiel

Talk about market specialization—Total Renal Care (TRC) is to healthcare what Saturday Night Live's Scotch Tape store was to retail. The Torrance, California, operation has built its entire business around a single very narrow element of the healthcare universe. There is, however, one big difference between TRC and the fictional tape shop on Saturday Night Live: at TRC, business is booming.

As its name implies, TRC specializes in the treatment of renal ailments. It is the nation's third largest provider of dialysis services for patients suffering from chronic kidney failure, known as end stage renal disease (ESRD).

ESRD is an advanced and irreversible stage of renal impairment that requires routine dialysis treatments or kidney transplants to sustain life. More than 200,000 Americans suffer from ESRD, up from 66,000 in 1982, and the company projects that the rate of growth will continue at about 9 percent per year through the next five years.

TRC treats more than 10,000 patients per year through its network of about 130 outpatient dialysis facilities in 16 states. It also provides in-patient dialysis services at about 85 hospitals. Since 1994, the firm has opened 10 new dialysis facilities and acquired 79 existing facilities.

The company plans to pursue an aggressive expansion program by focusing on several key growth strategies. It will continue to make additional acquisitions and construct new centers, it will form business alliances with hospitals, physicians and managed care organizations, and it will continue to expand the range of ancillary services it provides for renal care patients. Among the ancillary services it currently offers are ESRD laboratory and pharmacy facilities, vascular access management and kidney transplant services.

Formerly known as Medical Ambulatory Care, TRC reorganized and changed its name in 1994, and issued stock in October 1995. The company has about 3,000 employees.

Late developments

The company acquired 12 dialysis centers with 1,200 patients over a five-month period in 1996. The biggest was the Houston Kidney Centers, which included four facilities with 67 dialysis stations and about 350 patients.

Performance

Stock growth (past year through 12/31/96): 21% (from $30.00 to $39.25).
Revenue growth (past two years through 12/31/96): 239% (from $80.5 million to $273 million).
Earnings per share growth (past two years through 12/31/96): 148% (from $0.37 to $0.92).

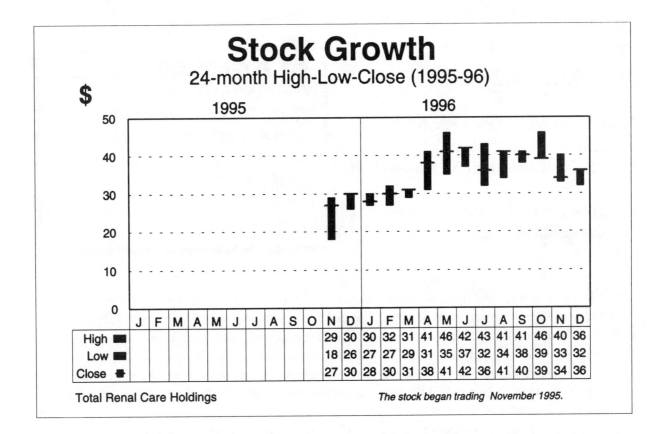

Stock Growth
24-month High-Low-Close (1995-96)

Total Renal Care Holdings

The stock began trading November 1995.

	J	F	M	A	M	J	J	A	S	O	N	D	J	F	M	A	M	J	J	A	S	O	N	D
High											29	30	30	32	31	41	46	42	43	41	41	46	40	36
Low											18	26	27	27	29	31	35	37	32	34	38	39	33	32
Close											27	30	28	30	31	38	41	42	36	41	40	39	34	36

Quick Fix

P/E range (past two years):	38 - 80
Earnings past four quarters:	$0.92 (through 12/31/96)
Projected 1997 earnings (median):	$1.21
International sales:	None
Total current assets:	$115.9 million (1996); $75.5 million (1995)
Total current liabilities:	$30.7 million (1996); $20.8 million (1995)
Net Income:	$26 million {1996); $8.2 million (1995)

Financial history

Fiscal year ended: Dec. 31
(Revenue in millions)

	1992	1993	1994	1995	1996
Revenue	$63.9	$71.6	$80.5	$89.7	$272.9
Earnings per share	NA	NA	0.31	0.36	0.92
Stock price: High	NA	NA	NA	30.00	46.38
Low	NA	NA	NA	18.00	27.00
Close	NA	NA	NA	30.00	36.25

46

Just For Feet, Inc.

153 Cahaba Valley Parkway North
Pelham, AL 35124
Phone: 210-403-8000; FAX: 205-403-8200

Chairman, President and CEO:
   Harold Ruttenberg

AT A GLANCE

Held by number of funds: 3
Industry: Retail shoe superstores
Earnings growth past 2 years: 757%
Stock price 1/1/97: $26.25
P/E ratio: 51
Year ago P/E: 58
NASDAQ: FEET

Now here's a concept Imelda Marcos couldn't resist. Just For Feet carries more than 4,000 different styles of shoes in its footwear superstores. By comparison, most mall-based shoe stores and department stores carry only about 200 to 700 different styles.

The company sells shoes for almost every sport and recreational activity, from wrestling to aerobics, from walking to football. In fact, the stores even carry in-line skates. Shoes are available in sizes from infants' size one to men's size 21.

Just For Fee currently operates about 45 company stores and seven franchise stores in 12 states—which means there is still plenty of room for growth. The company has been opening about 14 new stores per year.

The company's stores, which tend to be located in larger metropolitan areas, range in size from 15,000 to 20,000 square feet. That's about three to four times larger than the typical retail shoe store.

Just For Feet does not promote itself as a discounter, but it does offer special sales from time to time, and it regularly buys merchandise from leading vendors at close-out prices. Those specially-priced items are normally sold at prices ranging from 30 to 60 percent below list prices, and are featured in the front of the stores in an area called the "Combat Zone."

While shoes are the company's primary focus, its stores do carry a limited selection of apparel and accessories such as warm-up suits, T-shirts, athletic shorts, caps, socks and shoe care products.

The company opened its first store in 1977, and its first superstore in 1988. Just For Feet went public with its initial public offering in 1994. The Alabama-based retailer has about 1,000 full-time employees and 2,500 part-time employees.

Late developments

The company announced in late 1996 that it would accelerate its store expansion plans. The company will open a total of about 38 new stores during a 24-month period ending January 31, 1998. At that time, the company will have a total of 65 stores.

Performance

Stock growth (past two years through 12/31/96): 247% (from $7.56 to $26.25).
Revenue growth (past two years through 10/31/96): 380% (from $45 million to $215.7 million).
Earnings per share growth (past two years through 10/31/96): 757% (from $0.07 to $0.60).

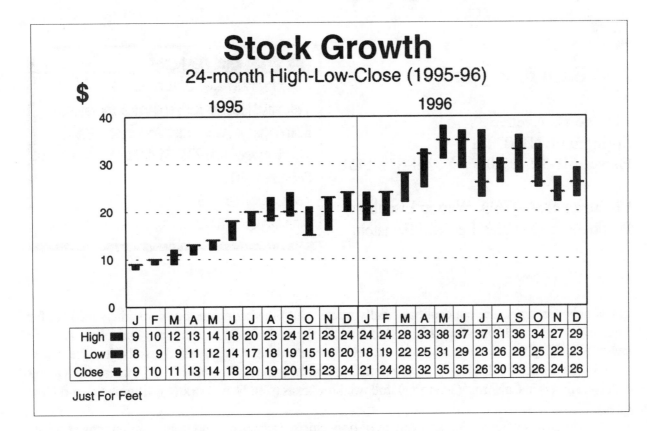

Stock Growth
24-month High-Low-Close (1995-96)

	J	F	M	A	M	J	J	A	S	O	N	D	J	F	M	A	M	J	J	A	S	O	N	D
High	9	10	12	13	14	18	20	23	24	21	23	24	24	24	28	33	38	37	37	31	36	34	27	29
Low	8	9	9	11	12	14	17	18	19	15	16	20	18	19	22	25	31	29	23	26	28	25	22	23
Close	9	10	11	13	14	18	20	19	20	15	23	24	21	24	28	32	35	35	26	30	33	26	24	26

Just For Feet

Quick Fix

P/E range (past two years):	20 - 65
Earnings past four quarters:	$0.60 (through 10/31/96)
Projected fiscal 1998 earnings:	$0.90
International sales:	None
Total current assets:	$224.4 million (7/31/96); $94.3 million (7/31/95)
Total current liabilities:	$51.8 million (7/31/96); $38.7 million (7/31/95)
Net Income:	$9.7 million (1996); $3.2 million (1995)

Financial history

Fiscal year ended: Jan. 31
(Revenue in millions)

	1992	1993	1994	1995	1996
Revenue	$8.5	$17.2	$23.7	$56.4	$119.8
Earnings per share	-0.02	0.05	-0.02	0.18	0.38
*Stock price: High	NA	NA	10.37	24.67	37.88
Low	NA	NA	3.19	7.61	17.56
Close	NA	NA	7.61	23.83	26.25

*Stock prices (only) reflect calendar year.

47

Bed Bath & Beyond, Inc.

715 Morris Avenue
Springfield, NJ 07081
Phone: 201-379-1520; FAX: 201-379-1731

Chairman & Co-CEO: Warren Eisenberg
President & Co-CEO: Leonard Feinstein

The warehouse superstore concept has finally made it into the bedroom. For consumers looking for a massive selection of home furnishings, Bed Bath & Beyond (BBB) is a shopping paradise. And for investors looking for a solid growth opportunity in the retail sector, BBB could also be just the ticket.

The Springfield, New Jersey, retailer operates about 107 stores in 25 states. Its leading concentration is in California (13 stores), followed by Texas (12), New York (8), Illinois (7) and New Jersey (7).

The stores offer a wide assortment of domestic merchandise and home furnishings at prices substantially below regular department store prices. The stores carry items such as bed linens, bath accessories, kitchen textiles, cookware, dinnerware and other basic housewares.

The selection is far greater than that generally available in department stores and other specialty retail stores. Its leading product line is bed linens, which accounts for about 20 percent of net sales.

BBB was founded in 1971 when Leonard Feinstein and Warren Eisenberg opened two stores – one in New York, one in New Jersey – under the name "Bed 'n Bath." Feinstein and Eisenberg continue to serve as co-CEOs of the company. Over the next 14 years, the pair opened additional stores in Connecticut and California. Then in 1985, they introduced a new superstore format, and changed the name two years later to "Bed Bath & Beyond."

The company opens about 20 to 30 new stores each year, and continues to expand its existing stores. Most of its stores range in size from 30,000 to 50,000 square feet, although some of the newer stores are as large as 85,000 square feet.

BBB has about 5,500 employees, including 3,500 full-time and about 2,000 part-time workers.

Late developments

The company opened stores in two new states in 1996, New Mexico and Tennessee.

Performance

Stock growth (past two years through 12/31/96): 62 % (from $15.00 to $24.25).
Revenue growth (past two years through 8/30/96): 91% (from $366.3 million to $700.8 million).
Earnings per share growth (past two years through 8/30/96): 76% (from $0.37 to $0.65).

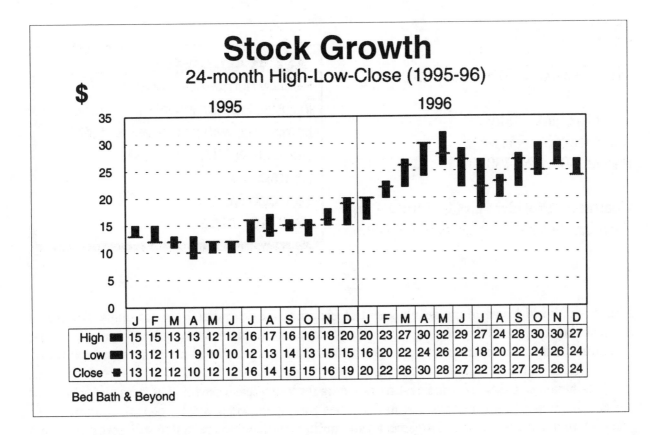

Stock Growth
24-month High-Low-Close (1995-96)

	J	F	M	A	M	J	J	A	S	O	N	D	J	F	M	A	M	J	J	A	S	O	N	D
High	15	15	13	13	12	12	16	17	16	16	18	20	20	23	27	30	32	29	27	24	28	30	30	27
Low	13	12	11	9	10	10	12	13	14	13	15	15	16	20	22	24	26	22	18	20	22	24	26	24
Close	13	12	12	10	12	12	16	14	15	15	16	19	20	22	26	30	28	27	22	23	27	25	26	24

Bed Bath & Beyond

Quick Fix

P/E range (past two years):	16 - 40
Earnings past four quarters:	$0.65 (through 8/30/96)
Projected 1997 earnings (median):	$0.75
International sales:	NA
Total current assets:	$206.1 million (8/30/96); $149.6 million (1995)
Total current liabilities:	$103.8 million (8/30/96); $160.3 million (1995)
Net Income:	$39.4 million (1996); $30.0 million (1995)

Financial history

Fiscal year ended: Feb. 28
(Revenue in millions)

	1992	1993	1994	1995	1996
Revenue	$167.6	$216.7	$305.7	$440.3	$601.2
Earnings per share	0.18	0.24	0.32	0.43	0.57
*Stock price: High	9.50	17.75	17.25	19.81	31.50
Low	3.50	6.50	11.38	9.00	16.38
Close	9.25	17.25	15.00	19.41	24.25

*Stock prices (only) reflect calendar year.

48
Altera Corp.

2610 Orchard Parkway
San Jose, CA 95134
Phone: 408-894-7000

Chairman, President and CEO:
  Rodney Smith

Altera is a world leader in the development of programmable computer "logic" chips that enable engineers to design and develop high technology electronic products more quickly and effectively. The semi-conductor chips are programmed with tools that run on personal computers or engineering workstations.

Altera also develops a line of software tools for logic development. The company's primary markets include manufacturers of communications equipment (61 percent of sales), computers (16 percent), industrial equipment (14 percent), and military and aerospace systems (5 percent). Altera chips are used in the electronic systems of high-speed trains, high definition television sets, professional videorecording systems, complex medical equipment, and a variety of other high-end, high-tech products.

The programmable chip market has been growing rapidly in recent years. Because the chips are programmable, they enable engineers to design products faster and manufacturers to bring them to market more quickly. Altera's programmable chips can be purchased "off the shelf" and configured by customers to their specific requirements.

The first logic chip, introduced by Altera in 1984, boasted a density of 300 gates (a unit of measurement for logic). Now the densities range as high as 100,000 gates, allowing dramatically faster and more complex programmable performance.

Altera also produces specialized software packages for engineering functions, and provides application assistance, design services, and customer training.

Founded in 1983, the San Jose, California, company has about 900 employees. About half of the company's sales are generated outside the U.S. market.

Late developments
The company's Flex 10K product line has been a leading contributor to its earnings and revenue growth. The Flex 10K chips are the company's largest devices, with approximately 100,000 useable gates.

Performance
Stock growth (past two years through 12/31/96): 247% (from $10.47 to $36.34).
Revenue growth (past two years through 12/31/96): 150% (from $199 million to $497 million).
Earnings per share growth (past two years through 12/31/96): 600% (from $0.17 to $1.19).

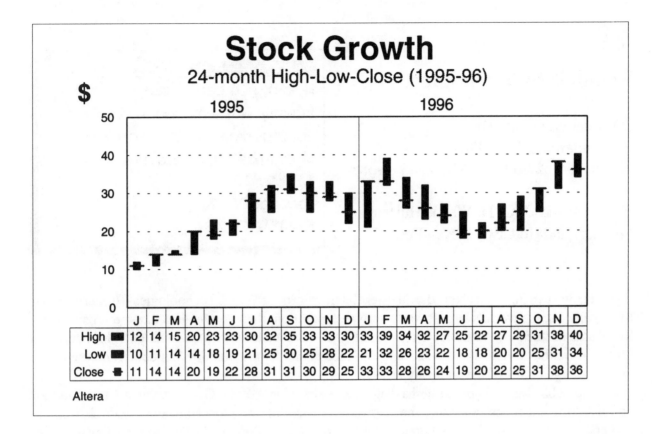

Stock Growth
24-month High-Low-Close (1995-96)

	J	F	M	A	M	J	J	A	S	O	N	D	J	F	M	A	M	J	J	A	S	O	N	D
High	12	14	15	20	23	23	30	32	35	33	33	30	33	39	34	32	27	25	22	27	29	31	38	40
Low	10	11	14	14	18	19	21	25	30	25	28	22	21	32	26	23	22	18	18	20	20	25	31	34
Close	11	14	14	20	19	22	28	31	31	30	29	25	33	33	28	26	24	19	20	22	25	31	38	36

Altera

Quick Fix

P/E range (past two years):	10 - 37
Earnings past four quarters:	$1.19 (through 12/31/96)
Projected 1997 earnings (median):	$2.79
International sales:	50% of total sales
Total current assets:	$475.6 million (1996); $518 million (1995)
Total current liabilities:	$194.9 million (1996); $171.8 million (1995)
Net Income:	$1.09.1 (1996); $86.8 million (1995)

Financial history

Fiscal year ended: Dec. 31

(Revenue in millions)

	1992	1993	1994	1995	1996
Revenue	$101.5	$140.3	$198.8	$401.6	$497.3
Earnings per share	0.14	0.25	0.17	0.95	1.19
Stock price: High	9.00	8.41	10.78	35.44	39.94
Low	2.03	2.97	3.81	9.81	13.13
Close	3.22	8.19	10.47	24.88	36.34

49

Republic Industries, Inc.

200 East Las Olas Blvd.
Ft. Lauderdale, FL 33301
Phone: 954-627-6000; FAX: 954-779-3884

Chairman and CEO: H. Wayne Huizenga
President and Co-CEO: Steven Berrard

AT A GLANCE

Held by number of funds: 3
Industry: Waste management services
Earnings growth past 2 years: 44%
Stock price 1/1/97: $31.19
P/E ratio: 135
Year ago P/E: 98
NASDAQ: RWIN

If you know anything at all about Blockbuster Entertainment or WMX Technologies (formerly Waste Management), the world's largest waste services operation, then you have to like the prospects for Republic Industries. H. Wayne Huizenga, the 58-year-old executive who co-founded WMX and later turned Blockbuster into the nation's largest video chain, is now running Republic Industries after buying a large chunk of the company in 1995.

Republic was a simple waste-hauling business based in Atlanta, Georgia, when Huizenga took control. But under his guidance, the company is changing rapidly. Huizenga, who also has an ownership stake in football's Miami Dolphins, baseball's Florida Marlins and hockey's Florida Panthers, immediately moved Republic's headquarters to Ft. Lauderdale, and began developing new core businesses.

Under Huizenga, the company will continue to expand its waste hauling business (primarily through acquisitions), and will actively build core businesses in home security systems and billboard advertising. Like Blockbuster's, both new areas are essentially rental businesses. In the security systems business, the company installs home alarm systems and collects a monthly monitoring fee—just as it collects monthly fees from billboard customers, and just as it collects a steady stream of income from dumpster rentals in the trash hauling business. Huizenga plans to build all three businesses through a rapid-fire series of acquisitions. The company is also expanding into the rental car and used car superstore business.

To help him shape Republic, Huizenga hired former Blockbuster president, Steven R. Berrard, as president and co-CEO. Republic, which operates landfill and trash collection operations in Texas, California, Florida, Michigan, North Carolina, South Carolina, Indiana and North Dakota, has about 5,000 employees.

Late developments

In late 1996, the company acquired Alamo Rent-A-Car, the nation's fourth largest car rental agency. Also in 1996, Republic acquired CarChoice and AutoNation USA, both of which operate a chain of used car superstores. Republic also acquired ADT, Ltd., the largest provider of electronic security services in North America and the United Kingdom.

Performance

Stock growth (past two years through 12/31/96): 1,460% (from $2.00 to $31.19).
Revenue growth (past two years through 12/31/96): 1,162% (from $187 million to $2.36 bllion).
Earnings per share growth (past two years through 12/31/96): 44% (from $0.16 to $0.23).

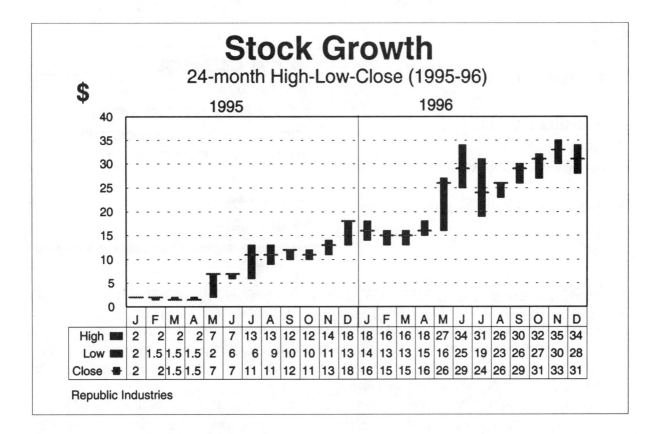

Stock Growth
24-month High-Low-Close (1995-96)

	1995												1996											
	J	F	M	A	M	J	J	A	S	O	N	D	J	F	M	A	M	J	J	A	S	O	N	D
High	2	2	2	2	7	7	13	13	12	12	14	18	18	16	16	18	27	34	31	26	30	32	35	34
Low	2	1.5	1.5	1.5	2	6	6	9	10	10	11	13	14	13	13	15	16	25	19	23	26	27	30	28
Close	2	2	1.5	1.5	7	7	11	11	12	11	13	18	16	15	15	16	26	29	24	26	29	31	33	31

Republic Industries

Quick Fix

P/E range (past two years):	8 - 138
Earnings past four quarters:	$0.23 (through 12/31/96)
Projected 1997 earnings (median):	$0.59
International sales:	Less than 5% of total sales
Total current assets:	$378.0 million (1996); $206.8 million (1995)
Total current liabilities:	$97.2 million (1996); $63.9 million (1995)
Net Income:	$53 million* (1996); $23.2 million (1995)

Financial history

Fiscal year ended: Dec. 31
(Revenue in millions)

	1992	1993	1994	1995	*1996
Revenue	$134.4	$154.3	$187.1	$1,791	$2,365
Earnings per share	0.08	-0.03	0.16	0.19	0.23*
Stock price: High	6.81	2.75	2.06	18.06	34.63
Low	2.25	1.38	1.25	1.50	13.19
Close	2.63	1.69	2.00	18.06	31.19

*1996 earnings and net income (above) exclude charges relating to Alamo acquisition and $31.6
million in early repayment of debt.

50

Solectron Corp.

777 Gibraltar Drive
Milpitas, CA 95035
Phone: 408-957-8500; FAX: 408-957-6075

President and CEO: Koichi Nishimura

Need it done? Can't do it. Outsource it. Electronics companies turn to Solectron to help with the design and manufacturing of products they can't make on their own.

The Milpitas, California, operation is a custom manufacturer of electronic systems and subsystems for companies in the avionics, communications, computer, consumer electronics, industrial, medical, semiconductor, software and related industries. The company can pitch in on product design, assembly and even warehousing.

Solectron's outsourcing services provide a number of benefits for its corporate customers:

- *Reduces time-to-market.* With the intense competitive pressures in the electronics industry, manufacturers have shorter product life cycles, and a greater need to shorten the time-to-market for their products. Solectron helps them get their new products out faster by providing the manufacturing capabilities and expertise.

- *Reduces capital investment.* Manufacturers don't have to invest in the latest manufacturing technology in order to put out advanced products. They can rely instead on Solectron's facilities.

- *Allows them to focus their resources.* Companies can put more of their resources into product development and marketing by letting Solectron handle the manufacturing.

Solectron markets its services worldwide, with international sales accounting for about 29 percent of total revenue. About 90 percent of its business comes from repeat customers.

In addition to its manufacturing capabilities, Solectron offers a variety of turnkey options, such as materials management, circuit board design, concurrent engineering, assembly of complex printed circuit boards and other electronic assemblies, test engineering, software manufacturing, and accessory packaging.

Founded in 1977, the company has about 11,000 employees. Solectron received the Malcom Baldrige National Quality Award in 1991.

Late developments

The company continues to stretch its international operations, opening facilities recently in Germany, Malaysia and China.

Performance

Stock growth (past two years through 12/31/96): 94% (from $27.50 to $53.38).
Revenue growth (past two years through 8/30/96): 93% (from $1.45 billion to $2.8 billion).
Earnings per share growth (past two years through 8/30/96): 68% (from $1.31 to $2.20).

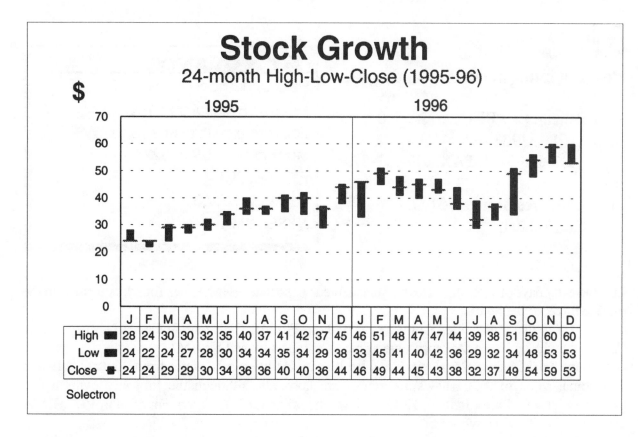

Stock Growth
24-month High-Low-Close (1995-96)

	1995												1996											
	J	F	M	A	M	J	J	A	S	O	N	D	J	F	M	A	M	J	J	A	S	O	N	D
High	28	24	30	30	32	35	40	37	41	42	37	45	46	51	48	47	47	44	39	38	51	56	60	60
Low	24	22	24	27	28	30	34	34	35	34	29	38	33	45	41	40	42	36	29	32	34	48	53	53
Close	24	24	29	29	30	34	36	36	40	40	36	44	46	49	44	45	43	38	32	37	49	54	59	53

Solectron

Quick Fix

P/E range (past two years):	12 - 27
Earnings past four quarters:	$2.20 (through 8/30/96)
Projected 1997 earnings (median):	$2.78
International sales:	29 percent of total sales (Asia/Pacific, 12%; Europe, 17%)
Total current assets:	$1.14 billion (1996); $726.3 million (1995)
Total current liabilities:	$358.4 million (1996); $370.7 million (1995)
Net Income:	$114.2 million (1996); $79.5 million (1995)

Financial history

Fiscal year ended: Aug. 31
(Revenue in millions)

	1992	1993	1994	1995	1996
Revenue	$406.9	$836.3	$1,456.8	$2,065.5	$2,817.2
Earnings per share	0.44	0.75	1.18	1.62	2.17
*Stock price: High	18.69	29.75	34.00	45.13	60.13
Low	4.66	16.56	23.38	22.13	29.00
Close	18.69	28.38	27.50	44.13	53.38

*Stock prices (only) reflect calendar year.

51

Health Management Associates, Inc.

5811 Pelican Bay Blvd., Suite 500
Naples, FL 33963
Phone: 813-598-3131; FAX: 813-597-5794

Chairman, President and CEO:
  William Schoen

Like the early days of Wal-Mart, Health Management Associates (HMA) has found its fortune in the rural hamlets of the South.

Burgs like Painteville, Kentucky; Marathon, Florida; Gadsden, Alabama; Gaffney, South Carolina, and Van Buren, Arkansas, are home to hospitals owned by HMA.

In all, HMA owns 25 hospitals and health care facilities in 11 states from South Carolina to Oklahoma. Most of the facilities are acute care hospitals, although the firm also owns a few psychiatric care facilities. In total, HMA facilities house about 3,000 beds. Founded in 1977, HMA has more than 7,000 employees.

Since becoming president of HMA in 1983, William Schoen's strategy of acquiring unprofitable and undervalued hospitals in small markets has paid off with a growing stream of revenue. Schoen uses a combination of cost controls, marketing and technological upgrading to quickly turn his losing acquisitions into winners.

HMA is able to cut costs by using cutting administrative and staffing costs, and by utilizing centralized, volume purchasing and streamlined, computerized record-keeping. To attract more patients, the Naples, Florida, operation renovates its newly-acquired facilities and equips them with the latest medical devices, such as magnetic resonance imagers. HMA also adds new medical services, such as cardiology care, and pursues an aggressive policy of recruiting and retaining top physicians and surgeons.

The combination of improved facilities and equipment, and broader medical services helps bring in a higher percentage of the locally-based patients. Rather than drive 50 to 100 miles to stay at a metropolitan hospital, local residents are more likely to chose to stay close to home at an HMA facility.

HMA plans to continue to add more hospitals to its growing stable – and with 2,500 rural-based hospitals nationwide, the prospects seem almost endless.

Late developments

HMA made two acquisitions in 1996, including the purchase of the 195-bed Northwest Mississippi Regional Medical Center in Clarksdale, Mississippi, and the 206-bed Midwest City Memorial Hospital in Midwest City, Oklahoma.

Performance

Stock growth (past two years through 12/31/96): 106% (from $10.94 to $22.50).
Revenue growth (past two years through 9/30/96): 63% (from $438.4 million to $714.3 million).
Earnings per share growth (past two years through 9/30/96): 65% (from $0.46 to $0.76).

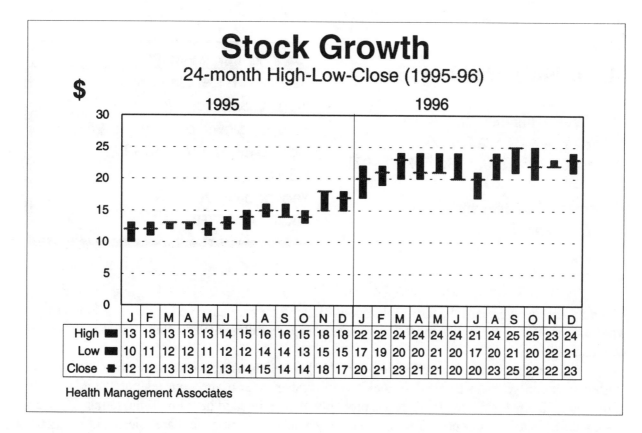

Stock Growth
24-month High-Low-Close (1995-96)

	1995												1996											
	J	F	M	A	M	J	J	A	S	O	N	D	J	F	M	A	M	J	J	A	S	O	N	D
High	13	13	13	13	13	14	15	16	16	15	18	18	22	22	24	24	24	24	21	24	25	25	23	24
Low	10	11	12	12	11	12	12	14	14	13	15	15	17	19	20	20	21	20	17	20	21	20	22	21
Close	12	12	13	13	12	13	14	15	14	14	18	17	20	21	23	21	21	20	20	23	25	22	22	23

Health Management Associates

Quick Fix

P/E range (past two years):	18 - 33
Earnings past four quarters:	$0.76 (through 9/30/96)
Projected 1997 earnings (median):	$0.91
International sales:	None
Total assets:	$559.2 million (6/30/96); $467 million (1995)
Total current liabilities:	$67million (6/30/96); $50.6 million (1995)
Net Income:	$84.1 million (1996); $63.3 million (1995)

Financial history

Fiscal year ended: Sept. 30
(Revenue in millions)

	1992	1993	1994	1995	1996
Revenue	$301.8	$346.7	$438.4	$531.1	$714.3
Earnings per share	0.23	0.32	0.46	0.58	0.76
*Stock price: High	5.66	8.67	11.85	18.00	24.88
Low	3.70	3.11	8.00	10.44	16.75
Close	5.14	8.67	11.11	17.42	22.50

*Stock prices (only) reflect calendar year.

52

Microchip Technology, Inc.

2355 West Chandler Boulevard
Chandler, AZ   85224-6199
Phone: 602-786-7200; FAX: 602-899-9210

Chairman, President and CEO:
    Steve Sanghi

You may never have heard the term "microcontroller." You may have no idea what it looks like or what it does. But if you're like most Americans, microcontrollers have become an intricate part of your daily life.

You may find microcontrollers in your TV channel changer, your garage door opener, your toaster, your car, your electronic door locks, your washer, your dryer, your telephone and in many of the toys you buy for your kids. They are probably also embedded in many of the items you use at work such as your fax, your computer and your copy machine. So prevalent are microcontrollers that nearly 2.5 billion of them are inserted into new products every year.

Microcontrollers are the tiny semiconductor chips inserted into this vast range of products that provide the intelligence to run those products.

Microchip Technology is a leader in the development and production of microcontrollers. Since 1990, the company's 8-bit field programmable microcontrollers have been inserted into nearly half a billion products. The company has more than 6,000 corporate customers around the world.

Microprocessors have become popular for several important reasons. They're very small, very powerful, they work well under low voltage and they're very cheap. The cost of Microchip's microcontrollers ranges from about 80 cents to $10 a piece.

Microchip also makes a line of specialty memory chips such as erasable programmable read-only memory chips (EPROMs).

The Phoenix area operation markets its products worldwide through a direct sales organization of about 130 people, and through independent distributors. About 65 percent of its revenue is generated outside the U.S.

Microchip Technology has about 1,700 employees.

Late developments

The company began production in late 1996 at its new final test facility in Bangkok, Thailand.

Performance

Stock growth (past two years through 12/31/96): 85% (from $18.33 to $33.92).
Revenue growth (past two years through 9/30/96): 75% (from $173.8 million to $303.8 million).
Earnings per share growth (past two years through 9/30/96): 25% (from $0.58 to $0.73).

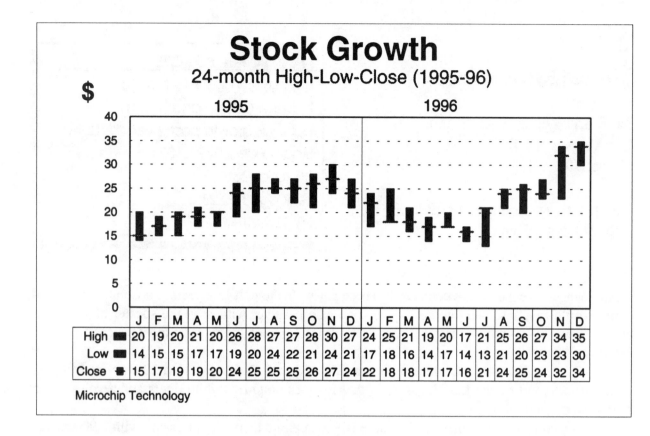

Stock Growth
24-month High-Low-Close (1995-96)

$

1995 | 1996

	J	F	M	A	M	J	J	A	S	O	N	D	J	F	M	A	M	J	J	A	S	O	N	D
High	20	19	20	21	20	26	28	27	27	28	30	27	24	25	21	19	20	17	21	25	26	27	34	35
Low	14	15	15	17	17	19	20	24	22	21	24	21	17	18	16	14	17	14	13	21	20	23	23	30
Close	15	17	19	19	20	24	25	25	25	26	27	24	22	18	18	17	17	16	21	24	25	24	32	34

Microchip Technology

Quick Fix

P/E range (past two years):	18 - 50
Earnings past four quarters:	$0.73 (through 9/30/96)
Projected 1997 earnings (median):	$1.04
International sales:	65 percent of total sales (Asia/Pacific)
Total current assets:	$149.2 million (9/30/96); $151.2 million (9/30/95)
Total current liabilities:	$150.6 million (9/30/96); $107.6 million (9/30/95)
Net Income:	$43.7 million (1996); $36.3 million (1995)

Financial history

Fiscal year ended: March 31
(Revenue in millions)

	1992	1993	1994	1995	1996
Revenue	$0.360	$4.22	$19.2	$36.3	$43.7
Earnings per share	0.02	0.12	0.42	0.70	0.80
*Stock price: High	NA	11.56	21.11	30.00	35.38
Low	NA	2.09	8.56	14.50	13.06
Close	NA	11.56	18.33	24.33	33.92

Stock prices (only) reflect calendar year.

53

Mirage Resorts, Inc.

3400 Las Vegas Blvd. South
Las Vegas, NV 89109
Phone: 702-791-7111; FAX: 702-792-7646

Chairman, President and CEO:
  Stephen A. Wynn

It's no mirage—the money this company has been pulling in the past few years is absolutely real (and, some would say, absolutely unreal—as anyone who has ever witnessed the specter of the Vegas casino scene would attest). Mirage Resorts operates some of the world's most successful casino resorts.

The Las Vegas-based company operates the Mirage Casino Hotel, a 29-story, 3.1 million-square-foot resort on the Las Vegas Strip that features dolphins, white tigers and a volcano that erupts every 15 minutes.

The company also operates Treasure Island, a pirate theme hotel-casino with 2,900 rooms, two gourmet restaurants and wealth of other extras that is also located on the Vegas Strip.

Mirage also owns the famous Golden Nugget in downtown Las Vegas, and the Golden Nugget-Laughlin in Laughlin, Nevada.

The company's newest venture is the Monte Carlo Resort & Casino, which is located near its other properties on the Vegas Strip. Mirage is a 50 percent owner of the resort, which opened June 21, 1996. The Mirage is a 3000-room, mid-priced hotel-casino resort that includes a variety of extras, such as health spa, a pool with waterfalls, tennis courts, restaurants, sunning decks, a cascading wave pool and an "easy river" water ride.

Mirage Resorts traces its roots back 52 years to the opening of the Golden Nugget in 1945. The company currently has about 15,000 full-time employees and 2,200 part-time employees.

Late developments

The company is currently constructing two wholly-owned hotel-casino resorts, including the Bellagio, a 3,000-room luxury resort scheduled to be completed in 1998 on 120 acres next to the Monte Carlo. Designed to be the most luxurious hotel in Las Vegas, it will overlook a 12-acre lake. Total development cost is expected to be about $1 billion.

The other project under construction is the Beau Rivage, an upscale 1,800-room resort in Biloxi, Mississippi, which is also scheduled to be completed in 1998. The company is also working with the New Jersey Casino Control Commission to receive clearance to build a large casino in Atlantic City.

Performance

Stock growth (past two years through 12/31/96): 111% (from $10.25 to $21.63).
Revenue growth (past two years through 9/30/96): 15% (from $1.22 billion to $1.4 billion).
Earnings per share growth (past two years through 9/30/96): 100% (from $0.51 to $1.02).

116

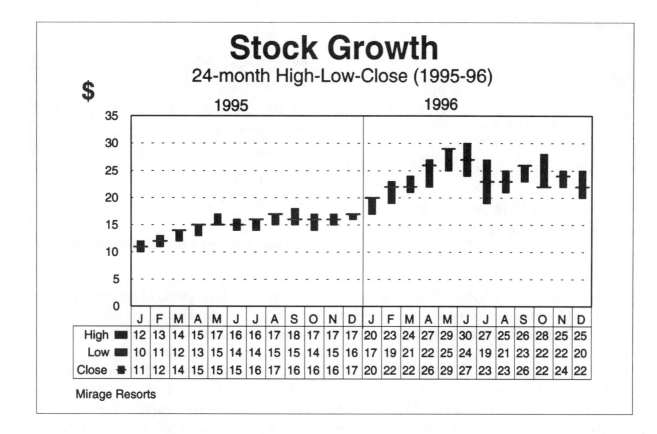

Stock Growth
24-month High-Low-Close (1995-96)

	J	F	M	A	M	J	J	A	S	O	N	D	J	F	M	A	M	J	J	A	S	O	N	D
High	12	13	14	15	17	16	16	17	18	17	17	17	20	23	24	27	29	30	27	25	26	28	25	25
Low	10	11	12	13	15	14	14	15	15	14	15	16	17	19	21	22	25	24	19	21	23	22	22	20
Close	11	12	14	15	15	15	16	17	16	16	16	17	20	22	22	26	29	27	23	23	26	22	24	22

Mirage Resorts

Quick Fix

P/E range (past two years):	11 - 27
Earnings past four quarters:	$1.02 (through 9/30/96)
Projected 1997 earnings (median):	$1.15
International sales:	none
Total current assets:	$193 million (1996); $169.7 million (1995)
Total current liabilities:	$151.4 million (1996); $133.3 million (1995)
Net Income:	$170 million (1995); $124.7 million (1994)

Financial history

Fiscal year ended: Dec. 31
(Revenue in millions)

	1992	1993	1994	1995	*1996
Revenue	$833	$953.3	$1,254	$1,331	$1,058*
Earnings per share	0.26	0.29	0.66	0.89	0.79*
Stock price: High	7.43	12.50	18.13	17.56	29.63
Low	4.40	6.55	8.31	9.88	15.56
Close	6.55	11.94	10.25	17.25	21.63

1996 revenue and earnings through Sept. 30 (nine months).

54

National Data Corp.

National Data Plaza
Atlanta, GA 30329-2010
Phone: 404-728-2000; FAX: 404-728-2551

Chairman President and CEO:
 Robert Yellowlees

National Data Corp. (NDC) doesn't dole out the medicine, but it handles the claims for about 3.5 million medical customers per day. In all, it processed 2.25 billion transactions in fiscal 1996.

NDC provides electronic claims processing and adjudication services, billing services, clinical data base information and related services for pharmacies, dentists, physicians, hospitals, health maintenance organizations, managed care companies, clinics, nursing homes and other health care providers. In all, the company serves a customer base of about 70,000 health care providers, 1,000 health care plans, more than 350,000 merchant locations, 35,000 corporations and 300 banking institutions. The Atlanta operation also provides related services for state and federal government agencies.

About 45 percent of the company's revenue comes from its healthcare claims processing and related services.

Through its Global Payment Systems subsidiary, the company provides transaction processing for banks and their merchant customers. Global also provides electronic information reporting and cash flow services to thousands of corporations and government agencies, and it recently introduced a purchase card processing program that provides electronic payment capabilities for business-to-business purchasing transactions. Global accounts for about 32 percent of the NDC's total revenue.

NDC's Integrated Payment Systems business provides merchant authorization, processing and settlement services for a broad range of merchants, healthcare providers, trade associations, universities and financial institutions. Integrated accounts for about 32 percent of NDC's annual revenue.

Founded in 1967, NDC has about 2,500 employees.

Late developments

In January 1997, the company reached an agreement with Georgia Hospital Health Services to market NDC's payment systems products, eligibility verification and electronic data interchange services to the 180 hospitals, clinics and physician practices in the Georgia Hospital Health network.

Performance

Stock growth (past two years through 12/31/96): 153% (from $17.19 to $43.50).

Revenue growth (past two years through 8/30/96): 59% (from $219 million to $349 million).

Earnings per share growth (past two years through 8/30/96): 82% {from $0.62 to $1.13 (excluding restructuring and acquisition charges)}.

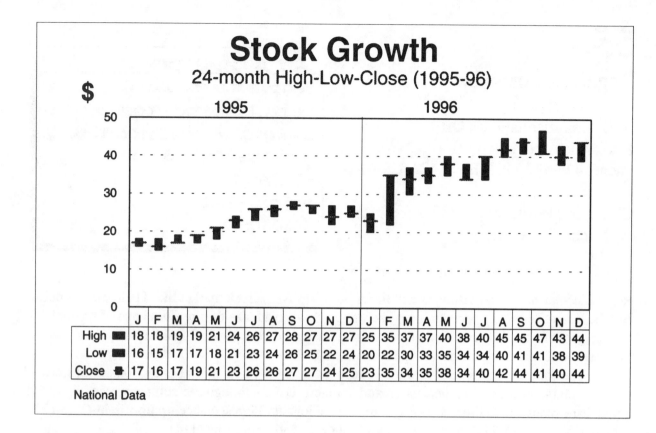

Stock Growth
24-month High-Low-Close (1995-96)

		J	F	M	A	M	J	J	A	S	O	N	D	J	F	M	A	M	J	J	A	S	O	N	D
High	■	18	18	19	19	21	24	26	27	28	27	27	27	25	35	37	37	40	38	40	45	45	47	43	44
Low	■	16	15	17	17	18	21	23	24	26	25	22	24	20	22	30	33	35	34	34	40	41	41	38	39
Close	■	17	16	17	19	21	23	26	26	27	27	24	25	23	35	34	35	38	34	40	42	44	41	40	44

National Data

Quick Fix

P/E range (past two years):	15 - 41*
Earnings past four quarters:	*$1.13 (through 8/30/96)
Projected 1997 earnings (median):	$1.34
International sales:	3 percent of total sales (Canada, England, Japan)
Total current assets:	$81.4 million (1996); $95.2 million (1995)
Total current liabilities:	$102.7 million (1996); $61.6 million (1995)
Net Income:	*$24.7 million (1996); $18.4 million (1995)

Excludes 1996 restructuring and acquisition charges

Financial history

Fiscal year ended: May 31

(Revenue in millions)

	1992	1993	1994	1995	1996
Revenue	$216.5	$206.2	$237.7	$278.1	$325.8
Earnings per share	0.41	0.45	0.55	0.75	1.01*
Dividends	0.29	0.29	0.29	0.30	0.30
**Stock price: High	11.83	12.83	17.58	28.00	46.63
Low	5.33	9.75	10.33	15.33	20.00
Close	9.00	11.25	17.17	24.75	43.50

Excludes restructuring and acquisition charges.   **Stock prices (only) reflect calendar year.*

55

Regal Cinemas, Inc.

7132 Commercial Park Drive
Knoxville, TN 37918
Phone: 423-922-1123; FAX: 423-922-6739

Chairman, President and CEO:
    Michael L. Campbell

Regal Cinemas has been blasting across the American silver screen market like Thelma and Louise. But the Knoxville-based operation is not likely to go down in a blaze of glory. It is one of the nation's fastest-growing motion picture theater companies. Founded in 1989, Regal has already grown to become the seventh largest theater operator in the U.S.

The company has about 150 multi-screen theaters with a total of about 1,300 screens. Most of its theaters are located in the eastern and southern U.S., although the company recently added about 70 screens in California through an acquisition. Its largest concentration is in Ohio (243 screens), Virginia (152), Georgia (181), Florida (116) and Tennessee (114).

The firm also operates two FunScape family entertainment centers. FunScapes are one-story operations that include 13 movie screens, and a 50,000-square-foot entertainment area with a food court, batting cages, arcade, miniature golf, a party room and a variety of games and other amusements. The FunScape centers, which are located in Chesapeake, Virginia, and Rochester, New York, cost about $5 million to build.

Regal has flourished through an aggressive four-pronged growth strategy:

- *Construction of new theaters in existing and target markets.* The company continues to add new multi-screen theaters both in its existing markets and in other mid-sized metropolitan and suburban markets.

- *Addition of new screens to existing theaters.* When possible the company adds new screens to existing theaters. Its average of eight screens per theater is the highest in the industry.

- *Acquisition of existing theaters.* Much of the company's growth has come through acquisitions of existing theaters, and the company plans to continue that strategy.

- *Development of complementary theater concepts.* The company will continue to consider new concepts such as the FunScape family entertainment centers to expand its operation.

Regal has about 4,000 employees, although only about 600 are full-time.

Late developments

The company is building at least two new FunScape family entertainment centers, with plans to add more centers in the near future.

Performance

Stock growth (past two years through 12/31/96): 173 % (from $11.25 to $30.75).

Revenue growth (past two years through 9/30/96): 71% (from $143.6 million to $245.5 million).

Earnings per share growth (past two years through 9/30/96): 174% (from $0.31 to $0.85).

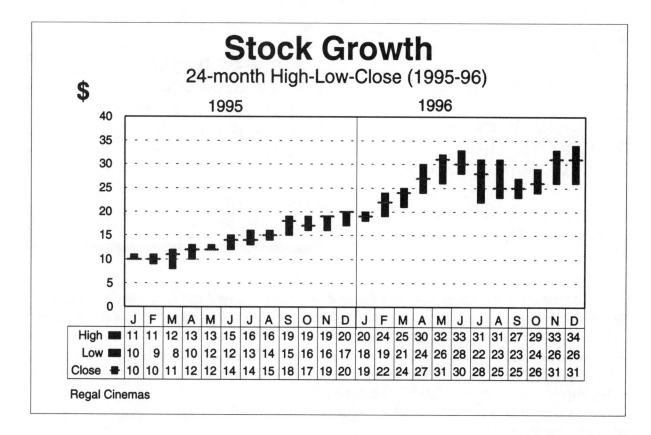

Stock Growth
24-month High-Low-Close (1995-96)

	J	F	M	A	M	J	J	A	S	O	N	D	J	F	M	A	M	J	J	A	S	O	N	D
High	11	11	12	13	13	15	16	16	19	19	19	20	20	24	25	30	32	33	31	31	27	29	33	34
Low	10	9	8	10	12	12	13	14	15	16	16	17	18	19	21	24	26	28	22	23	23	24	26	26
Close	10	10	11	12	12	14	14	15	18	17	19	20	19	22	24	27	31	30	28	25	25	26	31	31

Regal Cinemas

Quick Fix

P/E range (past two years):	12 - 37
Earnings past four quarters:	$0.92 (through 12/31/96)
Projected 1997 earnings (median):	$1.19
International sales:	NA
Total assets:	$307 million (1996); $235 million (1995)
Total current liabilities:	$18.9 million (1996); $31.6 million (1995)
Net Income:	$30 million (1996); $17.7 million (1995)

Financial history

Fiscal year ended: Dec. 31
(Revenue in millions)

	1992	1993	1994	1995	1996
Revenue	$98.7	$119.9	$159.7	$190.1	$270
Earnings per share	0.48	0.33	0.38	0.65	0.92
Stock price: High	NA	6.37	11.67	20.17	34.25
Low	NA	3.93	6.00	7.56	17.56
Close	NA	6.30	11.33	19.83	30.75

56

PMT Services, Inc.

Two Maryland Farms, Suite 200
Brentwood, TN   37027
Phone: 615-254-1539; FAX: 615-254-1549

Chairman and CEO: Richardson Roberts
President: Gregory Daily

The proliferation of plastic money over the past decade has played right into the hands of PMT Services. The firm provides electronic credit card authorization and payment equipment to retailers and restaurants throughout the United States.

The Tennessee operation has established a niche serving small merchants with a low volume of credit card transactions, which has long been an underserved sector of the market. In all, PMT has a customer base of more than 100,000 merchants.

In addition to its focus on small merchants, PMT's growth strategy revolves around several other key concepts:

- *Creating association relationships.* The company develops business relationships with national trade associations who help PMT reach small merchants that would otherwise be difficult to identify. PMT works with about 180 associations who provide leads, and endorse the company's processing systems.

- *Telemarketing.* The company uses telemarketing to solicit new customers, a technique PMT management believes is the most cost-effective means to reach the small merchant market.

- *Increasing operating efficiencies.* The company assigns its processing and network services to outside sources who can handle the duties more cost-effectively.

- *Acquiring additional merchant portfolios.* The firm pursues an ongoing policy of acquiring merchant portfolios from other operators. For instance, PMT recently purchased the portfolio of UMB Bank, which included about 15,000 merchant accounts with $1.4 billion in annual credit card charges. Since 1993, the company has made about 30 such acquisitions, including five portfolios in 1996 with a totaal of about 34,500 merchant accounts.

Founded in 1984 by Rich Roberts and Greg Daily (who still serve as chairman and president, respectively), PMT went public with its initial stock offering in 1994. The firm has about 350 employees.

Late developments

The company acquired five merchant portfolios with about 15,500 merchant accounts in the first quarter of fiscal 1997.

Performance

Stock growth (past two years through 12/31/96): 508% (from $2.88 to $17.50).
Revenue growth (past two years through 7/31/96):180% (from $53.5 million to $150 million).
Earnings per share growth (past two years through 7/31/96): 67% (from $0.20 to $0.30).

122

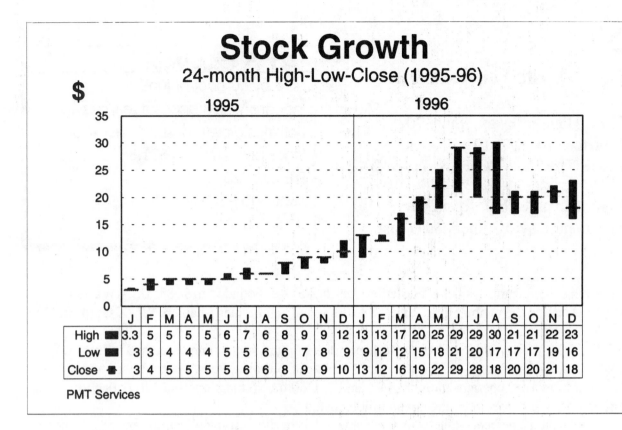

Stock Growth
24-month High-Low-Close (1995-96)

	J	F	M	A	M	J	J	A	S	O	N	D	J	F	M	A	M	J	J	A	S	O	N	D
High	3.3	5	5	5	5	6	7	6	8	9	9	12	13	13	17	20	25	29	29	30	21	21	22	23
Low	3	3	4	4	4	5	5	6	6	7	8	9	9	12	12	15	18	21	20	17	17	17	19	16
Close	3	4	5	5	5	5	6	6	8	9	9	10	13	12	16	19	22	29	28	18	20	20	21	18

PMT Services

Quick Fix

P/E range (past two years):	16 - 98
Earnings past four quarters:	$0.30 (through 7/31/96)
Projected 1997 earnings (median):	$0.44
International sales:	None
Total current assets:	$113.6 million (1996); $5.2 million (1995)
Total current liabilities:	$6.9 million (1996); $5.8 million (1995)
Net Income:	$8.6 million (1996); $3.6 million (1995)

Financial history

Fiscal year ended: July 31
(Revenue in millions)

	1992	1993	1994	1995	1996
Revenue	$29.5	$35.6	$61.2	$89.0	$149.8
Earnings per share	0.05	0.12	0.20	0.17	0.30
*Stock price: High	NA	NA	3.75	11.58	29.63
Low	NA	NA	2.58	2.79	9.19
Close	NA	NA	2.88	10.08	17.50

*Stock prices (only) reflect calendar year.

57

USA Waste Services, Inc.

2777 Allen Parkway, Suite 700
Houston, TX 77019
Phone: 713-942-6200; FAX: 713-942-6299

Chairman and CEO: John Drury
President: David Sutherland-Yoest

Refuse has its rewards, as USA Waste Services can attest. Founded in 1988, USA Waste has already become the nation's third largest waste service behind mega-haulers WMX Corp. and Browning-Ferris.

USA Waste, which serves the full spectrum of municipal, commercial and industrial customers, has operations in 35 states, the District of Columbia, Puerto Rico, Mexico and Canada. It owns or operates more than 90 landfills, 60 transfer stations and 120 collection operations, and serves more than two million customers.

About 52 percent of the company's revenue is derived from collection services, 32 percent comes from landfill operations, 10 percent comes from transfer operations, and the balance comes from a variety of related operations.

The company has grown quickly through an aggressive acquisition strategy. It buys both small independent operations and larger collection services such as Pittsburgh-based Chambers Development Company and California-based Western Waste Industries, both of which it acquired in 1995.

In addition to the standard waste services, the company has also began offering limited recycling collection services. And it has a 25 percent stake in Automated Recycling Technologies, which operates two recycling and sorting facilities in New Jersey.

USA Waste went public in 1993 with its initial stock offering. The company has about 3,000 employees.

Late developments

The company recently completed an acquisition of Sanifill, Inc., a Houston-based waste management company that specializes in disposal of nonhazardous wastes. It has operations in 23 states, Puerto Rico, Mexico and Canada. USA Waste also closed on its acquisition of Canadian-based Philip Environmental, a non-hazardous solid waste company with operations in Quebec, Ontario and Michigan.

Performance

Stock growth (past two years through 12/31/96): 154% (from $12.50 to $31.78).
Revenue growth (past two years through 9/30/96): 153% (from $358.7 million to $906 million).
Earnings per share growth (past two years through 9/30/96): 190% (from $0.21 to $0.61).

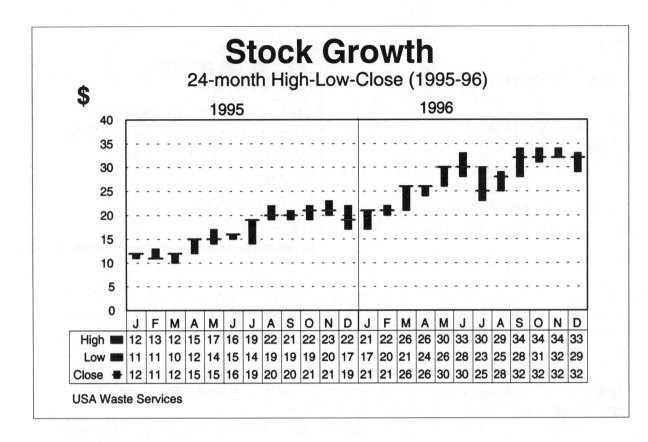

Stock Growth
24-month High-Low-Close (1995-96)

		1995											1996											
	J	F	M	A	M	J	J	A	S	O	N	D	J	F	M	A	M	J	J	A	S	O	N	D
High	12	13	12	15	17	16	19	22	21	22	23	22	21	22	26	26	30	33	30	29	34	34	34	33
Low	11	11	10	12	14	15	14	19	19	19	20	17	17	20	21	24	26	28	23	25	28	31	32	29
Close	12	11	12	15	15	16	19	20	20	21	21	19	21	21	26	26	30	30	25	28	32	32	32	32

USA Waste Services

Quick Fix

P/E range (past two years):	18 - 31
Earnings past four quarters:	$0.61 (through 9/30/96)
Projected 1997 earnings (median):	$1.54
International sales:	NA
Total current assets:	$216.8 million (6/30/96); $126.1 million (6/30/95)
Total current liabilities:	$123.5 million (6/30/96); $121.7 million (6/30/95)
Net Income:	$30.3 million (1995); -$76.3 million (1994)

Financial history

Fiscal year ended: Dec. 31
(Revenue in millions)

	1992	1993	1994	1995	*1996
Revenue	$57.0	$382.2	$434.2	$457.1	$963*
Earnings per share	-0.20	0.01	-1.55	0.55	0.01*
Stock price: High	NA	15	15.13	22.50	34.25
Low	NA	9.75	10.38	10.00	17.00
Close	NA	11.38	11.38	18.88	31.88

1996 revenue and earnings through Sept. 30 (nine months). Earnings per share reflect acquisition expenses.

58

Input/Output, Inc.

12300 Parc Crest Drive
Stafford, TX 77477
Phone: 713-933-3339; FAX: 713-879-3600

Chairman: Charles Selecman
President and CEO: Gary Owens

Input/Output (IO) helps researchers peer deep into the earth's surface. It is the leading manufacturer of seismic data acquisition equipment, which is used by seismic contractors and oil and gas companies around the world.

The company's advanced three-dimensional data collection equipment enables geoscientists to more accurately survey seismic areas for oil and gas reserves—particularly since 1991 when the company introduced its more advanced systems.

The company also produces marine data acquisition systems that collect seismic data in deep water environments.

IO has grown rapidly by pursuing a strategy that focuses on technological advances, product line acquisitions and innovative marketing. The company continues to offer new systems, expanding from from 14 systems in 1991 to 65 systems by 1996. One of its newest innovations is the "I/O System Two RSR," a radio telemetry system designed to collect data across a variety of difficult environments, including surf zones, marshes, swamps and mountain ranges.

IO is now working on the next generation of seismic survey devices, including some that go beyond 3-D to 4-D (or time lapse 3-D). The 4-D process measures the same length, depth and width of data collected in 3-D surveys, but it also offers the capability to record time intervals between two or more surveys. That method helps identify fluid movements and changes in the producing status of reservoirs.

The company's equipment sells for between $800,000 and $8 million. Its has customers around the world. About 45 percent of its revenue is generated outside the U.S.

Founded in 1968, IO went public with its initial stock offering in 1991. The company has about 1,300 employees.

Late developments
After 21 consecutive record quarters, the company saw its earnings drop for the quarter ended Nov. 30, 1996. The company blamed the drop on "unexpected delays in concluding negotiations for land seismic equipment."

Performance
Stock growth (past two years through 12/31/96): 55% (from $11.94 to $18.50).
Revenue growth (past two years through 8/30/96): 179% (from $106 million to $296.5 million).
Earnings per share growth (past two years through 11/30/96): 42% (from $0.62 to $0.88).

126

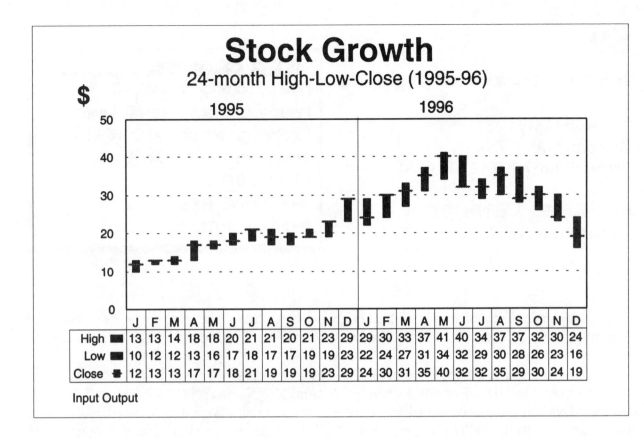

Stock Growth
24-month High-Low-Close (1995-96)

		J	F	M	A	M	J	J	A	S	O	N	D	J	F	M	A	M	J	J	A	S	O	N	D
High	■	13	13	14	18	18	20	21	21	20	21	23	29	29	30	33	37	41	40	34	37	37	32	30	24
Low	■	10	12	12	13	16	17	18	17	17	19	19	23	22	24	27	31	34	32	29	30	28	26	23	16
Close	■	12	13	13	17	17	18	21	19	19	19	23	29	24	30	31	35	40	32	32	35	29	30	24	19

Input Output

Quick Fix

P/E range (past two years):	12 - 43
Earnings past four quarters:	$0.88 (through 11/30/96)
Projected 1997 earnings (median):	$0.95
International sales:	45% of total sales
Total current assets:	$208.9 million (1996); $151.5 million (1995)
Total current liabilities:	$30.9 million (1996); $55.3 million (1995)
Net Income:	$38.7 million (1996); $24.5 million (1995)

Financial history

Fiscal year ended: May 31
(Revenue in millions)

	1992	1993	1994	1995	1996
Revenue	$45.5	$54.2	$95.7	$134.7	$278.3
Earnings per share	0.27	0.31	0.53	0.66	0.94
*Stock price: High	4.44	6.13	13.63	28.88	40.50
Low	2.38	2.44	5.94	11.00	16.00
Close	2.69	6.00	11.81	28.88	18.50

*Stock prices (only) reflect calendar year.

59

Security Dynamics Technologies, Inc.

20 Crosby Drive
Bedford, MA 01730
Phone: 617-687-7000; FAX: 617-687-7010

Chairman, President and CEO:
  Charles Stuckey Jr.

Security Dynamics Technologies is the hacker's biggest nightmare. The company makes a family of computer products designed to protect computer data bases from being opened by unauthorized users.

The company's software and hardware products address a crucial flaw in the majority of computer networks—the reliance on a reusable password for gaining access to computer data bases. Security Dynamics introduces an added element to the mix that makes unauthorized access much more difficult. Its technology requires a second access code that is randomly generated and automatically changes every 60 seconds.

The Bedford, Massachusetts, firm claims that the two-factor authentication code provides "crackproof" protection against unauthorized access, while preserving user convenience. Authorized users simply enter their secret password, followed by the code displayed on a special "SecurID" smart card, and that gives them quick, easy access.

Security Dynamics has a wholly-owned subsidiary, RSA Data Security, that is the world leader in cryptography and computer network security tools.

The company markets its products through a direct sales force in North America, the United Kingdom, France, Germany and Singapore. Elsewhere, it uses independent distributors to sell its products. Its principal customers are telecommunications, pharmaceutical, financial and medical companies, academic institutions, research laboratories and government agencies. In all, the company has more than 1,000 customers worldwide. About 16 percent of the company's revenues are generated outside of North America.

Founded in 1984, the company shipped its first products in 1987. It went public with its initial stock offering in 1994. Security Dynamics has about 170 employees.

Late developments
The company recently acquired a minority position in VPNet Technologies, a privately held company that develops products for creating virtual private networks.

Performance
Stock growth (past two years through 12/31/96): 572% (from $4.69 to $31.50).
Revenue growth (past year through 9/30/96): 72% (from $37 million to $63 million).
Earnings per share growth (past year through 9/30/96): 14% (from $0.22 to $0.25).

Stock Growth
24-month High-Low-Close (1995-96)

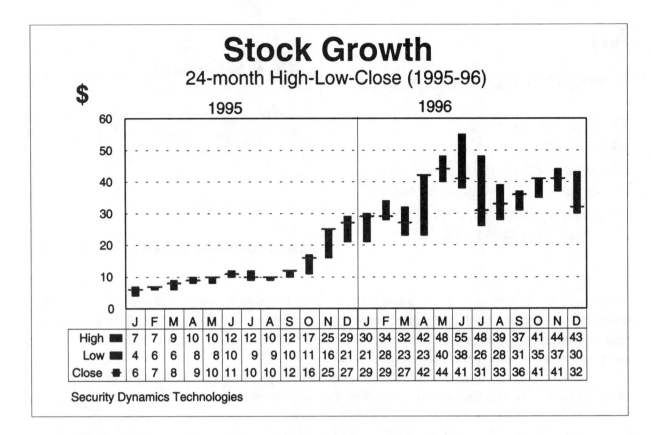

		1995											1996											
	J	F	M	A	M	J	J	A	S	O	N	D	J	F	M	A	M	J	J	A	S	O	N	D
High ■	7	7	9	10	10	12	12	10	12	17	25	29	30	34	32	42	48	55	48	39	37	41	44	43
Low ■	4	6	6	8	8	10	9	9	10	11	16	21	21	28	23	23	40	38	26	28	31	35	37	30
Close ✦	6	7	8	9	10	11	10	10	12	16	25	27	29	29	27	42	44	41	31	33	36	41	41	32

Security Dynamics Technologies

Quick Fix

P/E range (past two years):	19 - 100+
Earnings past four quarters:	$0.25 (through 9/30/96)
Projected 1997 earnings (median):	$0.59
International sales:	16% of total sales (outside North America)
Total current assets:	$121 million (1996); $98.4 million (1995)
Total current liabilities:	$20 million (1996); $6.5 million (1995)
Net Income:	$5.81 million (1995); $2.3 million (1994)

Financial history

Fiscal year ended: Dec. 31
(Revenue in millions)

	1992	1993	1994	1995	*1996
Revenue	$8.9	$12.1	$17.6	$33.8	$52.6*
Earnings per share	0.05	0.09	0.13	0.23	0.17*
Stock price: High	NA	NA	5.06	29.13	54.50
Low	NA	NA	3.50	4.41	21.25
Close	NA	NA	4.66	27.25	31.50

1996 revenue and earnings through Sept. 30 (nine months).

60

Vencor, Inc.

3300 Providian Center
400 West Market Street
Louisville, KY 40202
Phone: 502-596-7300; FAX: 502-596-4099

Chairman, President and CEO:
  Bruce Lunsford

Since it began operations in 1985, Vencor has built its business by specializing in the treatment of critically ill patients who require respiratory care over an extended period. Through a series of acquisitions, the Louisville-based operation has become the nation's largest intensive care hospital company, with 37 acute care hospitals in 17 states.

But with its 1995 acquisition of Hillhaven Corp., Vencor dramatically broadened its focus. In addition to its acute care facilities., Vencor now operates about 310 nursing centers, 53 institutional and retail pharmacies and 23 independent and assisted living communities.

In the future, the Louisville-based operation plans to grow through four key strategies:

• *Focus on long-term care.* Vencor plans to continue to expand its long-term care network through additional acquisitions.

• *Expansion of specialty care services.* Vencor plans to continue to expand its specialty care programs and services at its nursing centers. Services currently offered include physical rehabilitation, occupational and speech therapies, wound care, oncology treatment, brain injury care, stroke therapy and orthopedic therapy.

• *Expansion of contract services.* The company plans to continue to expand a service it began in 1993 of providing respiratory therapy and subacute care at facilities owned by other companies. In all, the company provides services to more than 2,000 nursing homes and subacute care centers.

• *Complete installation of the ProTouch record system.* By the end of 1997, the company expects to have its ProTouch electronic patient medical record system installed in all of its facilities. ProTouch gives the medical staff instant access to clinical data on all of its patients.

Vencor has about 45,000 full-time employees and 16,000 part-time employees. In all, the Vencor network has about 3,200 licensed beds, with about 500,000 total patient days per year.

Late developments
Vencor acquired four nursing centers, including a total of 377 beds from Excel Care Management of Marion Indiana, and sold 34 nursing centers to Lenox Healthcare in late 1996.

Performance
Stock growth (past two years through 12/31/96): 13% (from $27.88 to $31.63).
Revenue growth (past two years through 9/30/96): 60% (from $1.58 billion to $2.53 billion).
Earnings per share growth (past two years through 9/30/96): 43% (from $1.20 to $1.72).

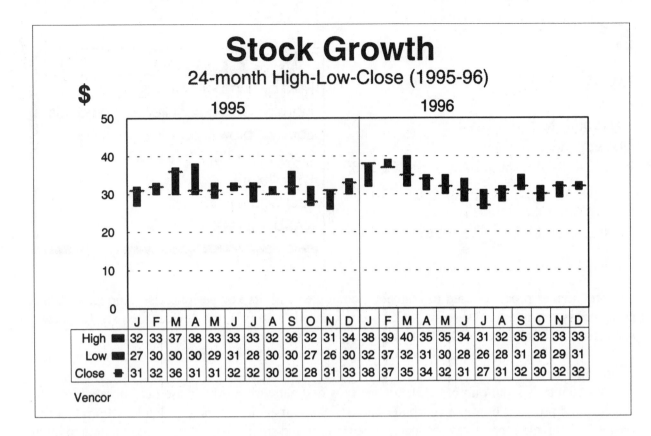

Stock Growth
24-month High-Low-Close (1995-96)

	J	F	M	A	M	J	J	A	S	O	N	D	J	F	M	A	M	J	J	A	S	O	N	D
High	32	33	37	38	33	33	33	32	36	32	31	34	38	39	40	35	35	34	31	32	35	32	33	33
Low	27	30	30	30	29	31	28	30	30	27	26	30	32	37	32	31	30	28	26	28	31	28	29	31
Close	31	32	36	31	31	32	32	30	32	28	31	33	38	37	35	34	32	31	27	31	32	30	32	32

Vencor

Quick Fix

P/E range (past two years):	18 - 178
Earnings past four quarters:	$1.72 (through 9/30/96)
Projected 1997 earnings (median):	$2.19
International sales:	none
Total current assets:	$641.6 million (1996); $524.7 million (1995)
Total current liabilities:	$324.8 million (1996; $285.0 million (1995)
Net Income:	$8.36 million** (1995); $86.14 million(1994)

Financial history

Fiscal year ended: Dec. 31
(Revenue in millions)

	1992	1993	1994	1995	*1996
Revenue	$214.7	$1,727	$2,033	$2,324	$1,911*
Earnings per share	0.63	1.22	1.37	0.21**	1.30*
Stock price: High	26.67	24.17	30.58	38.00	39.88
Low	14.67	13.00	19.17	26.00	25.50
Close	24.25	19.92	27.88	32.50	31.63

1996 revenue and earnings through Sept. 30 (nine months).
**1995 earnings reflect a $1.30 per share charge related to the Hillhaven acquisition*

61
Adaptec, Inc.

691 South Milpitas Blvd.
Milpitas, CA 95035
Phone: 408-945-8600; FAX: 408-262-2533

Chairman: John Adler
President and CEO: Grant Saviers

AT A GLANCE
Held by number of funds: 3
Industry: Computer interface products
Earnings growth past 2 years: 18%
Stock price 1/1/97: $40.00
P/E ratio: 48
Year ago P/E: 23
NASDAQ: ADPT

Adaptec makes products used to connect a computer with its key peripherals. Known as "small computer system interface" systems (SCSI – pronounced "scuzzy"), the devices are used to connect such items as hard drives, CD-ROMs and scanners to the computer processor.

The Milpitas, California, operation also makes networking products that connect computers to one another.

Adaptec's input/output (I/O), connectivity and network products are incorporated into the systems and products of major computer and peripheral manufacturers worldwide. Its product line ranges from simple connectivity products for single-user and small-office desktop computers to high-performance SCSI and related products for large computer networks. Among its leading customers are IBM, Digital Equipment, Dell Computer, Compaq, Samsung, NEC, Intel and Hewlett-Packard, all of whom install Adaptec products in their computers.

Adaptec's products put the company at the heart of a major growth segment of the computer industry. In addition to the growing popularity of computer networks within large corporations, many of the newest desktop and portable computers are being configured with a more diverse set of peripherals. Items such as CD-ROM drives and CD-R and digital audio tape (DAT) drives are being added to computers either in the manufacturing stage, at the time of purchase or after the original equipment sale.

Along with SCSI host adapters, the company's leading products include network interface cards, ASPI software, accelerator cards, enterprise computing systems, CD software, fast ethernet cards, programmable storage controllers and wireless networking connectors.

Founded in 1981, Adaptec went public with its initial stock offering in 1986. Adaptec is global in scope, with about 56 percent of its revenue generated outside the U.S. The company has about 2,300 employees.

Late developments
Sidus Systems recently reached an agreement with Adaptec to distribute Adaptec's complete product line to Sidus System's network of resellers and systems integrators. Sidus is an Ontario, Canada, based maker of personal computer systems and workstations.

Performance
Stock growth (past two years through 12/31/96): 239% (from $11.81 to $40.00).
Revenue growth (past two years through 9/30/96): 92% (from $410.5 million to $789.3 million).
Earnings per share growth (past two years through 12/31/96): 18% (from $0.77 to $0.91).

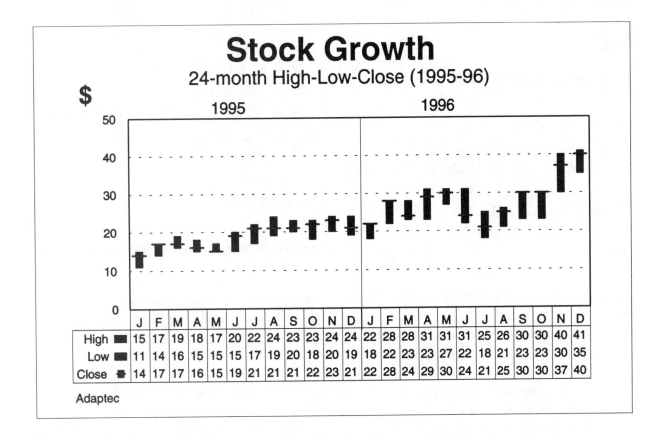

Stock Growth
24-month High-Low-Close (1995-96)

	J	F	M	A	M	J	J	A	S	O	N	D	J	F	M	A	M	J	J	A	S	O	N	D
High	15	17	19	18	17	20	22	24	23	23	24	24	22	28	28	31	31	31	25	26	30	30	40	41
Low	11	14	16	15	15	15	17	19	20	18	20	19	18	22	23	23	27	22	18	21	23	23	30	35
Close	14	17	17	16	15	19	21	21	21	22	23	21	22	28	24	29	30	24	21	25	30	30	37	40

Adaptec

Quick Fix

P/E range (past two years):	11 - 48
Earnings past four quarters:	$0.91 (through 12/31/96)
Projected fiscal 1998 earnings:	$2.05
International sales:	56% of total sales (Asia/Pacific, 325; Europe, 24%)
Total current assets:	$425.6 million (1996); $465.3 million (1995)
Total current liabilities:	$98.4 million (1996); $130.3 million (1995)
Net Income:	$104.3 million (1996); $93.4 million (1995)

Financial history

Fiscal year ended: March 31
(Revenue in millions)

	1992	1993	1994	1995	1996	*1997
Revenue	$150.3	$311.3	$372.2	$466.2	$659.3	$864.8*
Earnings per share	0.18	0.48	0.56	0.88	0.95	0.53*
**Stock price: High	7.75	9.97	12.19	24.19	41.13	NA
Low	2.14	4.63	7.00	10.88	17.50	NA
Close	6.50	9.94	11.81	20.50	40.00	NA

1997 revenue and earnings through Dec. 31, 1996 (nine months).
**Stock prices (only) reflect calendar year.*

62

Newbridge Networks Corp.

600 March Road
Kanata, Ontario, Canada   K2K 2E6
Phone: 613-591-3600; FAX: 613-591-3680

Chairman and CEO: Terence Matthews
President: Peter Sommerer

AT A GLANCE

Held by number of funds: 2

Industry: Computer networking products

Earnings growth past 2 years: 26%

Stock price 1/1/97: $28.13

P/E ratio: 28

Year ago P/E: 19

NYSE: NN

Newbridge Networks, which specializes in building bridges from one computer to another, has helped forge a cyber-superhighway around the globe. The Canadian manufacturer's computer networking products are used by the world's 200 largest telecommunications service providers, and more than 10,000 public and private enterprises, government organizations and other institutions.

Newbridge sells its networking products to customers in more than 100 countries. The company operates plants and sales offices in Canada, the U.S., Latin America, Europe, the Middle East, Africa, Asia and Australia

The company makes networking products designed for transmitting voice, data, image and video traffic. Its end-to-end networking products incorporate leading edge technologies, including asynchronous transfer mode (ATM), frame relay, and time division multiplexing (TDM) – all manageable by a single network system.

The Newbridge product line consists of broadband digital networking products that provide both wide and local area networking, and software-controlled desktop-to-desktop connectivity. Its products help companies and communications service providers build and manage wide area networks.

Newbridge has a 41 percent share of the ATM wide area network switching equipment market, making it the worldwide market leader. Nearly half of the company's total sales are generated outside of North America.

The company was founded in 1986 in Kanata, Ontario, and went public with its initial stock offering in 1989. Its stock is now traded on the New York Stock Exchange. Newbridge has more than 4,000 employees.

Late developments

Newbridge reached a strategic alliance agreement with Siemens of Germany in 1996 to develop products for ATM networks, and to market each other's telephone switching products. Newbridge also announced its intentions in late 1996 to acquire a majority interest in Coasin Chile S.A., a telecommunications engineering, distribution and marketing company that has operations in Chile, Argentina, Brazil, Costa Rica, Ecuador, Peru and Uruguay.

Performance

Stock growth (past two years through 12/31/96): 47% (from $19.13 to $28.13).
Revenue growth (past two years): 67% (from $410 million to $684 million).
Earnings per share growth (past two years): 26% (from $0.70 to $0.88).

Stock Growth
24-month High-Low-Close (1995-96)

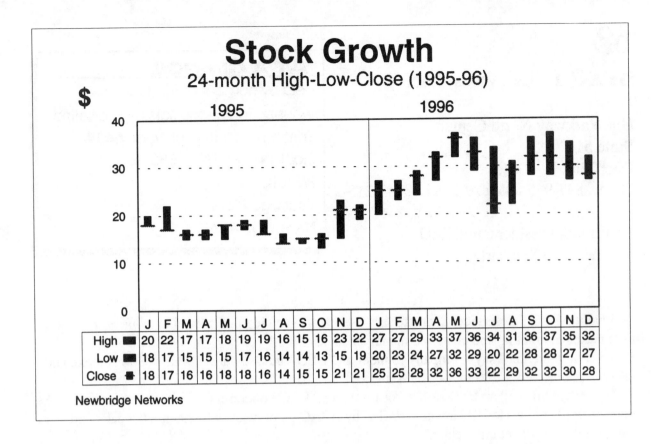

	J	F	M	A	M	J	J	A	S	O	N	D	J	F	M	A	M	J	J	A	S	O	N	D
High	20	22	17	17	18	19	19	16	15	16	23	22	27	27	29	33	37	36	34	31	36	37	35	32
Low	18	17	15	15	15	17	16	14	14	13	15	19	20	23	24	27	32	29	20	22	28	28	27	27
Close	18	17	16	16	18	18	16	14	15	15	21	21	25	25	28	32	36	33	22	29	32	32	30	28

Newbridge Networks

Quick Fix

P/E range (past two years):	14 - 41
Earnings past four quarters:	$0.98 (through 9/30/96)
Projected fiscal 1998 earnings:	$1.42
International sales:	46% of total sales (Asia/Pacific, 15%; Europe, 30%)
Total current assets:	$607 million (1996); $459 million (1995)
Total current liabilities:	$123 million (1996); $97 million (1995)
Net Income:	$152 million (1996); $141 million (1995)

Financial history

Fiscal year ended: April 30
(Revenue in millions)

	1993	1994	1995	1996	*1997
Revenue	$228	$410	$594	$684	$602*
Earnings per share	0.28	0.70	0.84	0.88	0.63*
** Stock price: High	36.94	34.38	22.69	37.25	NA
Low	9.56	13.25	12.50	20.13	NA
Close	27.38	19.13	20.69	28.13	NA

1997 revenue and earnings through Oct. 31 (six months).
Stock prices (only) reflect calendar years.

63

APAC Teleservices, Inc.

One Parkway North Center
Suite 510
Deerfield, IL 60015
Phone: 847-945-0055; FAX 847-374-3215

Chairman, President and CEO:
   Theodore Schwartz

Officially APAC Teleservices characterizes itself as a "growing provider of outsourced telephone-based sales, marketing and customer management services."

"In plain talk," says company founder and CEO Ted Schwartz, "what we do is make and take telephone calls -- 200 million calls a year."

When you call an FTD florist, for instance, APAC's operators answer the phones and take your order. The lines to UPS are also staffed by APAC employees, who handle the calls and send the UPS delivery fleet into action.

APAC works both ends of the phone lines for its growing list of corporate clients. Companies such as At&T and Discover Card contract with APAC to serve as their telemarketing unit, making sales calls to prospective customers. About 60 percent of APAC's business is outbound (making sales calls) and 40 percent is inbound (taking orders). But thanks to the new wave of 800 numbers, the inbound end of the business is growing at a much faster pace than the outbound, and is expected ultimately to become the larger part of the business.

The bulk of the company's telemarketing business involves making sales prospecting calls to customers for financial and insurance companies.

APAC (which is an acronym for All People Are Customers) was founded in 1973 by Schwartz, who still owns about 48 percent of the company stock. Initially, the company was in the business of selling radio time to advertisers, but in the 1980s Schwartz gradually transformed it into a teleservices operation.

APAC stock has been publicly traded only since October 1995. The company has about 7,000 employees, most of whom tend the phone lines in APAC's 41 telephone call centers.

Late developments
APAC has been gaining a growing share of telemarketing business from AT&T because of some strong results from APAC's "customer acquisition" work.

Performance
Stock growth (past year through 12/31/96): 130 % (from $16.69 to $38.38).
Revenue growth (past two years through 12/31/96): 493% (from $46.6 million to $276 million).
Earnings per share growth (past two years through 12/31/96): 540% (from $0.10 to $0.64).

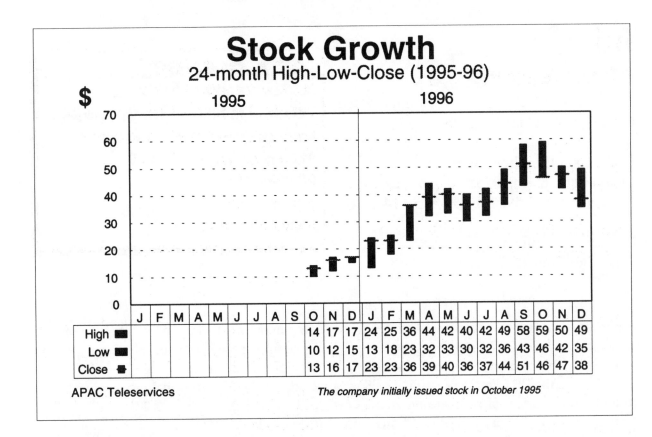

Stock Growth
24-month High-Low-Close (1995-96)

	J	F	M	A	M	J	J	A	S	O	N	D	J	F	M	A	M	J	J	A	S	O	N	D
High ■										14	17	17	24	25	36	44	42	40	42	49	58	59	50	49
Low ■										10	12	15	13	18	23	32	33	30	32	36	43	46	42	35
Close ■										13	16	17	23	23	36	39	40	36	37	44	51	46	47	38

APAC Teleservices

The company initially issued stock in October 1995

Quick Fix

P/E range (past two years):	21 - 97
Earnings past four quarters:	$0.64 (through 12/31/96)
Projected 1997 earnings (median):	$0.92
International sales:	None
Total current assets:	$53.3 million (1996); $50.7 million (1995)
Total current liabilities:	$26.2 million (1996); $17.7 million (1995)
Net Income:	$31 million (1996); $7.5 million (1995)

Financial history

Fiscal year ended: Dec. 31
(Revenue in millions)

	1992	1993	1994	1995	1996
Revenue	$13.5	$28.9	$46.6	$101.7	$276.4
Earnings per share	0.04	0.12	0.19	0.36	0.64
Stock price: High	NA	NA	NA	17.44	59.00
Low	NA	NA	NA	12.00	13.31
Close	NA	NA	NA	16.69	38.38

64

CBT Group, PLC

2 Clonskeagh Square
Dublin 14, Ireland

USA: 1005 Hamilton Court
Menlo Park, CA 94025
Phone: 415-614-5900; FAX: 415-614-5901

Chairman: William G. McCabe
President: James J. Buckley

AT A GLANCE

Held by number of funds: 2
Industry: interactive software designs
Earnings growth past 2 years: 472%
Stock price 1/1/97: $54.25
P/E ratio: 86
Year ago P/E: 77
NASDAQ: CBTSY

For anyone who has ever experienced the drudgery of using a training manual to learn how to operate computer software, CBT Group brings welcome relief. The firm specializes in developing interactive computer software designed specifically to help people run their computers.

In all, the CBT library of training packages includes about 250 titles that provide interactive training for a variety of software programs developed by such companies as Microsoft, Oracle, Netscape, Cisco, Lotus, Novell and Powersoft. CBT's training software is used by more than a thousand major corporations around the world.

For instance, CBT's JavaScript Object Model courseware helps computer program developers and programmers who are new to scripting languages learn the basics of designing internet applications.

Based in Dublin, Ireland, CBT's stock trades in the U.S. on the NASDAQ Exchange. About 81 percent of the firm's revenue is generated in the U.S.

There are several advantages to interactive training software. Users can run through the training programs on their own schedule at their own computer – no travel and no special schedules to meet. And users learn at their own pace.

CBT derives its revenues primarily from agreements under which customers license its software for periods of one, two or three years. The multi-year agreements also generally allow customers to exchange training titles for other titles in the CBT library on an annual basis.

The company also generates revenue by forming development and marketing alliances with some of the leading software companies to develop training software for their newer products. For instance, the company recently reached an agreement with Informix Software to jointly develop education software for the Informix databases.

Late developments

The company recently reached agreements to provide training software for Unisys Corp. and Compaq Computer Corp. The company also recently acquired Applied Learning Ltd. of New South Wales, Australia.

Performance

Stock growth (past year through 12/31/96): 104 % (from $26.50 to $54.25).
Revenue growth (past two years through 12/31/96): 208% (from $21.5 million to $66.3 million).
Earnings per share growth (past two years through 12/31/96): 472% (from $0.11 to $0.63).

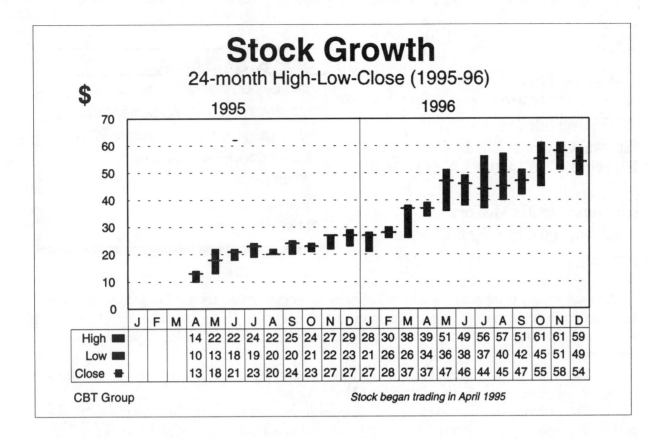

Stock Growth
24-month High-Low-Close (1995-96)

$	J	F	M	A	M	J	J	A	S	O	N	D	J	F	M	A	M	J	J	A	S	O	N	D
High ■				14	22	22	24	22	25	24	27	29	28	30	38	39	51	49	56	57	51	61	61	59
Low ■				10	13	18	19	20	20	21	22	23	21	26	26	34	36	38	37	40	42	45	51	49
Close ✦				13	18	21	23	20	24	23	27	27	27	28	37	37	47	46	44	45	47	55	58	54

1995   1996

CBT Group   *Stock began trading in April 1995*

Quick Fix

P/E range (past two years):	29 -112
Earnings past four quarters:	$0.51 (through 9/30/96)
Projected 1997 earnings (median):	$0.89
Non-U.S. sales:	19% (Europe 17.5%; other 1.5%)
Total current assets:	$66.3 million (1996); $63.9 million (1995)
Total current liabilities:	$17.9 million (1996); $15.5 million (1995)
Net Income:	$6.0 million (1995); $1.6 million (1994)

Financial history

Fiscal year ended: Dec. 31
(Revenue in millions)

	1992	1993	1994	1995	1996
Revenue	$6.1	$12.1	$21.5	$36.9	$66.3
Earnings per share	-0.22	- 0.03	0.11	0.34	0.63
Stock price: High	NA	NA	NA	28.50	61.00
Low	NA	NA	NA	10.00	21.13
Close	NA	NA	NA	26.50	54.25

65

Cognos, Inc.

3755 Riverside Drive
Ottawa, Ontario, Canada
Phone: 613-738-1440; FAX: 613-738-0002

Chairman: James M. Tory
President and CEO: Ron Zambonini

AT A GLANCE

Held by number of funds: 2

Industry: integrated software tools

Earnings growth past 2 years: 392%

Stock price 1/1/97: $28.13

P/E ratio: 53

Year ago P/E: 37

NASDAQ: COGNF

In the increasingly competitive world of business, corporate managers need to gather and analyze information faster than ever to get a jump on the competition. Cognos specializes in developing software designed to help corporate managers and analysts extract and analyze information vital to their operations.

Based in Ottawa, Ontario, Cognos has more than 600 customers around the world. About 45 percent of its revenue is generated outside of North America.

The company's business intelligence software gives users the ability to independently access, analyze and report corporate data from their desktop personal computers. It also makes application development tools that are used by software developers to create software application programs for corporate information systems.

The company offers four main products:

• *PowerPlay*. This business intelligence software product provides high-speed graphical navigation of multidimensional data. With PowerPlay, users can perform their own ad hoc analysis by investigating all critical success factors that drive business, in any combination at any level.

• *Impromptu*. This visual and interactive query reporting software allows users to easily access, manipulate and integrate detailed corporate data into useful reports.

• *PowerHouse*. This server-based application development tool allows developers to work in character-based development environment on UNIX and proprietary operating systems.

• *Asiant 4GL*. This core client/server tool offers built-in application intelligence, optimized deployment and integrated business analysis and reporting in the Windows environment.

Founded in 1969, Cognos has about 1,000 employees.

Late developments

The company has been pushing a new application development tool, RealObjects, that was designed to enable software developers to create complex client/server applications more quickly and easily than with standard development tools.

Performance

Stock growth (past two years through 12/31/96): 76% (from $ 15.94 to $28.13).

Revenue growth (past two years through 8/30/96): 49% (from $118 million to $176 million).

Earnings per share growth (past two years through 8/30/96): 392% (from $0.12 to $0.59).

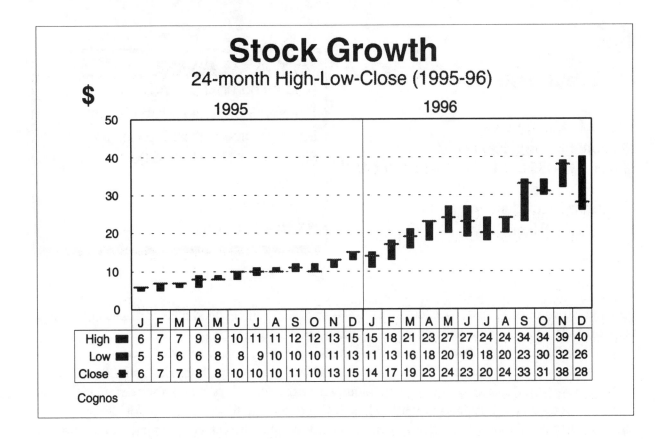

Stock Growth
24-month High-Low-Close (1995-96)

		1995											1996											
		J	F	M	A	M	J	J	A	S	O	N	D	J	F	M	A	M	J	J	A	S	O	N	D
High		6	7	7	9	9	10	11	11	12	12	13	15	15	18	21	23	27	27	24	24	34	34	39	40
Low		5	5	6	6	8	8	9	10	10	10	11	13	11	13	16	18	20	19	18	20	23	30	32	26
Close		6	7	7	8	8	10	10	10	11	10	13	15	14	17	19	23	24	23	20	24	33	31	38	28

Cognos

Quick Fix

P/E range (past two years):	13 - 65
Earnings past four quarters:	$0.59 (through 8/30/96)
Projected 1997 earnings (median):	$0.75
International sales:	U.S., 46%; Canada, 9%; Europe, 37%; other, 8%.
Total current assets:	$120.5 million (1996); $108.4 million (1995)
Total current liabilities:	$54.3 million (1996); $48.7 million (1995)
Net Income:	$17.6 million (1996); $8.4 million (1995)

Financial history

Fiscal year ended: Feb. 29
(Revenue in millions)

	1992	1993	1994	1995	1996
Revenue	$107.0	$108.8	$110.6	$123.9	$152.9
Earnings per share	0.11	-0.15	0.08	0.21	0.43
*Stock price: High	4.38	3.71	6.29	15.21	39.50
Low	1.88	2.00	3.25	5.33	11.13
Close	2.25	3.67	5.96	14.88	28.13

Stock prices (only) reflect calendar year.

66

JLG Industries, Inc.

One JLG Drive
McConnellsburg, PA 17233
Phone: 717-485-5161; FAX: 717-485-6417

Chairman, President and CEO:
  L. David Black

AT A GLANCE

Held by number of funds: 2

Industry: Mobile elevated platforms

Earnings growth past 2 years: 262%

Stock price 1/1/97: $16.00

P/E ratio: 18

Year ago P/E: 14

NYSE: JLG

JLG Industries puts its customers on a pedestal—or at least an elevated platform. The company is the world's leading manufacturer of mobile aerial work platforms.

The Pennsylvania-based operation manufactures three primary types of lifts:

- *Boom lifts.* Because of their ability to bend in any direction, boom lifts are often used for reaching over machinery and equipment mounted on factory floors, and for reaching elevated positions not accessible to ladders or vertical lifts. JLG markets the lifts worldwide for use by a broad range of customers, including mechanical, electrical, utility and painting contractors, automotive and aircraft plants, petroleum and chemical refineries, entertainment facilities, and textile, food processing and fabricating plants.

- *Scissor lifts.* Designed to accommodate larger work areas and to support heavier loads, scissor lifts are often used in factories, warehouses, hotels, recreational centers and educational facilities.

- *Vertical lifts.* These lower-cost machines, in their retracted position, can fit through standard door openings, yet reach platform heights of up to 36 feet. They are used for general maintenance applications in factories, distribution and retail centers, theaters, airports and public buildings.

JLG sells its lifts primarily to independent distributors who rent or resell them to end users. In North America, the lifts are marketed by about 100 distributors. Internationally, the lifts are sold in eight countries in Asia as well as in Australia, Japan and Latin America through a network of independent distributors. About 24 percent of the company's revenue comes from its foreign sales.

Founded in 1969, JLG has about 2,700 employees.

Late developments

The company introduced an industry record 20 new and redesigned products during 1996. The new products, which included self-propelled vertical lifts, electric-powered scissor lifts and a rough terrain scissor model, accounted for about 27 percent of the JLG's total sales in fiscal 1996.

Performance

Stock growth (past two years through 12/31/96): 423% (from $3.06 to $16.00).

Revenue growth (past two years through 9/30/96): 131% (from $193.4 million to $447 million).

Earnings per share growth (past two years through 9/30/96): 262% (from $0.29 to $1.05).

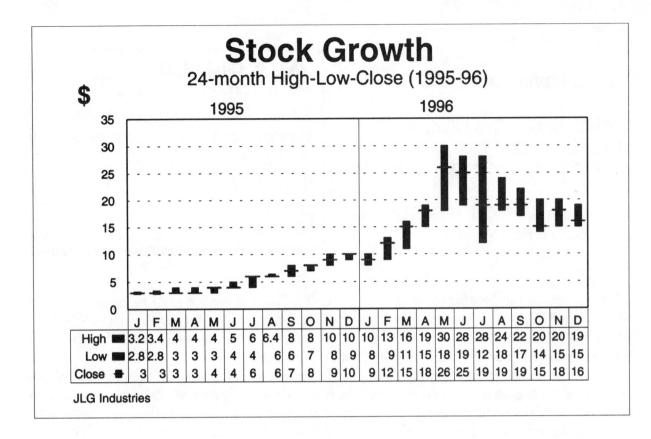

Stock Growth
24-month High-Low-Close (1995-96)

	1995												1996											
	J	F	M	A	M	J	J	A	S	O	N	D	J	F	M	A	M	J	J	A	S	O	N	D
High	3.2	3.4	4	4	4	5	6	6.4	8	8	10	10	10	13	16	19	30	28	28	24	22	20	20	19
Low	2.8	2.8	3	3	3	4	4	6	6	7	8	9	8	9	11	15	18	19	12	18	17	14	15	15
Close	3	3	3	3	4	4	6	6	7	8	9	10	9	12	15	18	26	25	19	19	19	15	18	16

JLG Industries

Quick Fix

P/E range (past two years):	12 - 31
Earnings past four quarters:	$1.05 (through 9/30/96)
Projected 1997 earnings (median):	$1.24
International sales:	24% of total sales
Total current assets:	$129 million (1996); $85 million (1995)
Total current liabilities:	$57 million (1996); $39.2 million (1995)
Net Income:	$42.1 million (1996); $20.7 million (1995)

Financial history

Fiscal year ended: July 31
(Revenue in millions)

	1992	1993	1994	1995	1996
Revenue	$110.5	$123.0	$176.4	$269.2	$413.4
Earnings per share	-0.07	0.07	0.23	0.49	0.95
*Stock price: High	1.02	2.10	3.48	10.17	29.50
Low	0.65	0.88	2.02	2.83	7.75
Close	0.94	2.06	3.04	9.92	16.00

Stock prices (only) reflect calendar year.

67

LCI International, Inc.

8180 Greensboro Drive Suite 800
McLean, VA 22102
Phone: 703-442-0220; FAX: 703-448-6792

Chairman and CEO: H. Brian Thompson
President: Thomas Wynne

LCI International isn't looking to become the next AT&T. It just wants a growing share of the $70 billion-a-year U.S. long-distance telephone business. Currently, the big three in the industry, AT&T, Sprint and MCI, generate nearly 90 percent of the total long-distance revenue, while LCI battles it out for the other 10 percent with a few hundred other carriers.

But as a small fish in a very big pond, LCI has grown rapidly, and would seem to have plenty of room for future growth. Its marketing theme "simple, fair and inexpensive"—with customers being billed based on time of day rather than distance—has brought a lot of new customers into the fold.

The company generates its revenue through four basic services:

• Commercial long-distance service accounts for about 50 percent of the company's $1 billion in annual revenue. LCI has expanded its marketing efforts from primarily small and mid-sized businesses in the Midwest to a full range of large and small businesses throughout the U.S.

• Residential long-distance service accounts for about 25 percent of the company's revenue, up from 8 percent in 1993. The company has made a strong push into the residential market through its "simple, fair and inexpensive" campaign.

• Wholesale and reseller services—the sale of transmission capacity and services to other long-distance wholesalers—accounts for about 15 percent of total revenue.

• Private line service accounts for about 10 percent of revenue. Private line services are dedicated lines for a single customer's use, connected to customer locations at both ends.

Originally formed in 1983, LCI has expanded rapidly through a series of acquisitions of smaller long-distance networks. LCI is now the six largest long-distance carrier in the country. The Virginia-based operation went public with its initial stock offering in 1993. The company has about 1,700 employees.

Late developments

The company recently announced plans to lease a new 156,000-square foot facility in Dublin, Ohio, to house many of its core functions. The facility has a capacity for 750 to 1,000 employees.

Performance

Stock growth (past two years through 12/31/96): 61% (from $13.88 to $21.50).
Revenue growth (past two years through 9/30/96): 137% (from $426.3 million to $1 billion).
Earnings per share growth (past two years through 9/30/96): 257% (from $0.21 to $0.75).

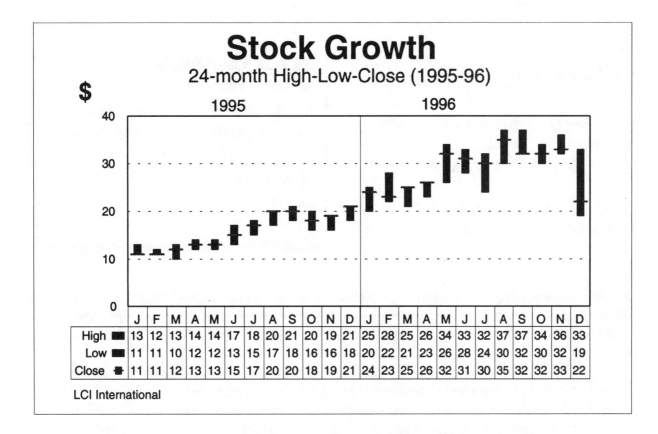

Stock Growth
24-month High-Low-Close (1995-96)

	J	F	M	A	M	J	J	A	S	O	N	D	J	F	M	A	M	J	J	A	S	O	N	D
High	13	12	13	14	14	17	18	20	21	20	19	21	25	28	25	26	34	33	32	37	37	34	36	33
Low	11	11	10	12	12	13	15	17	18	16	16	18	20	22	21	23	26	28	24	30	32	30	32	19
Close	11	11	12	13	13	15	17	20	20	18	19	21	24	23	25	26	32	31	30	35	32	32	33	22

LCI International

Quick Fix

P/E range (past two years):	18 - 50
Earnings past four quarters:	$0.75 (through 9/30/96)
Projected 1997 earnings (median):	$1.14
International sales:	none
Total current assets:	$128.5 million (9/30/96); $189.2 million (9/30/95)
Total current liabilities:	$189.8 million (9/30/95); $110.5 million (9/30/95)
Net Income:	$50.8 million (1995); $6.8 million (1994)

Financial history

Fiscal year ended: Dec. 31
(Revenue in millions)

	1992	1993	1994	1995	*1996
Revenue	$260.5	$341.2	$463.9	$672.8	$809.2*
Earnings per share	-0.72	-0.28	0.02	0.63	0.58*
Stock price: High	NA	10.56	13.38	20.75	37.25
Low	NA	4.56	6.38	10.13	18.50
Close	NA	9.25	13.38	20.50	21.50

1996 revenue and earnings through Sept. 30 (nine months).

145

68

Cadence Design Systems, Inc.

555 River Oaks Parkway
San Jose, CA 95134
Phone: 408-943-1234; FAX: 408-943-0513

Chairman: Donald L. Lucas
President and CEO: Joseph B. Costello

AT A GLANCE

Held by number of funds: 2
Industry: Electronic design software
Earnings growth past 2 years: 246%
Stock price 1/1/97: $39.50
P/E ratio: 30
Year ago P/E: 26
NYSE: CDN

The computer revolution is locked in an eternal tug-of-war. The demand for greater power and performance continues to grow, while at the same time, the size of the chips and components continues to shrink. The Cadence challenge is to help strained developers succeed at both ends of the tug-of-war.

Cadence Design Systems makes software that is used to design semiconductors, computer systems and peripherals, telecommunications and networking equipment, mobile and wireless devices, automotive components, consumer products and other advanced electronics.

The San Jose-based firm combines its technology with expert services to aid in its customer's product development.

Electronic design automation (EDA) software tools are used primarily by electronic designers to develop electronic circuits and systems. Cadence's tools are used to analyze, simulate, implement and verify electronic designs. By using these tools to automate significant parts of the design process, electronic engineers can focus their time on developing the intellectual content of the integrated circuit or electronic system. Cadence's tools can also be used by design architects to build abstract models of chips, simulate their behavior and analyze their physical attributes for acceptable performance.

Cadence not only supplies the EDA software, it can also send in a team of experts to help companies with the design and development process. For instance, in 1995, Unisys Corp. hired Cadence, at a cost of $75 million, to help with the company's internal silicon design operations.

Cadence was formed in 1988 as a result of a merger of SDA Systems and ECAD. It bought out its largest competitor, Valid Logic Systems, in 1991 to become the leading company in the design field.

Nearly half of the company's revenue is generated outside the U.S. Cadence has about 3,000 employees.

Late developments

In late 1996, Cadence acquired High Level Design Systems, a leading supplier of integrated circuit design tools for complex submicron (very small) computer chips.

Performance

Stock growth (past two years through 12/31/96): 330% (from $9.19 to $39.50).
Revenue growth (past two years through 9/30/96): 68% (from $413.5 million to $693.0 million).
Earnings per share growth (past two years through 9/30/96): 246% (from $0.38 to $1.28).

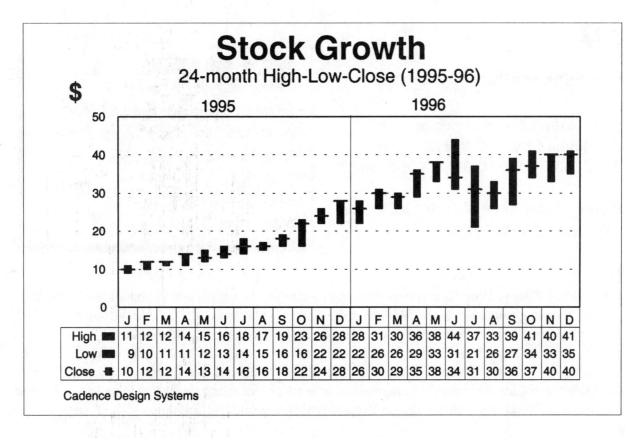

Stock Growth
24-month High-Low-Close (1995-96)

	J	F	M	A	M	J	J	A	S	O	N	D	J	F	M	A	M	J	J	A	S	O	N	D
High	11	12	12	14	15	16	18	17	19	23	26	28	28	31	30	36	38	44	37	33	39	41	40	41
Low	9	10	11	11	12	13	14	15	16	16	22	22	22	26	26	29	33	31	21	26	27	34	33	35
Close	10	12	12	14	13	14	16	16	18	22	24	28	26	30	29	35	38	34	31	30	36	37	40	40

Cadence Design Systems

Quick Fix

P/E range (past two years):	8 - 32
Earnings past four quarters:	$1.28 (through 9/30/96)
Projected 1997 earnings (median):	$1.66
International sales:	48% of total sales (Europe, 17%; Asia, 31%)
Total current assets:	$221.5 million (1996); $206.9 million (1995)
Total current liabilities:	$219.7 million (1996); $200.4 million (1995)
Net Income:	$97.3 million (1995); $36.6 million (1994)

Financial history

Fiscal year ended: Dec. 31
(Revenue in millions)

	1992	1993	1994	1995	*1996
Revenue	$418.7	$368.6	$429.1	$548.4	$529.2*
Earnings per share	0.53	-0.13	0.37	1.05	0.95*
Stock price: High	13.28	10.83	9.63	28.25	44.38
Low	5.83	3.67	4.56	8.56	21.68
Close	9.50	5.17	9.17	28.00	39.50

1996 revenue and earnings through Sept. 29 (nine months).

69

Chesapeake Energy Corp.

6100 North Western Avenue
Oklahoma City, OK 73118
Phone: 405-848-8000; FAX: 405-843-0573

Chairman and CEO: Aubrey McClendon
President: Tom L. Ward

Chesapeake Energy Corp. is a young, growing oil and gas company with a phenomenal record of success in drilling new wells. Since 1989 when the company was founded, Chesapeake has drilled 562 wells of which 529 have been commercially successful – a 94 percent success rate.

Since its inception, most of Chesapeake's drilling activity has been in the Giddings Field of southern Texas and the Golden Trend Field of southern Oklahoma. But in the past couple of years, the Oklahoma City operation has also moved into other promising fields including the Louisiana Austin Chalk Trend, the Williston Basin in eastern Montana and the Lovington area in eastern New Mexico.

The company's operating areas are generally characterized by fractured carbonate reservoirs of oil and gas that cover a wide geographic area. Recent advances in drilling technologies – and the resulting lower exploration costs – have given Chesapeake an opportunity to develop large new reserves of oil and natural gas at a relatively low cost. That success has lead to explosive growth of the company revenue and earnings.

Other keys to the Chesapeake's success include:

• *Technological leadership.* The firm has developed expertise in the rapidly evolving technologies of horizontal drilling, 3-D seismic evaluation and deep fracture stimulation.

• *Superior operating margin.* The company maintains one of the lowest operating cost structures in the industry.

During fiscal 1996, the company produced 1.413 million barrels of oil and 52 billion cubic feet of natural gas – an increase of 88 percent over the previous year.

The company went public with its initial stock offering in 1993. Founders Aubrey K. McClendon and Tom L. Ward each own about 22 percent of the company's stock. Chesapeake has about 350 employees.

Late developments
The company recently entered an agreement with Koch Oil Company to sell some of its crude oil and condensate production.

Performance
Stock growth (past two years through 12/31/96): 681% (from $3.56 to $27.81).
Revenue growth (past two years through 6/30/96): 401% (from $29.8 million to $149.4 million).
Earnings per share growth (past two years through 9/30/96): 313% (from $0.12 to $0.48).

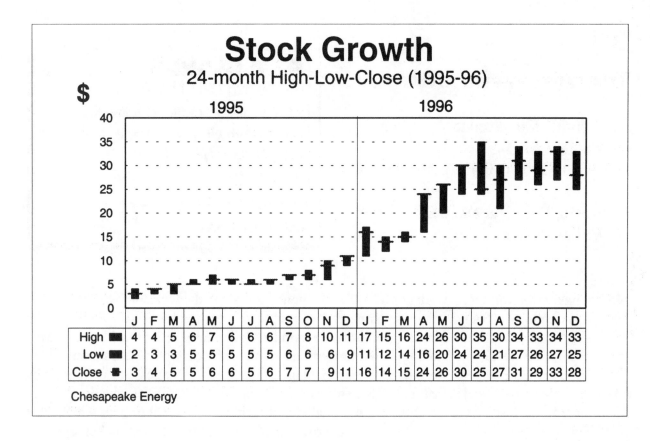

Stock Growth
24-month High-Low-Close (1995-96)

		1995												1996										
		J	F	M	A	M	J	J	A	S	O	N	D	J	F	M	A	M	J	J	A	S	O	N	D
High		4	4	5	6	7	6	6	6	7	8	10	11	17	15	16	24	26	30	35	30	34	33	34	33
Low		2	3	3	5	5	5	5	5	6	6	6	9	11	12	14	16	20	24	24	21	27	26	27	25
Close		3	4	5	5	6	6	5	6	7	7	9	11	16	14	15	24	26	30	25	27	31	29	33	28

Chesapeake Energy

Quick Fix

P/E range (past two years):	11 - 88
Earnings past four quarters:	$0.48 (through 9/30/96)
Projected 1997 earnings (median):	$0.78
International sales:	None
Total current assets:	$109.2 million (1996); $106.4 million (1995)
Total current liabilities:	$108.8 million (1996); $74.9 million (1995)
Net Income:	$23.3 million (1996); $11.7 million (1995)

Financial history

Fiscal year ended: June 30
(Revenue in millions)

	1992	1993	1994	1995	1996
Revenue	$18.7	$18.0	$29.8	$67.3	$149.4
Earnings per share	0.05	-0.03	0.08	0.21	0.40
*Stock price: High	NA	1.42	3.84	11.09	35.13
Low	NA	0.50	0.47	2.25	10.69
Close	NA	1.42	3.84	11.09	27.81

*Stock prices (only) reflect calendar year.

70

Transaction Systems Architects, Inc.

330 South 108th Avenue
Omaha, NE 68154
Phone: 402-390-7600; FAX: 402-390-8077

Chairman, President and CEO:
   William Fisher

AT A GLANCE

Held by number of funds: 2
Industry: Electronic fund software
Earnings growth past 2 years: NA
Stock price 1/1/97: $33.25
P/E ratio: 65
Year ago P/E: 60
NASDAQ: TSAI

Money makes the world go 'round, and TSA makes money go 'round the world—fast. Transaction Systems Architects (TSA) develops software that is used to process transactions involving credit cards, smart cards, debit cards, checks, point-of-sale terminals, automated teller machines (ATMs), manned teller devices, home banking, wire transfers and automated clearing house transactions

TSA software keeps those transactions moving at high speed. A typical ATM transaction takes just eight seconds, and in that time, TSA software reads the card, determines whether the card has been reported lost or stolen, validates a personal identification number, determines which bank issued the card, checks the account balance, approves or denies the transaction and charges the account. Often the transaction will travel across several regional, national and international networks before arriving at the issuing institution—and all in less than 10 seconds. That's fast money.

The Omaha-based operation plays some part in about 40 percent of the 700 million ATM transactions made in the U.S. each month. TSA's customer base includes more than 150 of the world's 1,000 largest banks, as well as hundreds of retailers (such as JC Penny, Texaco and Safeway) and third party processors. In all, the company has about 1,000 customers in 65 countries on six continents. About 53 percent of TSA's revenue is generated outside the U.S.

TSA was formed in November 1993 as a successor to Applied Communications, which had been a subsidiary of Tandem Computers. William Fisher, who is now TSA's chairman, CEO and president, led a management buy-out of the company from Tandem for an investment of about $5.5 million. The company now has a market capitalization of about $900 million. TSA stock has been publicly traded since February 1995.

TSA has about 900 employees.

Late developments

The company recently acquired Grapevine Systems, a Nebraska-based maker of transaction processing software used for mission critical applications in finance, healthcare, manufacturing and on-line services.

Performance

Stock growth (past 23 months through 12/31/96): 272% (from $8.94 to $33.25).
Revenue growth (past two years through 9/30/96): 68% (from $92.9 million to $156.0 million).
Earnings per share growth (past two years through 9/30/96): NA (from -$1.74 to $0.51).

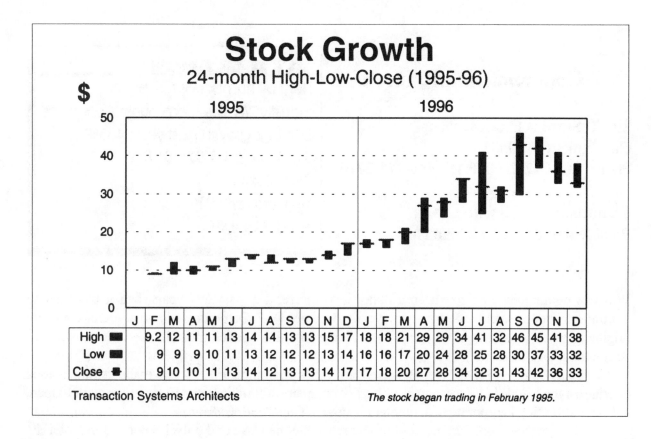

Stock Growth
24-month High-Low-Close (1995-96)

$		1995												1996										
	J	F	M	A	M	J	J	A	S	O	N	D	J	F	M	A	M	J	J	A	S	O	N	D
High ■		9.2	12	11	11	13	14	14	13	13	15	17	18	18	21	29	29	34	41	32	46	45	41	38
Low ■		9	9	9	10	11	13	12	12	12	13	14	16	16	17	20	24	28	25	28	30	37	33	32
Close ■		9	10	10	11	13	14	12	13	13	14	17	17	18	20	27	28	34	32	31	43	42	36	33

Transaction Systems Architects

The stock began trading in February 1995.

Quick Fix

P/E range (past two years):	31 - 300
Earnings past four quarters:	$0.51 (through 9/30/96)
Projected 1997 earnings (median):	$0.75
International sales:	53% of total sales
Total current assets	$76.7 million (1996); $78.8 million (1995)
Total current liabilities:	$40.2 million (1996); $40.1 million (1995)
Net Income:	$13.5 million (1996); $6.5 million (1995)

Financial history

Fiscal year ended: Sept. 30
(Revenue in millions)

	1992	1993	1994	1995	1996
Revenue	$65.1	$71.2	$92.9	$114.9	$156.1
Earnings per share	NA	-0.22	-1.74	0.29	0.51
*Stock price: High	NA	NA	NA	16.88	45.75
Low	NA	NA	NA	8.88	16.38
Close	NA	NA	NA	16.88	33.25

***Stock prices (only) reflect calendar year.**

71

DSP Communications, Inc.

20300 Stevens Creek Blvd.
Cupertino, CA 95014
Phone: 408-777-2700; FAX: 408-777-2770

Chairman: Davidi Gilo
President and CEO: Nathan Hod

AT A GLANCE

Held by number of funds: 2
Industry: Wireless communications chips
Earnings growth past year: 433%
Stock price 1/1/97: $19.38
P/E ratio: 41
Year ago P/E: 91
NASDAQ: DSPC

Wireless communications has been a major growth area the past few years, and it promises to continue to boom worldwide for many years to come. DSP Communications, a young company originally based in Israel, has enjoyed skyrocketing growth by developing chip sets for the wireless communications market.

Founded in 1987, DSP first registered as a U.S. corporation in 1994, and made its initial stock offering on the NASDAQ Exchange in 1995. The company still maintains offices in Israel and Japan, although its official corporate headquarters is now in Cupertino, California.

DSP generates only 2.5 percent of its revenue in the U.S., and only 1.3 percent in Israel. Its biggest market by far is Japan, which accounts for about 94 percent of its revenue. The vast majority of its business involves the sale of chip sets to cellular and other wireless communications manufacturers in Japan, such as Kendwood, Kyocera, Sanyo and Sharp.

The company's leading products are low power integrated circuit chip sets for cellular phones and other wireless communications products. The firm has developed baseband chip sets that support a broad range of frequency modulation standards such as the Personal Digital Cellular standards, the Advanced Mobile Phone System standards and the Total Access Communication System standards.

The company keeps its overhead down by using independent foundries to manufacture its products. It orders products from its foundries only upon receipt of orders from its customers, eliminating the need for product inventories.

Because of its use of independent foundries and a marketing and distribution system that relies on outside distributors, DSP has kept its staff to a minimum. Prior to a recent merger with Proxim, the company had only about 110 employees – which is almost unheard of for a company with annual revenues of more than $60 million.

Late developments

DSP acquired Proxim in late 1996 through a stock exchange valued at about $400 million. Proxim, based in Mountain View, California, makes wireless local area data networking products based on spread spectrum radio frequency technology.

Performance

Stock growth (past 22 months through 12/31/96): 485% (from $3.31 to $39.38).
Revenue growth (past two years through 12/31/96): 445% (from $16.0 million to $88.9 million).
Earnings per share growth (past two years through 12/31/96): 433% (from $0.09 to $0.48).

152

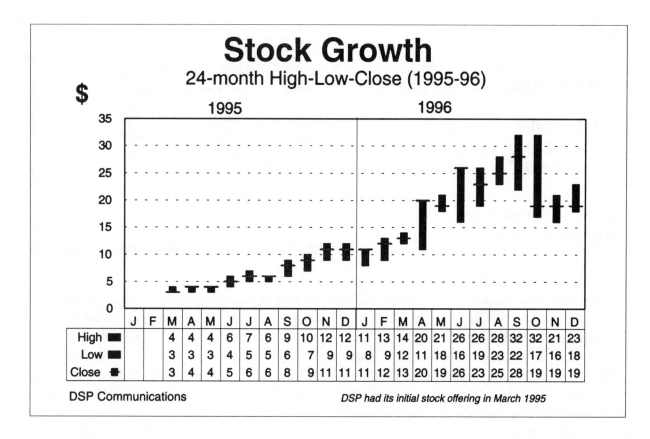

Stock Growth
24-month High-Low-Close (1995-96)

$	J	F	M	A	M	J	J	A	S	O	N	D	J	F	M	A	M	J	J	A	S	O	N	D
High ■			4	4	4	6	7	6	9	10	12	12	11	13	14	20	21	26	26	28	32	32	21	23
Low ■			3	3	3	4	5	5	6	7	9	9	8	9	12	11	18	16	19	23	22	17	16	18
Close ■			3	4	4	5	6	6	8	9	11	11	11	12	13	20	19	26	23	25	28	19	19	19

DSP Communications

DSP had its initial stock offering in March 1995

Quick Fix

P/E range (past two years):	16 - 100
Earnings past four quarters:	$1.00 (through 9/30/96)
Projected 1997 earnings (median):	$1.40
International sales:	97.5% of total sales (Asia/Pacific, 94%; other, 3.5%)
Total current assets:	$140.7 million (1996); $47.5 million (1995)
Total current liabilities:	$16.5 million (1996); $9.1 million (1995)
Net Income:	$21.8 million (1996); $8.5 million (1995)

Financial history

Fiscal year ended: Dec. 31
(Revenue in millions)

	1992	1993	1994	1995	1996
Revenue	$2.6	$4.1	$16.0	$40.9	$88.9
Earnings per share	-0.22	-0.08	0.09	0.24	0.48
Stock price: High	NA	NA	NA	12.25	31.75
Low	NA	NA	NA	2.50	7.50
Close	NA	NA	NA	10.94	19.38

72
Atmel Corp.

2325 Orchard Parkway
San Jose, CA 95131
Phone: 408-441-0311; FAX: 408-436-4200

Chairman, President and CEO:
George Perlegos

Atmel makes smart chips that allow home appliances and other devices to maintain their memory even when you turn them off. Known as nonvolatile memory chips, they are used to control the functions in toasters, dishwashers, portable phones, microwaves and other appliances. They are also used in automobiles for a variety of functions. For instance, even when the battery in your car dies, the radio may still remember the station lineup because it is programmed into the nonvolatile memory chip.

Most of the nonvolatile chips produced by Atmel are known as EPROMs—erasable programmable read-only memory chips—and EEPROMs—electrically erasable programmable read-only memory chips, which are more advanced than the EPROMs. Their common thread is that they can all be altered or reprogrammed. The company also makes "flash memory" chips that can be used to store operating programs in telecommunications devices, graphics or networking systems, and home video game systems.

The San Jose manufacturer also produces the four basic types of user-programmable logic chips, typically used by manufacturers of electronics systems to program standard functions.

About 40 percent of Atmel's revenue comes from the sale of chips to the telecommunications industry. The rest are sold to computer makers (25 percent), industrial and military manufacturers (10 percent), networking companies (10 percent), and consumer goods and automotive manufacturers (15 percent).

The company markets its products worldwide through nine North American and 12 international sales offices. It has manufacturing plants in Colorado Springs and Rousset, France.

Founded in 1984, Atmel has about 3,000 employees.

Late developments

In 1996, Atmel produced the industry's first "flash combo chip," an integrated circuit chip that combines two different memory functions on a single chip, and has the ability to do both read and write functions simultaneously. The chips will be used in products such as cellular phones, networks, point-of-sale terminals, small computers and modems. In the past, manufacturers have had to use two or more chips to achieve the same results.

Performance

Stock growth (past two years through 12/31/96): 98% (from $16.75 to $33.13).

Revenue growth (past two years through 9/30/96):195% (from $335 million to $989.5 million).

Earnings per share growth (past two years through 9/30/96): 210% (from $0.60 to $1.86).

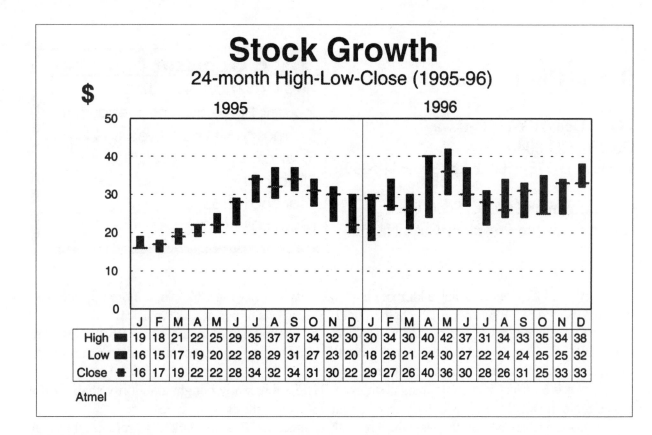

Stock Growth
24-month High-Low-Close (1995-96)

	J	F	M	A	M	J	J	A	S	O	N	D	J	F	M	A	M	J	J	A	S	O	N	D
High	19	18	21	22	25	29	35	37	37	34	32	30	30	34	30	40	42	37	31	34	33	35	34	38
Low	16	15	17	19	20	22	28	29	31	27	23	20	18	26	21	24	30	27	22	24	24	25	25	32
Close	16	17	19	22	22	28	34	32	34	31	30	22	29	27	26	40	36	30	28	26	31	25	33	33

Atmel

Quick Fix

P/E range (past two years):	13 - 32
Earnings past four quarters:	$1.86 (through 9/30/96)
Projected 1997 earnings (median):	$2.38
International sales:	52% of total sales
Total current assets:	$404.5 million (1996); $289.1 million (1995)
Total current liabilities:	$329.6 million (1996); $142.5 million (1995)
Net Income:	$113.7 million (1995); $59.4 million (1994)

Financial history

Fiscal year ended: Dec. 31
(Revenue in millions)

	1992	1993	1994	1995	*1996
Revenue	$139.8	$221.7	$375.1	$634.2	$789.2*
Earnings per share	0.19	0.37	0.67	1.16	1.48*
Stock price: High	4.25	9.66	18.81	36.75	42.38
Low	1.91	3.88	8.25	15.38	18.13
Close	4.09	8.66	16.75	22.38	33.13

1996 revenue and earnings through Sept. 30 (nine months).

73

Boston Chicken, Inc.

14103 Denver West Parkway
Golden, CO 80401
Phone: 303-278-9500; FAX: 303-384-5339

Cochairman and CEO: Scott Beck
Cochairman and President: Saad Nadhir

Kentucky Fried Chicken is feeling a lot more heat these days as Boston Chicken, a more upscale-but-similarly-priced fast food restaurant chain, quickly spreads its wings across America.

The upstart franchise operation has already opened about a thousand Boston Market restaurants in 38 states, and the company's growth is just beginning. It recently announced plans to add another 2,700 stores in the near future.

Nor is Boston Chicken stopping at chicken. The firm recently bought a majority share of the Einstein/Noah Bagel Corp., which operates about 250 bagel shops in 19 states.

Boston Chicken's restaurants, which recently changed to "Boston Market" to reflect a broader menu selection, offer rotisserie-roasted chicken, chicken pot pies and a variety of side dishes, such as corn, green beans, salads, beans, potatoes and dressing. The restaurants also recently began serving ham, turkey, meat loaf and special Boston Carver sandwiches.

Boston Market stores feature a clean, bright environment with ample in-store seating (plus carry-out).

Most of its stores are owned by franchisees who typically pay an up-front franchise fee of about $35,000, plus a 5 percent royalty on gross revenue, a 2 percent national advertising fund contribution, a 4 percent local advertising fund contribution, and a $10,000 minimum grand opening expenditure. Franchisees may also be charged for special computer hardware at a cost of $22,000 and software at a cost of $15,000.

The company generally offers secured debt financing to franchisees to assist them in raising start-up capital.

Founded in 1985, the Golden, Colorado, operation has about 560 corporate employees. The company went public with its initial stock offering in 1993.

Late developments

Einstein/Noah Bagel Corp. a partially-owned subsidiary of Boston Chicken, completed a public offering in late 1996 for 3 million common shares of stock to finance additional store openings. Boston Chicken maintained about 53 percent ownership share of the company.

Performance

Stock growth (past two years through 12/31/96): 106% (from $17.38 to $35.88).
Revenue growth (past two years through 9/30/96): 179% (from $83.3 million to $232.1 million).
Earnings per share growth (past two years through 9/30/96): 191% (from $0.32 to $0.93).

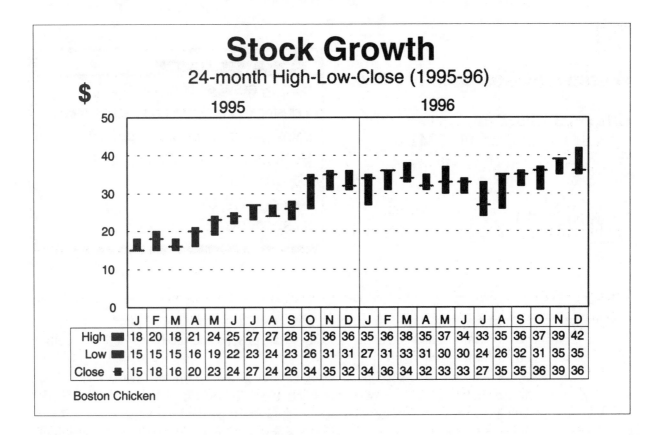

Stock Growth
24-month High-Low-Close (1995-96)

	J	F	M	A	M	J	J	A	S	O	N	D	J	F	M	A	M	J	J	A	S	O	N	D
High ■	18	20	18	21	24	25	27	27	28	35	36	36	35	36	38	35	37	34	33	35	36	37	39	42
Low ■	15	15	15	16	19	22	23	24	23	26	31	31	27	31	33	31	30	30	24	26	32	31	35	35
Close ➤	15	18	16	20	23	24	27	24	26	34	35	32	34	36	34	32	33	33	27	35	35	36	39	36

Boston Chicken

Quick Fix

P/E range (past two years):	22 - 60
Earnings past four quarters:	$0.93 (through 9/30/96)
Projected 1997 earnings (median):	$1.29
International sales:	none
Total current assets:	$150.5 million (1996); $92.5 million (1995)
Total current liabilities:	$45.2 million (1996); $23.6 million (1995)
Net Income:	$33.5 million (1995); $16.2 million (1994)

Financial history

Fiscal year ended: Dec. 31
(Revenue in millions)

	1992	1993	1994	1995	*1996
Revenue	$8.3	$42.5	$96.1	$159.5	$186.2*
Earnings per share	-0.21	0.07	0.38	0.66	0.74*
Stock price: High	NA	25.50	24.25	35.88	41.50
Low	NA	17.75	13.50	14.50	24.13
Close	NA	18.00	17.38	32.13	35.88

1996 revenue and earnings through Sept. 30 (nine months).

74

Wackenhut Corrections Corp.

4200 Wackenhut Drive
Palm Beach Gardens, FL 33410
http://www.wackenhut.com
Phone: 561-622-5656

Chairman: Timothy Cole
President : George Zoley

Wackenhut Corrections certainly has its share of repeat "customers," but not of their own volition. Wackenhut manages correctional and detention facilities—jails, prisons and the like—so its customers are not exactly itching for a return visit.

The private corrections business has been a tremendous growth industry for the past decade, growing at a rate of about 42 percent per year since 1986 (based on privatized prison beds). Wackenhut's growth has eclipsed that rate, expanding at about 66 percent per year, from 167 beds in 1986 to more than 16,000 now. The company holds about a 30 percent share of the worldwide private corrections market.

There's little reason to believe that the industry growth rate will subside anytime soon. Demand for prison beds already dramatically exceeds supply, and that trend is expected to continue well into the next century at a projected annual growth rate of about 35 percent.

Founded in 1984, Wackenhut Corrections is a division of Wackenhut Corp., which is a leader in security services and training. Wackenhut Corrections became a publicly-traded company in 1994, and its stock trades on the New York Stock Exchange.

Wackenhut Corrections offers a wide range of prison services to federal, state, local and foreign government agencies, including consulting, integrated design, financing and construction, and management and staffing of correctional facilities.

The Palm Beach Gardens, Florida, operation also provides health services, institutional food service and all other logistical support to operate the facilities. In addition, it offers rehabilitative and educational programs such as chemical dependency counseling, remedial education, job training and life skills instruction.

The firm currently operates about 25 facilities in the U.S., Puerto Rico, Great Britain and Australia. Wackenhut has about 3,000 employees.

Late developments

In 1996, the company began operating a prisoner transport business in England servicing about 25 percent of the country.

Performance

Stock growth (past two years through 12/31/96): 139 % (from $8.38 to $20.00).

Revenue growth (past two years through 9/30/96): 67% (from $76.1 million to $127.3 million).

Earnings per share growth (past two years through 9/30/96): 136% (from $0.14 to $0.33).

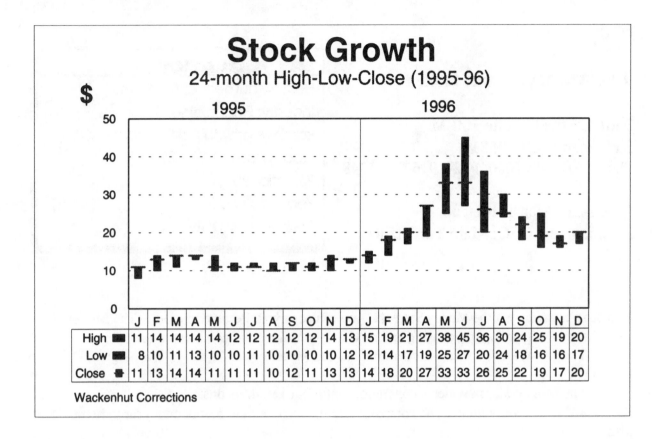

Stock Growth
24-month High-Low-Close (1995-96)

	J	F	M	A	M	J	J	A	S	O	N	D	J	F	M	A	M	J	J	A	S	O	N	D
High	11	14	14	14	14	12	12	12	12	14	13	15	19	21	27	38	45	36	30	24	25	19	20
Low	8	10	11	13	10	10	11	10	10	10	10	12	12	14	17	19	25	27	20	24	18	16	16	17
Close	11	13	14	14	11	11	11	10	12	11	13	13	14	18	20	27	33	33	26	25	22	19	17	20

Wackenhut Corrections

Quick Fix

P/E range (past two years):	33 - 75
Earnings past four quarters:	$0.33 (through 9/30/96)
Projected 1997 earnings (median):	$0.52
International sales:	18% of total sales
Total current assets:	$212.1 million (1996); $122.2 million (1995)
Total current liabilities:	$71.2 million (1996); $70.3 million (1995)
Net Income:	$5.9 million (9/30/96); $5.3 million (1995)

Financial history

Fiscal year ended: Dec. 31
(Revenue in millions)

	1992	1993	1994	1995	*1996
Revenue	$47.2	$58.8	$84.0	$99.4	$99.6*
Earnings per share	0.05	0.06	0.15	0.25	0.26*
Stock price: High	NA	NA	8.44	14.63	45.00
Low	NA	NA	4.50	8.25	11.63
Close	NA	NA	8.44	12.63	20.00

1996 revenue and earnings through Sept. 30 (nine months).

75

The Money Store, Inc.

3301 C Street, Suite 100-M
Sacramento, CA 95816
Phone: 916-446-5000; FAX: 916-979-7348

Chairman: Alan Turtletaub
President and CEO: Marc Turtletaub

You can't buy money at the Money Store, but you can borrow it. Founded in 1967, The Money Store specializes in originating, purchasing and servicing consumer and commercial loans.

The Sacramento, California, operation has branch offices in 44 states, Washington, D.C. and Puerto Rico.

The Money Store divides its operations into four key divisions:

- *Home equity loans.* The company originates more than $3 billion a year in home equity loans.

- *Small Business Administration (SBA) loans.* The Money Store is the nation's leading SBA lender – as it has been for the past 13 years. The company originated $441 million in SBA loans in 1995.

- *Student loans.* The company is one of the nation's 10 largest originators of government-guaranteed student loans, with about $400 million a year in loan originations.

- *Auto loans.* The Money Store's newest division originated about $54 million in new and used auto loans in 1995, with substantial growth projected for 1996 and 1997. The company has auto loan offices in more than 20 states.

Nearly all the loans originated by The Money Store are sold to institutional investors or pledged to the company's lenders until the loans can be sold and the lenders repaid.

The company went public with its initial stock offering in 1991. It has about 2,600 employees who help staff its nearly 200 branch offices. In all, the firm has about 350,000 customers, with a total serviced loan portfolio of about $9 billion.

Late developments

The Money Store continues to try to find profitable new niches in which to expand. On the heels of its success with auto leasing, the company is exploring the possibility of entering the hotel franchise business.

Performance

Stock growth (past two years through 12/31/96): 466% (from $ 4.88 to $27.63).
Revenue growth (past two years through 9/30/96): 128% (from $306 million to $698 million).
Earnings per share growth (past two years through 9/30/96): 130% (from $0.57 to $1.31).

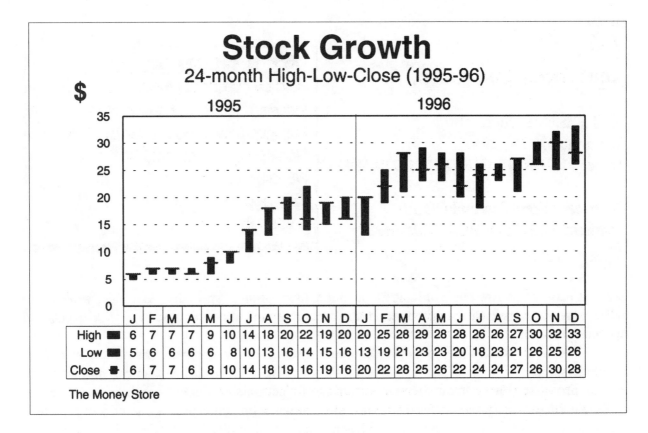

Stock Growth
24-month High-Low-Close (1995-96)

$

	1995												1996											
	J	F	M	A	M	J	J	A	S	O	N	D	J	F	M	A	M	J	J	A	S	O	N	D
High	6	7	7	7	9	10	14	18	20	22	19	20	20	25	28	29	28	28	26	26	27	30	32	33
Low	5	6	6	6	6	8	10	13	16	14	15	16	13	19	21	23	23	20	18	23	21	26	25	26
Close	6	7	7	6	8	10	14	18	19	16	19	16	20	22	28	25	26	22	24	24	27	26	30	28

The Money Store

Quick Fix

P/E range (past two years):	5 - 23
Earnings past four quarters:	$1.31 (through 9/30/96)
Projected 1997 earnings (median):	$1.62
International sales:	None
Total assets:	$1,792.2 million (1995); $1,165.1 million (1994)
Total liabilities:	$1,527.1 million (1995); $946.9 million (1994)
Net Income:	$48.7 million (1995); $31.3 million (1994)

Financial history

Fiscal year ended: Dec. 31
(Revenue in millions)

	1992	1993	1994	1995	*1996
Revenue	$1,007.4	$1,699.0	$2,779.4	$3,823.0	$535.3*
Earnings per share	0.34	0.48	0.62	0.95	0.97*
Dividends	0.01	0.04	0.05	0.07	0.12
Stock price: High	4.02	4.89	5.93	22.10	32.50
Low	1.82	2.76	4.13	4.73	13.00
Close	2.89	4.29	4.93	15.63	27.63

1996 revenue and earnings through Sept. 30.

76
Kent Electronics Corp.

7433 Harwin Drive
Houston, TX 77036
Phone: 713-780-7770; FAX: 713-978-5892

Chairman, President and CEO:
  Morrie K. Abramson

Kent has carved a narrow but profitable niche in the distribution of specialty electronics products to industrial users and original manufacturers in the data communications, computer, capital goods and medical industries.

Through its Kent Components Distribution division, the company distributes electronic connectors, electronic wire and cable and other passive and electromechanical products and interconnect assemblies used in the manufacturing of electronic products. It is the nation's largest publicly-traded specialty electronics distributor of interconnection and passive component products.

The Houston-based operation also has a manufacturing division, K*TEC Electronics, that makes custom electronic interconnect assemblies, specially fabricated battery power packs and other related products built to the customers' specifications.

Kent also operates another division, Kent Datacomm, that distributes a broad range of wiring products, such as fiber optic cables, patch panels and enclosures and local area network (LAN) and wide area network (WAN) equipment such as modems, hubs, bridges and routers. Its customer base is made up primarily of commercial end-users and companies that install and service voice and data communications networks.

Kent has sales offices in 18 states, and operates manufacturing plants in Houston, Dallas and San Jose, California.

Founded in 1973, the company went public with its initial stock offering in 1986. Kent has about 1,200 employees.

Late developments
In early 1997, the company completed the acquisition of Futronix Corp. of Houston, and Wire & Cable Specialties Corp. of Atlanta. Kent plans to merge the two companies to create a new Kent Electronics unit. The combined company, which will specialize in distributing specialty wire and cable, will serve more than 1,000 electrical distributors through 13 distribution centers and sales offices.

Performance
Stock growth (past two years through 12/31/96): 95% (from $13.19 to $25.75).
Revenue growth (past two years through 9/30/96): 88% (from $219.6 million to $412.8 million).
Earnings per share growth (past two years through 9/30/96): 132% (from $0.56 to $1.30).

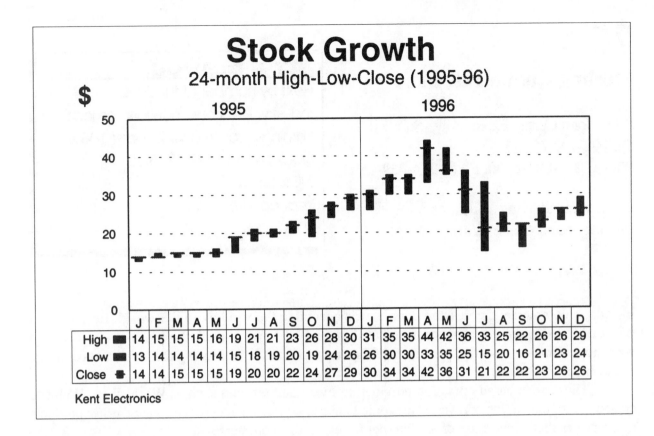

Stock Growth
24-month High-Low-Close (1995-96)

	J	F	M	A	M	J	J	A	S	O	N	D	J	F	M	A	M	J	J	A	S	O	N	D
High	14	15	15	15	16	19	21	21	23	26	28	30	31	35	35	44	42	36	33	25	22	26	26	29
Low	13	14	14	14	14	15	18	19	20	19	24	26	26	30	30	33	35	25	15	20	16	21	23	24
Close	14	14	15	15	15	19	20	20	22	24	27	29	30	34	34	42	36	31	21	22	22	23	26	26

Kent Electronics

Quick Fix

P/E range (past two years):	11 - 31
Earnings past four quarters:	$0.61 (through 9/30/96)
Projected 1997 earnings (median):	$1.11
International sales:	None
Total current assets:	$200 million (9/28/96); $189 million (9/30/95)
Total current liabilities:	$45 million (9/28/96); $34.5 million (9/30/95)
Net Income:	$28 million (1996); $13.4 million (1995)

Financial history

Fiscal year ended: March 31
(Revenue in millions)

	1992	1993	1994	1995	1996
Revenue	$94.7	$154.7	$192.9	$253.5	$372.0
Earnings per share	0.34	0.40	0.48	0.66	1.22
*Stock price: High	8.63	9.58	13.50	29.94	43.75
Low	5.67	6.67	8.83	12.83	15.25
Close	8.46	9.50	13.21	29.19	25.75

Stock prices (only) reflect calendar year.

77

Sterling Commerce, Inc.

8080 North Central Expressway, Suite 1100
Dallas, TX 75206
Phone: 214-891-8600; FAX: 214-739-0535

Chairman: Sterling Williams
President and CEO: Warner Blow

In today's commerce, the desktop computer is becoming the window to the world. Business and financial transactions are being consummated instantly through E-mail, the Internet and local and wide area computer networks. Sterling Commerce specializes in facilitating the give and take of the electronic marketplace.

The Dallas-based operation provides software and services such as World Wide Web site creation, data translation software, electronic banking services, data encryption and other products and services that support use of the Internet for electronic commerce.

The company groups its operations into four businesses: network services, interchange software, communications software and banking systems. Sterling Commerce is the premier provider of electronic payment systems for banks in the U.S

The firm's "Connect" family of products provides an infrastructure for managing electronic commerce and business applications such as electronic funds transfer, data warehousing, mobile computing and other data exchanges across diverse network systems.

Sterling's Gentran family of interchange products include software for a wide range of electronic commerce functions, from point-and-click electronic data interchange translators to cross-platform messaging systems. Its "Commerce" family of network services include network processing and messaging capabilities, and access to electronic forms, E-mail, and other related information sources.

Sterling Commerce had been a wholly-owned division of Sterling Software, Inc., until March 1996, when the parent company spun it off into a new company through an initial public stock offering. Sterling Software was founded in 1981.

Late developments

Sterling Commerce and National Wholesale Druggists' Association Service Corp. jointly introduced a Web-based service in early 1997 that provides drug manufacturers and wholesalers with industry news and reference information, including new product approvals, recalls, mergers and acquisitions, and related information. The service is available on a subscription basis.

Performance

Stock growth (past nine months through 12/31/96): 17% (from $30 to $35.25).
Revenue growth (past two years through 9/30/96): 72% (from $155.9 million to $267.8 million).
Earnings per share growth (past two years through 9/30/96): 108% (from $0.38 to $0.79).

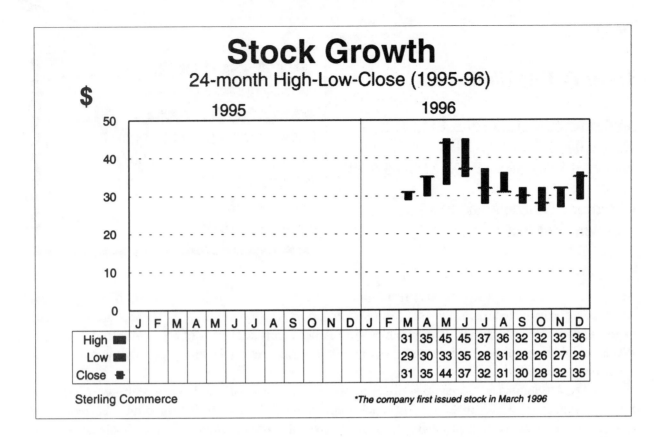

Stock Growth
24-month High-Low-Close (1995-96)

	J	F	M	A	M	J	J	A	S	O	N	D
High			31	35	45	45	37	36	32	32	32	36
Low			29	30	33	35	28	31	28	26	27	29
Close			31	35	44	37	32	31	30	28	32	35

Sterling Commerce

*The company first issued stock in March 1996

Quick Fix

P/E range (past year):	32 - 57
Earnings past four quarters:	$0.79 (through 9/30/96)
Projected 1997 earnings (median):	$1.00
International sales:	None
Total current assets:	$150 million (1996); $56 million (1995)
Total current liabilities:	$73 million (1996); $52 million (1995)
Net Income:	$58 million (1996); $43 million (1995)

Financial history

Fiscal year ended: Sept. 30
(Revenue in millions)

	1992	1993	1994	1995	1996
Revenue	NA	$117.8	$155.9	$203.6	$267.8
Earnings per share	NA	0.21	0.38	0.59	0.79
*Stock price: High	NA	NA	NA	NA	$45.00
Low	NA	NA	NA	NA	$25.50
Close	NA	NA	NA	NA	$35.25

*Stock prices (only) reflect calendar year.

165

78

Logan's Roadhouse, Inc.

565 Marriott Drive, Suite 490
Nashville, TN 37214
Phone: 615-885-9056; FAX: 615-885-9058

Chairman, President and CEO:
  Edwin W. Moats

Stepping into a Logan's Roadhouse restaurant is like stepping back in time. Built of rough-hewn cedar siding, corrugated metal and wooden planked floors, the Roadhouse restaurants are decorated with hand-painted murals depicting scenes from American roadhouses of the 1940s and 1950s. A Wurlitzer jukebox in the corner cranks out country hits, while the cooks toil in plain view over a gas-fired mesquite grill.

The restaurants feature steaks, ribs, seafood and salads at prices that are inviting to families. Prices range from $3.95 to $7.25 for lunch items and $7.25 to $16.95 for dinner entrees. The restaurants also have an express lunch menu of specially priced sandwiches and salads that are guaranteed to be served in 15 minutes or less. The restaurants are open seven days a week for lunch and dinner, and include full bar service.

For investors, one attractive feature of Logan's restaurants is that there aren't very many of them. Through late 1996, there were a total of 12 restaurants, scattered across Alabama, Georgia, Kentucky, Indiana and the chain's home state of Tennessee. But the company plans an accelerated expansion program, with plans for seven or eight new stores in 1997.

The company prefers to locate its restaurants in mid-sized metropolitan markets such as Memphis, Nashville, Lexington, Evansville and Birmingham, although it will build in smaller markets if the competition is scant and the cultural environment is favorable, such as Clarksville, Indiana; Johnson City, Tennessee; and Paducah, Kentucky.

The first Logan's Roadhouse opened in 1991 in Lexington. It was acquired by the present management in 1992, which then began opening new restaurants in the surrounding states. The company has been profitable since its initial year. The average sales per restaurant per year is about $4 million.

The company currently owns all of its restaurants, but it has indicated that it will probably open some franchised restaurants in the near future.

Logan's went public with its initial stock offering in July, 1995. It has about 1,200 employees.

Late developments

The company recently opened new restaurants in Oklahoma City and Huntington, West Virginia.

Performance

Stock growth (past year through 12/31/96): 104% (from $11.50 to $23.50).
Revenue growth (past two years through 9/30/96): 187% (from $13.2 million to $37.8 million).
Earnings per share growth (past two years through 9/30/96): 100% (from $0.32 to $0.64).

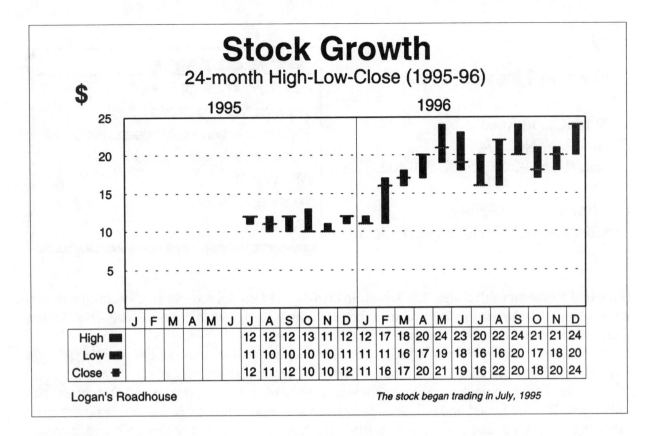

Stock Growth
24-month High-Low-Close (1995-96)

$

	J	F	M	A	M	J	J	A	S	O	N	D	J	F	M	A	M	J	J	A	S	O	N	D
High ■							12	12	12	13	11	12	12	17	18	20	24	23	20	22	24	21	21	24
Low ■							11	10	10	10	10	11	11	11	16	17	19	18	16	16	20	17	18	20
Close ■							12	11	12	10	10	12	11	16	17	20	21	19	16	22	20	18	20	24

Logan's Roadhouse

The stock began trading in July, 1995

Quick Fix

P/E range (past two years):	40 - 19
Earnings past four quarters:	$0.64 (through 9/30/96)
Projected 1997 earnings (median):	$0.90
International sales:	None
Total current assets:	$18 million (1996); $1.2 million (1995)
Total current liabilities:	$2.6 million (1996); $4.4 million (1995)
Net Income:	$2.9 million (through 3rd quarter, 1996); $1.9 million (1995)

Financial history

Fiscal year ended: Dec. 31
(Revenue in millions)

	1992	1993	1994	1995	*1996
Revenue	NA	$8.8	$15.0	$27.9	$30.1*
Earnings per share	NA	0.12	0.34	0.50	0.51*
Stock price: High	NA	NA	NA	12.50	24.00
Low	NA	NA	NA	9.50	11.00
Close	NA	NA	NA	11.50	23.50

1996 revenue and earnings through Sept. 30 (nine months).

79

Oakwood Homes Corp.

7800 McCloud Road
Greensboro, NC 27409
Phone: 910-664-2400; FAX: 910-632-3224

Chairman: Ralph Darling
President and CEO: Nicholas St. George

AT A GLANCE

Held by number of funds: 2
Industry: Manufactured homes
Earnings growth past 2 years: 88%
Stock price 1/1/97: $22.88
P/E ratio: 15
Year ago P/E: 20
NYSE: OH

Oakwood Homes manufacturers the American dream. The Greensboro, North Carolina, operation is the nation's third largest producer of manufactured homes, and, with 255 sales offices in 27 states, it sells more homes than any other retailer.

The company has 16 manufacturing plants, including five in North Carolina, four in Georgia, three in Texas, and one each in California, Colorado, Oregon and Tennessee.

Part of the company's success has come as a result of its broad depth of added services. Not only does Oakwood build and sell its manufactured and mobile homes, it also offers homebuyers financing, insurance, and even a site to place the home. The company develops and manages manufactured housing communities.

Oakwood manufactures 14-foot and 16-foot wide single section homes (formerly known as "mobile homes"), and 24-foot and 28-foot wide multi-section homes with two floors that are joined at the homesite. The firm also manufactures a few multi-section homes with three or four floors. Most of its home range from 40 to 80 feet in length.

Many of the homes are furnished with carpeting, draperies, curtains, furniture, lamps and a dinette set. Other options include beds, a fireplace, washing machine, dryer, microwave oven, dishwasher, air conditioning, intercom, wet bar, vaulted ceilings and skylights.

Oakwood has bolstered its growth the past three years through the acquisition of two other housing manufacturers. In 1994, it acquired California-based Golden West, and in 1995, it bought Georgia-based Destiny Industries.

Founded in 1946, Oakwood went public with its initial stock offering in 1971. The compnay has about 6,200 employees.

Late developments

Oakwood has been shifting its manufacturing emphasis in the past year from single-section homes to multi-section homes, which have been in greater demand recently. In the quarter ended January 1, 1997, single section home sales were down 12 percent, while multi-section home sales rose 27 percent.

Performance

Stock growth (past two years through 12/31/96): 88% (from $12.19 to $22.88).
Revenue growth (past two years through 9/30/96): 46% (from $664.6 million to $973.9 million).
Earnings per share growth (past two years through 9/30/96): 88% (from $0.78 to $1.47).

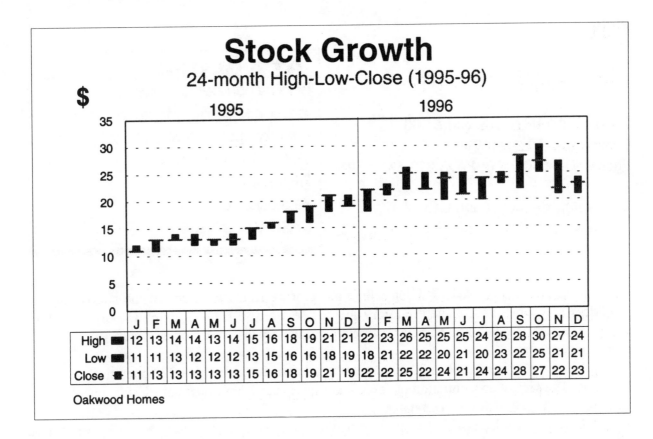

Stock Growth
24-month High-Low-Close (1995-96)

	1995												1996											
	J	F	M	A	M	J	J	A	S	O	N	D	J	F	M	A	M	J	J	A	S	O	N	D
High	12	13	14	14	13	14	15	16	18	19	21	21	22	23	26	25	25	25	24	25	28	30	27	24
Low	11	11	13	12	12	12	13	15	16	16	18	19	18	21	22	22	20	21	20	23	22	25	21	21
Close	11	13	13	13	13	13	15	16	18	19	21	19	22	22	25	22	24	21	24	24	28	27	22	23

Oakwood Homes

Quick Fix

P/E range (past two years):	11 - 22
Earnings past four quarters:	$1.47 (through 9/30/96)
Projected 1997 earnings (median):	$1.72
International sales:	None
Total assets:	$836.3 million (1996); $634.2 million (1995)
Total liabilities:	$467.3 million (1996); $331.2 million (1995)
Net Income:	$68.2 million (1996); $45.3 million (1995)

Financial history

Fiscal year ended: Sept. 30
(Revenue in millions)

	1992	1993	1994	1995	1996
Revenue	$306.2	$483.7	$664.6	$821.4	$973.9
Earnings per share	0.48	0.61	0.78	0.99	1.47
*Stock price: High	10.69	14.38	14.94	21.25	30.25
Low	5.06	8.56	9.63	10.81	19.63
Close	10.06	13.50	12.19	19.19	22.88

Stock prices (only) reflect calendar year.

80

Lincare Holdings, Inc.

19337 U.S. 19 North, Suite 500
Clearwater, FL 34624
Phone: 813-530-7700; FAX: 813-532-9692

Chairman, President and CEO:
   James T. Kelly

This is a company that makes a living selling air. Lincare Holdings is one of the nation's largest providers of oxygen and other respiratory therapy services to patients living at home. Most of Lincare's customers suffer from chronic obstructive pulmonary diseases such as emphysema, chronic bronchitis or asthma.

Lincare serves more than 90,000 home-based patients from about 220 operating centers in 37 states. The largest concentration of centers are in Lincare's home state of Florida, plus Indiana, Ohio and the East and West coast states.

Lincare's service enables pulmonary patients to spend more time at home rather than in hospitals or nursing homes. Lincare staff members train patients or their families in the use of the equipment, such as ventilators, oxygen concentrators, nebulizers and oximeters. Lincare patients have a low 8 percent hospital readmission rate compared with a 29 percent readmission rate for other patients.

In addition to oxygen and respiratory therapy, the company also provides infusion therapies (such as chemotherapy, intravenous antibiotic therapy and continuous pain management) in some of its markets. The company also sells hospital beds, wheelchairs and other medical equipment required by its home-based customers.

The Clearwater, Florida, operation has grown quickly the past few years through internal growth and a series of acquisitions. In 1995, for instance, Lincare acquired 22 local and regional competitors in the respiratory therapy business.

Lincare collects most of its revenue (60 percent) through Medicare and Medicaid. Private insurance pays about 24 percent and direct payments account for 16 percent.

Lincare was founded in 1972, and reorganized in 1990 after the current management group lead a buy-out of the company. Lincare has about 2,200 employees.

Late developments

The company completed three acquisitions in late 1996, including Buffalo Oxygen Services in Buffalo, New York, Southwestern Medical Supply in Carlsbad, New Mexico, and the home care division of the New Mexico Steel Company in Albuquerque, New Mexico.

Performance

Stock growth (past two years through 12/31/96): 41% (from $29.00 to $41.00).
Revenue growth (past two years through 9/30/96): 75% (from $188.2 million to $328.7 million).
Earnings per share growth (past two years through 9/30/96): 77% (from $1.26 to $2.25).

Stock Growth
24-month High-Low-Close (1995-96)

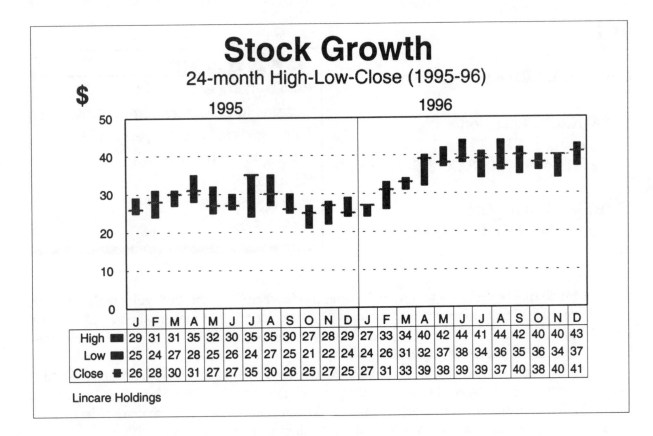

	J	F	M	A	M	J	J	A	S	O	N	D	J	F	M	A	M	J	J	A	S	O	N	D
High	29	31	31	35	32	30	35	35	30	27	28	29	27	33	34	40	42	44	41	44	42	40	40	43
Low	25	24	27	28	25	26	24	27	25	21	22	24	24	26	31	32	37	38	34	36	35	36	34	37
Close	26	28	30	31	27	27	35	30	26	25	27	25	27	31	33	39	38	39	39	37	40	38	40	41

Lincare Holdings

Quick Fix

P/E range (past two years):	12 - 20
Earnings past four quarters:	$1.74 (through 9/30/96)
Projected 1997 earnings (median):	$2.64
International sales:	none
Total current assets:	$48.2 million (1996); $38.9 million (1995)
Total current liabilities:	$30 million (1996); $27.1 million (1995)
Net Income:	$51 million (1995); $37.9 million (1994)

Financial history

Fiscal year ended: Dec. 31
(Revenue in millions)

	1992	1993	1994	1995	*1996
Revenue	$117.4	$154.5	$201.1	$274.8	$254.4*
Earnings per share	0.64	1.01	1.34	1.79	1.74*
Stock price: High	15.25	25.50	29.00	35.25	43.75
Low	6.38	8.44	18.75	21.00	24.00
Close	15.25	24.88	29.00	25.00	41.00

1996 revenue and earnings through Sept. 30 (nine months).

81

Catalina Marketing Corp.

11300 Ninth Street North
St. Petersburg, FL 33716
Phone: 813-579-5000; FAX: 813-570-8507

Chairman: Tommy Greer
President and CEO: George Off

Catalina Marketing has found a way to target consumers where they are most vulnerable—right at the cash register. The company helps hundreds of consumer product makers such as Coca-Cola, Bristol-Myers, General Mills and Campbell Soup get their coupons in the hands of specifically-targeted consumers just as they leave the grocery store.

Traditionally, consumer products companies have used mailers and newspaper ads to attempt to reach consumers with special offers and coupons. But consumers redeem less than 2 percent of the 300 billion coupons distributed annually—and 80 percent of the coupons that are redeemed are done so by shoppers who would have bought the product without a coupon.

Catalina has been able to significantly bolster the return on coupons by offering consumer products companies a more precise way to target customers. The company installs coupon printers at checkout scanners and cash registers in thousands of grocery stores. Catalina's computerized system evaluates scanner data (the items purchased by each shopper), matches it with manufacturer or retailer programmed promotions and directs its printer (which is located at the checkout counter) to print out the appropriate coupon or promotional message. The coupons are handed to shoppers as they pay for their groceries.

Consumer products companies can enter four-week promotional blocks during which their coupons are printed and distributed to specific consumers. For instance, Coca-Cola may contract to have coupons printed for all shoppers who buy their product—or a competing product. When a shopper with a six-pack of Pepsi goes through the check-out line, the scanner reads the bar code, recognizes that the shopper is buying a competing soft drink, and prints out a coupon for Coca-Cola that the shopper can use next time he or she is in the store.

Catalina's network is installed in more than 10,000 supermarkets across the U.S. and 650 stores abroad. In all, the company reaches about 150 million shoppers per week.

Founded in 1983, the St. Petersburg, Florida, operation has about 600 employees.

Late developments
Catalina introduced a "Checkout CallCard" in late 1996 that allows retailers to sell prepaid calling card "certificates" that are printed out at the store on the Catalina checkout printers.

Performance
Stock growth (past two years through 12/31/96): 98% (from $27.81 to $55.13).
Revenue growth (past two years through 9/30/96): 46% (from $104.3 million to $152.3 million).
Earnings per share growth (past two years through 9/30/96): 65% (from $0.75 to $1.24).

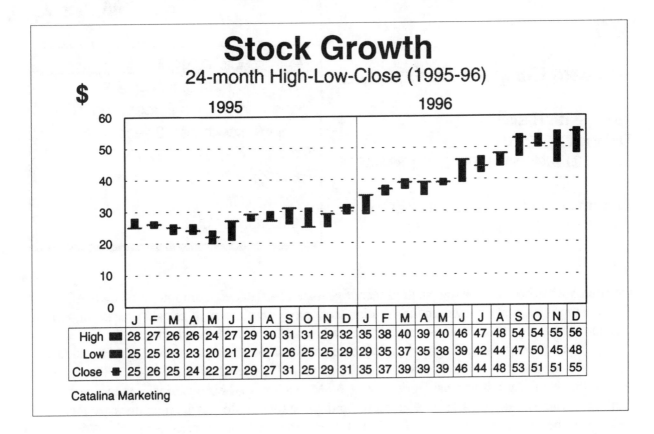

Stock Growth
24-month High-Low-Close (1995-96)

	J	F	M	A	M	J	J	A	S	O	N	D	J	F	M	A	M	J	J	A	S	O	N	D
High	28	27	26	26	24	27	29	30	31	31	29	32	35	38	40	39	40	46	47	48	54	54	55	56
Low	25	25	23	23	20	21	27	27	26	25	25	29	29	35	37	35	38	39	42	44	47	50	45	48
Close	25	26	25	24	22	27	29	27	31	25	29	31	35	37	39	39	39	46	44	48	53	51	51	55

Catalina Marketing

Quick Fix

P/E range (past two years):	18 - 44
Earnings past four quarters:	$1.24 (through 9/30/96)
Projected 1997 earnings (median):	$1.41
International sales:	Approximately 5 percent
Total current assets:	$50.3 million (6/30/96); $57.9 million (6/30/95)
Total current liabilities:	$37 million (6/30/96); $43.9 million (6/30/95)
Net Income:	$22.0 million (1996); $17.2 million (1995)

Financial history

Fiscal year ended: March 31
(Revenue in millions)

	1992	1993	1994	1995	1996
Revenue	$51.7	$71.9	$91.4	$113.2	$134.2
Earnings per share	0.25	0.41	0.62	0.86	1.11
*Stock price: High	19.63	25.13	28.13	32.44	55.50
Low	12.13	14.25	20.63	20.00	29.19
Close	19.13	25.00	27.81	31.38	55.13

*Stock prices (only) reflect calendar year.

173

82

Affiliated Computer Services, Inc.

2828 North Haskell
Dallas, TX 75204
Phone: 214-841-6111; FAX: 214-821-8315

Chairman and CEO: Darwin Deason
President: Jeffrey Rich

Outsourcing has been a growing trend in recent years, and Affiliated Computer Services (ACS) has carved a profitable niche providing information technology services such as data processing, image management and professional services for a broad range of corporate customers.

The company also has a growing electronic funds transfer transaction processing division, and operates a MoneyMaker automated teller machine (ATM) network of more than 3,000 machines. ACS is the second largest non-bank operator of ATM machines. Their machines are located in non-bank areas such as supermarkets, retail stores and gas stations. Most of its machines are located in Texas and the Southwest region, although it also operates a group of machines in New York.

Electronic funds transfer accounts for about 21 percent of the company's annual revenue. Image management accounts for another 21 percent and professional services makes up 3 percent.

ACS's leading source of revenue is its outsourcing business, which accounts for about 55 percent of total revenue. The company provides a broad range of outsourcing programs for commercial businesses and the financial services industry. Normally, the company does data processing duties from its data center using mainframe computers, which provides cost savings and improved quality for its customers.

The Dallas-based operation also provides a wide range of outsourcing services to commercial banks, thrifts and credit unions, including core processing of commercial and mortgage loans, financial accounting and reporting, deposits and information file processing.

ACS was founded in 1988 by Darwin Deason, who continues to serve as the company chairman. The company went public with its initial stock offering in 1994.

Late developments

In late 1996, ACS acquired Pinpoint Marketing, a New York-based marketing services company that specializes in administrating and analyzing the effectiveness of a wide range of marketing support and marketing fund programs including co-op advertising, marketing development, incentive programs and added-value promotions.

Performance

Stock growth (past two years through 12/31/96): 177% (from $10.75 to $29.75).
Revenue growth (past two years through 9/30/96): 63.3% (from $277 million to $451.5 million).
Earnings per share growth (past two years through 9/30/96): 56% (from $1.09 to $1.70).

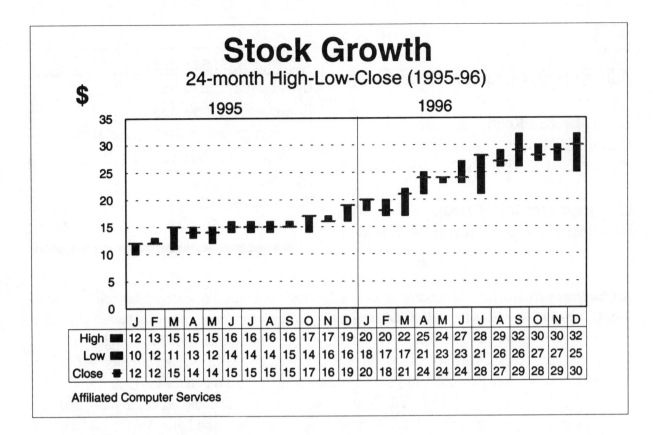

Stock Growth
24-month High-Low-Close (1995-96)

$

	1995												1996											
	J	F	M	A	M	J	J	A	S	O	N	D	J	F	M	A	M	J	J	A	S	O	N	D
High	12	13	15	15	15	16	16	16	16	17	17	19	20	20	22	25	24	27	28	29	32	30	30	32
Low	10	12	11	13	12	14	14	14	15	14	16	16	18	17	17	21	23	23	21	26	26	27	27	25
Close	12	12	15	14	14	15	15	15	15	17	16	19	20	18	21	24	24	24	28	27	29	28	29	30

Affiliated Computer Services

Quick Fix

P/E range (past two years):	14 - 38
Earnings past four quarters:	$1.70 (through 9/30/96)
Projected 1997 earnings (median):	$2.06
International sales:	None
Total current assets:	$168.8 million (1996); $114.4 million (6/30/95)
Total current liabilities:	$118.9 million (1996); $62.8 million (6/30/95)
Net Income:	$30.6 million (1996); $8.7 million (1995)

Financial history

Fiscal year ended: June 30
(Revenue in millions)

	1992	1993	1994	1995	1996
Revenue	$150.0	$189.1	$271.1	$313.2	$396.5
Earnings per share	0.46	0.82	1.08	1.37	1.65
*Stock price: High	NA	NA	11.75	19.25	32.00
Low	NA	NA	8.50	9.88	15.75
Close	NA	NA	10.75	18.75	29.75

*Stock price (only) reflects calendar year.

175

83

Air Express International Corp.

120 Tokeneke Road
Darien, CT 06820
Phone: 203-655-7900; FAX: 203-655-5779

Chairman: Hendrik Hartong
President and CEO: Guenter Rohrmann

Air Express gets around. The Connecticut-based hauler ships cargo to nearly 3,000 cities in more than 180 countries. AEI is the oldest and largest international airfreight company based in the U.S.

The company has established a profitable niche within the crowded shipping business by focusing primarily on international transportation of heavy cargo. AEI's average package weighs just over 500 pounds. More than half of its shipments are from locations outside the U.S.

AEI has set up a global network to handle its payloads, including offices in more than 800 cities in the U.S., Europe, Asia, Africa, Australia, the Middle East and Latin America. Most of its offices are managed by nationals of the countries in which they serve.

For AEI, the job of hauling heavy freight around the world is less a matter of muscle than it is logistics and documentation. In fact, AEI owns no ships or aircraft. Rather, the company arranges for transportation of its customer's shipments by steamship lines, commercial airlines and air cargo carriers. It also prepares the shipping documents, and arranges for clearance of its cargo through customs at the final destination. The company processes about a million customs entries a year.

In addition to its freight forwarding services, AEI also offers some ancillary services, such as door-to-door pick-up and delivery of freight, purchase order management, warehousing and distribution, inventory management, cargo assembly, protective packing and consolidation services.

About 62 percent of the company's revenue is generated outside the U.S. It continues to expand its international base through a series of acquisitions of small foreign freight haulers. AEI has about 6,000 employees.

Late developments

The company recently acquired Muller Air Freight BV, a Dutch airfreight and logistics company. The firm has a staff of 140, and annual revenues of $35 million.

Performance

Stock growth (past two years through 12/31/96): 61 % (from $20.00 to $32.25).
Revenue growth (past two years through 12/31/96): 34% (from $977 million to $1.34 billion).
Earnings per share growth (past two years through 12/31/96): 41% (from $1.28 to $1.81).

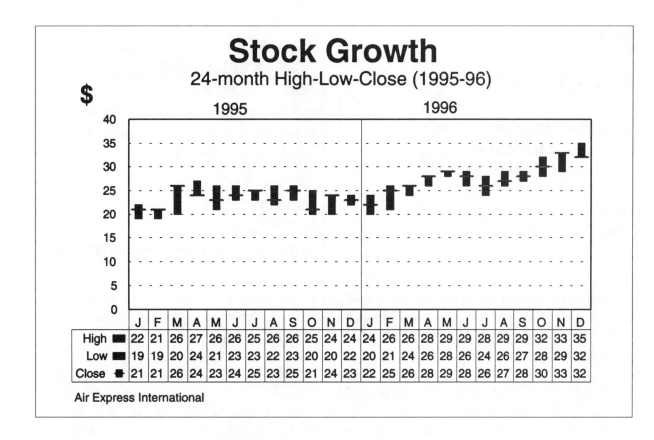

Stock Growth
24-month High-Low-Close (1995-96)

	J	F	M	A	M	J	J	A	S	O	N	D	J	F	M	A	M	J	J	A	S	O	N	D
High	22	21	26	27	26	26	25	26	26	25	24	24	24	26	26	28	29	29	28	29	29	32	33	35
Low	19	19	20	24	21	23	23	22	23	20	20	22	20	21	24	26	28	26	24	26	27	28	29	32
Close	21	21	26	24	23	24	25	23	25	21	24	23	22	25	26	28	29	28	26	27	28	30	33	32

Air Express International

Quick Fix

P/E range (past two years):	11 - 19
Earnings past four quarters:	$1.81 (through 12/31/96)
Projected 1997 earnings (median):	$2.05
International sales:	62% of total sales (Asia/Pacific, 30%; Europe, 32%)
Total current assets:	$350.9 million (1996); $327.5 million (1995)
Total current liabilities:	$259.6 million (1996); $250.6 million (1995)
Net Income:	$38.5 million (1996); $29.0 million (1995)

Financial history

Fiscal year ended: Dec. 31
(Revenue in millions)

	1992	1993	1994	1995	1996
Revenue	$672.3	$725.7	$997.4	$1,222	$1,335
Earnings per share	1.08	0.97	1.21	1.48	1.81
Stock price: High	18.42	19.67	20.00	26.50	34.50
Low	8.72	12.00	12.25	18.50	20.00
Close	18.08	13.25	20.00	23.00	32.25

84

JP Foodservice, Inc.

9830 Patuxent Woods Drive
Columbia, MD 21046
Phone: 410-312-7110; FAX: 410-312-7591

Chairman, President and CEO:
  James L. Miller

Variety is the spice of life—and spices are among the *huge* variety of products JP Foodservice distributes to its broad base of commercial customers. In all, the company handles more than 30,000 food brands and related items, including paper products, soaps, cosmetics and other supermarket items.

The company distributes products to about 35,000 restaurants, hotels, healthcare facilities, cafeterias and schools located primarily in the Midwest and East. Among the company's leading customers are Perkins Family Restaurants, Subway, Eurest Dining Services and Ruby Tuesday restaurants. Restaurants account for about 70 percent of the company's total sales, healthcare institutions account for 5 percent, schools make up 3 percent, and limited menu establishments account for 11 percent.

JP Foodservice's leading products include canned and dry foods (27 percent of total sales), meats (20 percent), frozen foods (18 percent), poultry (9 percent), seafood (8 percent) and dairy products (7 percent). National brands account for about 83 percent of the company's net sales, while lower price private brands and signature brands make up the balance.

The Columbia, Maryland, distributor ships its products out of nine distribution centers located in Baltimore, Minneapolis, Boston, Hartford, Des Moines, Fort Wayne, Streator, Illinois; and Allentown and Altoona, Pennsylvania.

JP, which once was a division of Sara Lee, has about 3,000 employees. Sara Lee still owns about 38 percent of the company.

Late developments

The company recently acquired Arrow Paper and Supply Company, a distributor of about 6,000 food service products in the New England area, and Valley Industries, a distributor of about 4,000 products in Las Vegas, Nevada. Arrow had annual sales of about $75 million, and Valley had annual sales of about $122 million.

The company's stock was recently moved from the NASDAQ exchange to the New York Stock Exchange. Its new symbol is JPF.

Performance

Stock growth (past two years through 12/31/96): 201% (from $9.25 to $27.88).
Revenue growth (past two years through 9/30/96): 26% (from $1.04 billion to $1.3 billion).
Earnings per share growth (past two years through 9/30/96): 108% (from $0.36 to $0.75).

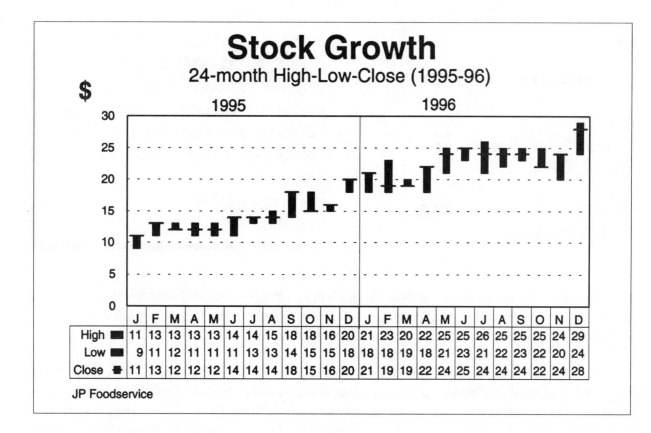

Stock Growth
24-month High-Low-Close (1995-96)

	J	F	M	A	M	J	J	A	S	O	N	D	J	F	M	A	M	J	J	A	S	O	N	D
High	11	13	13	13	13	14	14	15	18	18	16	20	21	23	20	22	25	25	26	25	25	25	24	29
Low	9	11	12	11	11	11	13	13	14	15	15	18	18	18	19	18	21	23	21	22	23	22	20	24
Close	11	13	12	12	12	14	14	14	18	15	16	20	21	19	19	22	24	25	24	24	24	22	24	28

JP Foodservice

Quick Fix

P/E range (past two years):	16 - 36
Earnings past four quarters:	$0.75 (through 9/30/96)
Projected 1997 earnings (median):	$1.23
International sales:	None
Total current assets:	$228.6 million (1996); $215.3 million (1995)
Total current liabilities:	$114 million (1996); $111.6 million (1995)
Net Income:	$14 million (1996); $ 6.6 million (1995)

Financial history

Fiscal year ended: June 30

(Revenue in millions)

	1992	1993	1994	1995	1996
Revenue	$1,014.7	$1,025.8	$1,029.0	$1,108.2	$1,242.7
Earnings per share	-2.86	- 2.55	- 0.59	0.59	0.88
*Stock price: High	NA	NA	11.50	19.75	28.75
Low	NA	NA	9.25	9.25	18.00
Close	NA	NA	9.25	19.50	27.88

Stock prices (only) reflect calendar year.

179

85

Sun International Hotels

Coral Towers
Paradise Island, The Bahamas
Phone: 809-363-2516

Chairman, President and CEO:
 Solomon Kerzner

Sun, fun and slot machines—that's the special allure of Sun International. The Bahamas-based operation runs a global chain of casinos and hotels that stretch from the Mohegan Indian Reservation in Connecticut to the tropical Indian Ocean island of Mauritius.

Sun's largest attraction is the Atlantis Resort and Casino, a 1,147-room property on Paradise Island in The Bahamas. The company recently poured $140 million into renovating and upgrading the property, converting it into an ocean-theme destination resort. In late 1996, Sun began a second stage of expansion at the resort that will ultimately cost an additional $375 million. The latest upgrade will include a new 1,200-room deluxe hotel, some new ocean adventure attractions, and a greatly expanded casino and convention capacity.

Other Sun International operations include:

- *The Mohegan Sun Casino.* Located in Montville, Connecticut, the facility has 3,000 slot machines, 180 table games and parking for 7,500 cars. The casino, which opened in October 1996, was developed for the Mohegan Indian Tribe by a partnership in which Sun holds a 50 percent share.

- *The Ocean Club Golf and Tennis Resort.* Located in The Bahamas, this luxury resort has 59 guest rooms and deluxe sports facilities.

- *Paradise Paradise Beach Resort.* Also located in The Bahamas, the resort has 100 guest rooms, and an 18-hole golf course.

- *Pirate's Cove Hotel.* Sun recently acquired this 562-room property, located adjacent to the Atlantis Resort. The company plans a $16 million renovation to be completed in 1998.

- *Indian Ocean resorts.* Sun operates (and owns a 23 percent share of) six resort hotels on the tropical Indian Ocean islands of Mauritius and Comoros.

- *French casinos.* Sun owns a 25 percent share of Societe de Participation et d'Investissements dans les Casinos, a French firm that operates four locals-oriented casinos in France.

In all, Sun manages 10 hotels and six casinos. The company, which had its initial stock offering in 1996, has about 3,200 employees.

Late developments
Sun International acquired Griffen Gaming & Entertainment, Inc., in late 1996.

Performance
Stock growth (past eleven months through 12/31/96): 1% (from $36 to $36.50).
Revenue growth (past year through 12/31/96): 12% (from $213.9 million to $240.1 million).
Earnings per share growth (past year through 12/31/96): 92% (from $0.87 to $1.60).

Stock Growth
24-month High-Low-Close (1995-96)*

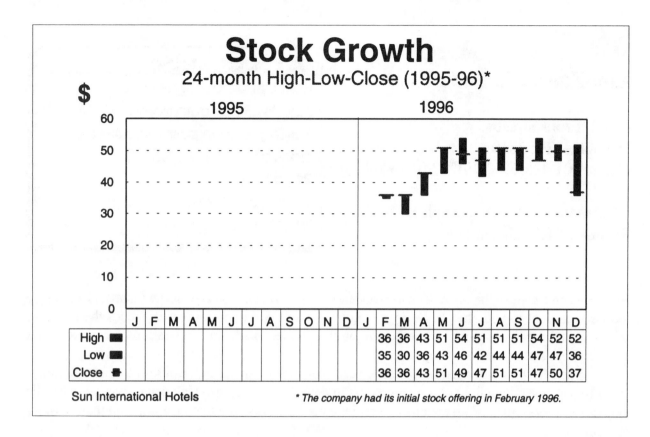

	J	F	M	A	M	J	J	A	S	O	N	D	J	F	M	A	M	J	J	A	S	O	N	D
High ◼														36	36	43	51	54	51	51	51	54	52	52
Low ◼														35	30	36	43	46	42	44	44	47	47	36
Close ◼														36	36	43	51	49	47	51	51	47	50	37

Sun International Hotels

The company had its initial stock offering in February 1996.

Quick Fix

P/E range (past two years):	16 - 34
Earnings past four quarters:	$1.60 (1996)
Projected 1997 earnings (median):	$2.30
International sales:	NA
Total current assets:	$190.6 million (3/31/96); $45.4 million (3/31/95)
Total current liabilities:	$42.4 million (3/31/96); $76.4 million (3/31/95)
Net Income:	$45.7 million (1996); $18.4 million (1995)

Financial history

Fiscal year ended: Dec. 31

(Revenue in millions)

	1992	1993	1994	1995	1996
Revenue	NA	NA	NA	$213.9	$240.1
Earnings per share	NA	NA	NA	$0.87	1.60
Stock price: High	NA	NA	NA	NA	54.25
Low	NA	NA	NA	NA	30.25
Close	NA	NA	NA	NA	36.50

86

AutoZone, Inc.

123 S. Front Street
Memphis, TN 38103
Phone: 901-495-6500; FAX: 901-495-8300

Chairman, and CEO: Joseph Hyde
President: T.S. Hanemann

It's long been a bane of the trade. You're in an auto parts store, next in line at the counter. But before the clerk can get to you, the phone rings, and instead of taking your order, he spends the next five minutes tracking down parts for the person on the phone. That's one frustration of the auto parts business that AutoZone is zoning out.

The Memphis-based retailer has set up call centers in Memphis and Houston to take calls from customers at several hundred of the company's highest volume stores. Call center operators handle inquiries and take orders from the customers, leaving the clerks free to concentrate on their in-store customers.

That's one of a series of new innovations the company has implemented to improve service. Another improvement was the installation of a chain-wide satellite system that gives each store the ability to instantly search and locate parts at neighboring AutoZone stores.

AutoZone, which is nation's largest retail auto parts store chain, competes in the crowded parts market by offering "everyday low prices" and convenience. The company has about 1,450 stores in 27 states, and it opens, on average, about one new store per day.

Each store carries about 15,000 new and remanufactured parts, such as alternators, starters, brake shoes and pads, antifreeze, engine additives, waxes, brake fluids and floor mats. While most stores carry basically the same parts, there are some regional differences based on climate, demographics and age, makes and models of the vehicles in each store's trade area.

AutoZone opened its first store in Forrest City, Arkansas, in 1979 as "Auto Shack." Now based in Memphis, AutoZone has its greatest concentration of stores in Texas (211 stores), Ohio (95), Georgia (72) and Tennessee (87).

The company has about 20,000 employees, including 14,000 full-time workers.

Late developments

AutoZone has recently begun test marketing a parts delivery program directed at commercial customers such as service stations and garages. That's a major departure for AutoZone, which has always focused on the do-it-yourself consumer.

Performance

Stock growth (past two years through 12/31/96): 13% (from $24.25 to $27.50).
Revenue growth (past two years through 8/30/96): 49% (from $1.5 billion to $2.2 billion).
Earnings per share growth (past two years through 8/30/96): 41% (from $0.78 to $1.10).

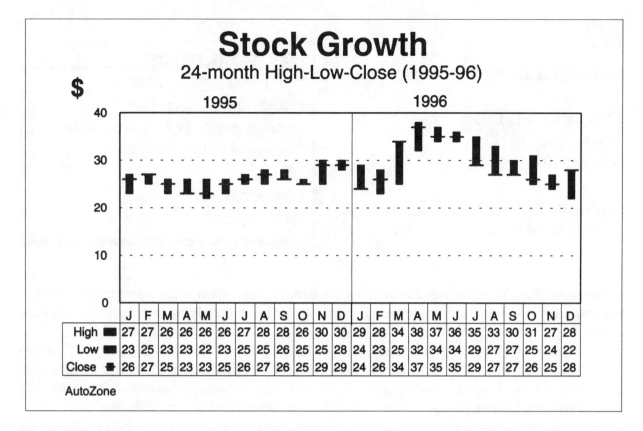

Stock Growth
24-month High-Low-Close (1995-96)

		J	F	M	A	M	J	J	A	S	O	N	D	J	F	M	A	M	J	J	A	S	O	N	D
High	■	27	27	26	26	26	26	27	28	28	26	30	30	29	28	34	38	37	36	35	33	30	31	27	28
Low	■	23	25	23	23	22	23	25	25	26	25	25	28	24	23	25	32	34	34	29	27	27	25	24	22
Close	✚	26	27	25	23	23	25	26	27	26	25	29	29	24	26	34	37	35	35	29	27	27	26	25	28

AutoZone

Quick Fix

P/E range (past two years):	20 - 34
Earnings past four quarters:	$1.10 (through 8/30/96)
Projected 1997 earnings (median):	$1.35
International sales:	None
Total current assets:	$592.7 million (1996); $426.1 million (1995)
Total current liabilities:	$589.8 million (1996); $373 million (1995)
Net Income:	$167.2 million (1996); $138.8 million (1995)

Financial history

Fiscal year ended: Aug. 31
(Revenue in millions)

	1992	1993	1994	1995	1996
Revenue	$1,002.3	$1,216.8	$1,508.0	$1,808.1	$2,242.6
Earnings per share	0.43	0.59	0.78	0.93	1.11
*Stock price: High	21.00	29.50	30.75	30.13	37.63
Low	12.56	16.88	21.63	22.00	22.13
Close	19.63	28.63	24.25	28.88	27.50

Stock prices (only) reflect calendar year.

87

SunGard Data Systems, Inc.

1285 Drummers Lane
Wayne, PA 19087
Phone: 610-341-8700

Chairman, President and CEO:
    James L. Mann

It may sound like a lotion for the ocean, but SunGard really has nothing to do with protecting tender skin from the hot sun. The company makes software for use primarily by investment and financial institutions.

The Wayne, Pennsylvania operation provides both software and support services for companies and government agencies around the world. About 18 percent of its revenue comes from outside the U.S. SunGard is a loosely organized group of business units managed under a philosophy of "controlled entrepreneurship." It breaks its offerings into six key groups, including:

- *Financial systems.* The firm offers portfolio management and securities trading and accounting systems for financial institutions, brokers, insurance companies, government agencies and corporations.

- *Trading systems.* SunGard makes software systems for trading, risk management and accounting relating to derivative instruments, securities and foreign exchange for international financial institutions, brokerage firms and corporations.

- *Trust and shareholder systems.* The company offers systems for investment accounting, portfolio management and administration, securities trading, and custody and employee benefit plans.

- *Recovery services.* The company offers business recovery services and software for mainframe and midrange computer platforms.

- *Computer services.* SunGard provides remote-access computer processing and outsourcing, and automated mailing services.

- *Healthcare information systems.* The firm offers work-flow management and document-imaging systems for healthcare and financial institutions.

SunGard has about 3,000 employees.

Late developments
SunGard signed an agreement in early 1997 to acquire GMI Software, which makes software for exchange-traded derivatives. Cost of the acquistion was about $30 million.

Performance
Stock growth (past two years through 12/31/96): 105% (from $19.25 to $39.50).
Revenue growth (past two years through 9/30/96): 49% (from $421.8 million to $631.0 million).
Earnings per share growth (past two years through 9/30/96): 35% (from $1.07 to $1.44).

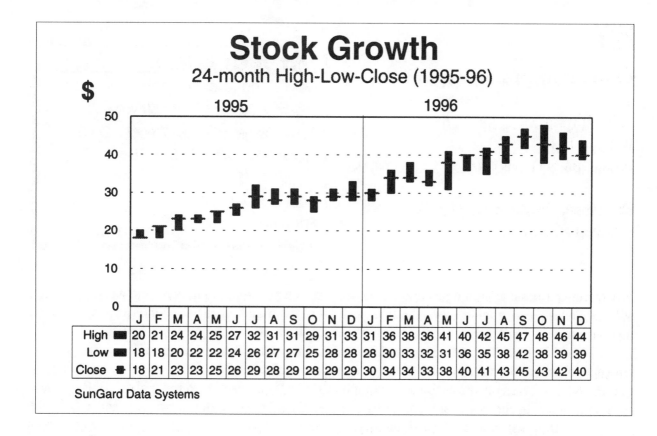

Stock Growth
24-month High-Low-Close (1995-96)

$

		J	F	M	A	M	J	J	A	S	O	N	D	J	F	M	A	M	J	J	A	S	O	N	D
High	■	20	21	24	24	25	27	32	31	31	29	31	33	31	36	38	36	41	40	42	45	47	48	46	44
Low	■	18	18	20	22	22	24	26	27	27	25	28	28	28	30	33	32	31	36	35	38	42	38	39	39
Close	✦	18	21	23	23	25	26	29	28	29	28	29	29	30	34	34	33	38	40	41	43	45	43	42	40

SunGard Data Systems

Quick Fix

P/E range (past two years):	14 - 52
Earnings past four quarters:	$1.44 (through 9/30/96)
Projected 1997 earnings (median):	$1.85
International sales:	18% percent of total sales
Total current assets:	$223 million (9/30/96); $223 million (9/30/95)
Total current liabilities:	$163 million (9/30/96); $110 million (9/30/95)
Net Income:	$49 million (1995); $43 million (1994)

Financial history

Fiscal year ended: Dec. 31
(Revenue in millions)

	1992	1993	1994	1995	*1996
Revenue	$324.6	$381.4	$437.2	$532.6	$477*
Earnings per share	0.83	1.07	1.12	1.23	1.13*
Stock price: High	15.63	21.38	20.50	32.50	47.50
Low	9.00	14.00	15.75	17.75	27.50
Close	14.88	20.63	19.25	28.50	39.50

1996 revenue and earnings through Sept. 30 (nine months).

185

88

SystemSoft, Corporation

2 Vision Drive
Natwick, MA 01760
Phone: 508-651-0088; FAX: 508-651-8188

Chairman, President and CEO:
  Robert F. Angelo

There are four basic technologies in the architecture of a personal computer—the basic hardware, which includes the microprocessors, the keyboard, the monitor and other peripherals; the application software, such as word processing and spreadsheet software; the operating system software, such as Windows and DOS; and a little-understood fourth level known as system-level software. It is on this fourth level where SystemSoft's software performs its vital role.

System-level software enables the computer's operating systems to recognize, configure and communicate with the hardware, including peripherals such as modems, printers and CD-ROM drives. SystemSoft specializes in designing system-level software for the growing mobile computer market, including laptops, notebooks, subnotebooks and personal computing devices. The company breaks its product line into five main categories:

- *PC card software*. PC cards are slide-in, credit-card-size peripherals that expand the functionality of notebook computers. SystemSoft's PC card software slots support more than 500 different PC cards, dominating the rapidly expanding market.
- *Plug and Play software*. SystemSoft's Plug and Play software permits PCs to automatically recognize and configure add-on peripherals and components.
- *Power management software*. This software is used on portable computers to reduce power consumption and extend the battery by monitoring the computer's operating system.
- *BIOS software*. The company's BIOS software permits PC hardware components to accept commands from and deliver commands to the computer's operating system software.
- *Call-avoidance software*. This new software category automatically diagnoses and fixes the most common problems that plague PC users before they need to call for support.

Founded in 1990, the company went public with its initial stock offering in 1994. SystemSoft has about 140 employees.

Late developments

The company signed an agreement in late 1996 to acquire Radish Communications Systems, a privately-held maker of VoiceView, the industry standard for integrated voice and data communications using a telephone and a personal computer.

Performance

Stock growth (past two years through 12/31/96): 231% (from $4.50 to $14.88).
Revenue growth (past two years through 9/30/96): 148% (from $14.1 million to $35 million).
Earnings per share growth (past two years through 9/30/96): 300% (from $0.06 to $0.24).

Stock Growth
24-month High-Low-Close (1995-96)

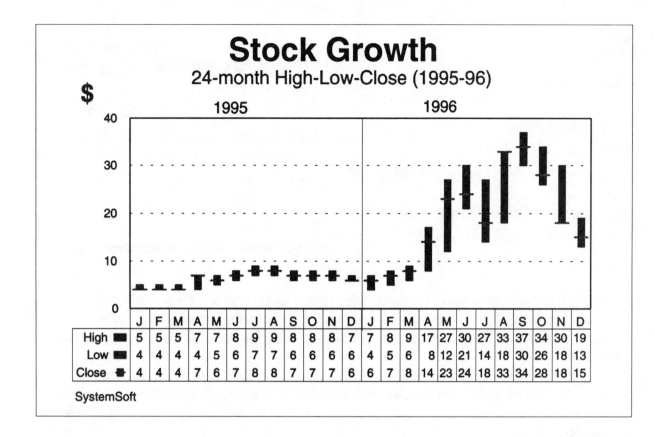

	J	F	M	A	M	J	J	A	S	O	N	D	J	F	M	A	M	J	J	A	S	O	N	D
High	5	5	5	7	7	8	9	9	8	8	8	7	7	8	9	17	27	30	27	33	37	34	30	19
Low	4	4	4	4	5	6	7	7	6	6	6	6	4	5	6	8	12	21	14	18	30	26	18	13
Close	4	4	4	7	6	7	8	8	7	7	7	6	6	7	8	14	23	24	18	33	34	28	18	15

SystemSoft

Quick Fix

P/E range (past two years):	22 - 170
Earnings past four quarters:	$0.18 (through 9/30/96)
Projected 1997 earnings (median):	$0.27
International sales:	28 percent of total sales (Asia/Pacific, 27%; Europe, 1%)
Total current assets:	$26 million (7/31/96); $20.8 million (7/31/95)
Total current liabilities:	$4.6 million (7/31/96); $2.9 million (7/31/95)
Net Income:	$3.6 million (1/31/96); $2.0 million (1/31/95)

Financial history

Fiscal year ended: Jan. 31
(Revenue in millions)

	1992	1993	1994	1995	*1996
Revenue	$2.9	$6.3	$9.1	$15.7	$24.6*
Earnings per share	-0.49	-0.44	-0.07	0.11	0.16*
**Stock price: High	NA	NA	5.38	9.06	26.50
Low	NA	NA	2.75	3.50	4.38
Close	NA	NA	4.50	5.63	14.88

1996 revenue and earnings through Oct 31, 1996 (nine months).
**Stock price reflects calendar year.*

89

Culp, Inc.

101 S. Main Street
High Point, NC 27261
Phone: 910-889-5161; FAX: 910-889-8339

Chairman and CEO: Robert Culp
President: Howard L. Dunn, Jr.

You may not know Culp by name, but there's a fair chance that you've slept with Culp or taken a seat on one of its products. Culp is the nation's second leading manufacturer of upholstery fabrics and one of the nation's top four manufacturers of mattress ticking (the fabric used for covering mattresses and box springs.)

The company's largest market is residential furniture and bedding, but Culp has also been aggressively marketing its fabrics for use in institutional furnishings, children's furniture, outdoor furniture and bed furnishings. The company produces a broad range of fabrics, including flat wovens, velvets and prints.

The High Point, North Carolina, manufacturer sells its products worldwide, with customers throughout Asia, North and South America, the Middle East and Europe. About 22 percent of its total revenue is generated outside the U.S.

The company markets its products in the U.S. through its own direct sales staff, and internationally through a combination of its own small internal sales staff and a network of outside sales agents.

Culp has been one of the fastest-growing, most consistent companies in the textile industry. Through 1996, the company had posted 16 consecutive quarters of increased earnings (versus the comparable year-earlier period). Its stock has risen about 29 percent per year, on average, over the past five years. The firm's growth has come through a combination of internal expansion and acquisitions of smaller related manufacturers.

Culp manufactures about 99 percent of all the products it sells. It has 10 manufacturing plants, most of which are in North and South Carolina. The company was founded in 1972 by Robert Culp, Jr., whose son, Robert Culp, III, currently serves as company chairman and CEO. Culp has about 3,000 employees.

Late developments

Culp stock recently moved from the NASDAQ over-the-counter exchange to the New York Stock Exchange. Its new symbol is CFI

Performance

Stock growth (past two years through 12/31/96): 53% (from $10.00 to $15.25).
Revenue growth (past two years through 10/30/96): 33% (from $289 million to $384.4 million).
Earnings per share growth (past two years through 10/30/96): 34% (from $0.83 to $1.11).

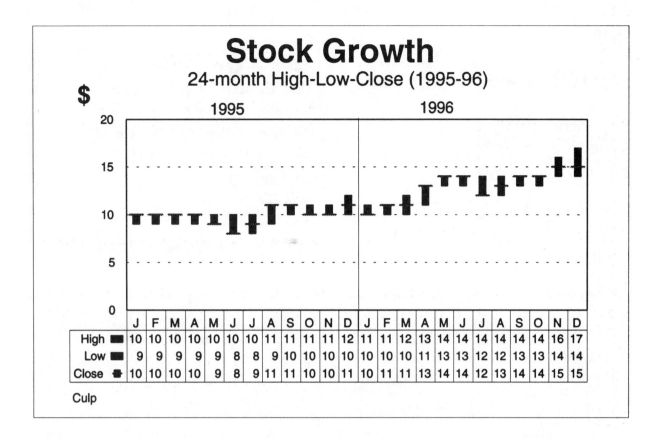

Stock Growth
24-month High-Low-Close (1995-96)

	J	F	M	A	M	J	J	A	S	O	N	D	J	F	M	A	M	J	J	A	S	O	N	D
High	10	10	10	10	10	10	10	11	11	11	11	12	11	11	12	13	14	14	14	14	14	14	16	17
Low	9	9	9	9	9	8	8	9	10	10	10	10	10	10	10	11	13	13	12	12	13	13	14	14
Close	10	10	10	10	9	9	8	9	11	11	10	10	11	10	11	11	13	14	14	12	13	14	14	15	15

Culp

Quick Fix

P/E range (past two years):	8 - 15
Earnings past four quarters:	$1.11 (through 10/30/96)
Projected 1997 earnings (median):	$1.15
International sales:	22% of total sales
Total assets:	$211.6 million (1996); $195 million (1995)
Total current liabilities:	$47.2 million (1996); $56.0 million (1995)
Net Income:	$11.0 million (1996); $9.8 million (1995)

Financial history

Fiscal year ended: April 28
(Revenue in millions)

	1992	1993	1994	1995	1996
Revenue	$191.3	$200.8	$245	$308	$351.7
Earnings per share	0.27	0.41	0.69	0.87	0.98
*Stock price: High	7.27	17.33	17.00	11.50	17.00
Low	3.60	4.27	7.25	7.75	10.00
Close	4.67	16.67	10.00	11.13	15.25

*Stock prices (only) reflect calendar year.

189

90

Quorum Health Group, Inc.

103 Continental Place
Brentwood, TN 37027
Phone: 615-371-7979

Chairman: R.L. Carson
President and CEO: J.E. Dalton Jr.

Budgets have been getting squeezed in the healthcare industry in recent years, and Quorum Health Group has been helping hospitals across the country cope with the new cost restraints. The Brentwood, Tennessee, operation specializes in hospital management, and is currently under contract to manage more than 250 hospitals. Quorum also provides consulting services for 213 hospitals. It is the largest contract manager of non-profit hospitals in the U.S.

Quorum also owns 16 acute care hospitals located in small cities in the South and the Midwest. The company acquired its first hospital in 1991, bought three more in 1992, and acquired a group of 10 hospitals in 1994. The company plans to continue to pursue acquisitions of hospitals ranging in size from 100 to 400 beds in medium-sized markets with populations of 50,000 to 500,000 people.

Under its management program, Quorum provides hospital owners with a hospital administrator and a chief financial officer. This management tandem is supported by Quorum's regional and corporate management staff, who have extensive experience in managing hospitals efficiently. The company also provides a comprehensive range of management and professional services, such as setting up new financial and operating systems, establishing a local or regional provider network, and identifying areas of possible cost savings.

The company's consulting services address many of the strategic and operational needs of hospitals, such as integration and integrated delivery system strategies, business office management, continuous quality improvement and re-engineering programs, health information management, human resources, surgical and nursing services, facilities design and other operational services.

Quorum went public with its initial stock offering in 1994. The company has about 15,000 employees.

Late developments
In late 1996, Quorum purchased a majority stake in Barberton Citizens Hospital in Barberton, Ohio.

Performance
Stock growth (past two years through 12/31/96): 57% (from $19.00 to $29.75).
Revenue growth (past two years through 9/30/96): 56% (from $743.6 million to $1.2 billion).
Earnings per share growth (past two years through 9/30/96): 32% (from $1.10 to $1.45).

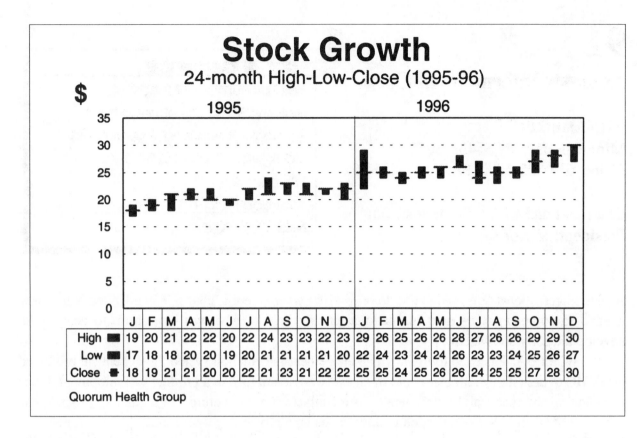

Stock Growth
24-month High-Low-Close (1995-96)

$

		J	F	M	A	M	J	J	A	S	O	N	D	J	F	M	A	M	J	J	A	S	O	N	D
High	■	19	20	21	22	22	20	22	24	23	23	22	23	29	26	25	26	26	28	27	26	26	29	29	30
Low	■	17	18	18	20	20	19	20	21	21	21	21	20	22	24	23	24	24	26	23	23	24	25	26	27
Close	◆	18	19	21	21	20	20	22	21	23	21	22	22	25	25	24	25	26	26	24	25	25	27	28	30

Quorum Health Group

Quick Fix

P/E range (past two years):	15 - 21
Earnings past four quarters:	$1.45 (through 9/30/96)
Projected 1997 earnings (median):	$1.55
International sales:	None
Total current assets:	$303.2 million (9/30/96); $218.4 million (1995)
Total current liabilities:	$127.1 million (9/30/96); $85.1 million (1995)
Net Income:	$69.2 million (1996); $56.0 million (1995)

Financial history

Fiscal year ended: June 30
(Revenue in millions)

	1992	1993	1994	1995	1996
Revenue	$173.2	$343.1	$641.0	$850.2	$1,098.5
Earnings per share	0.02	0.50	0.96	1.14	1.39
*Stock price: High	NA	NA	23.00	24.00	29.75
Low	NA	NA	16.25	17.00	21.75
Close	NA	NA	19.00	22.00	29.75

Stock prices (only) reflect calendar year.

91

Analysts International Corp.

7615 Metro Blvd.
Minneapolis, MN 55439-3050
Phone: 612-835-5900; FAX: 612-835-4924

Chairman and CEO: Frederick Lang
President: Victor Benda

AT A GLANCE

Held by number of funds: 2
Industry: Software-related services
Earnings growth past 2 years: 56%
Stock price 1/1/97: $28.25
P/E ratio: 30
Year ago P/E: 19
NASDAQ: ANLY

Analysts International Corp. (AIC) tries to bring order where there is chaos. When United Van Lines needed to computerize its new international pricing system, AIC was brought in to design and develop the software system.

When BASF needed to update its management information system, the chemical producer hired AIC to design a system that could track every twist and turn in a product's development, from its biological and chemical development to its manufacturing, marketing and regulatory procedures.

And when U.S. West needed to upgrade its data processing operations, AIC put together a team of 920 programmers and technicians—220 AIC employees and 700 subcontractors—to handle the massive high tech overhaul.

AIC specializes in designing and developing customized software systems for large and small corporate clients in a broad range of industries. The Minneapolis-based operation works with about 1,000 companies, handling more than 6,000 custom programming projects per year. Its largest clients are IBM and U.S. West, both of which account for more than 10 percent of AIC's total revenue.

Telecommunications is the leading industry served by AIC, accounting for about 30 percent of the company's revenue. The electronics industry is a close second at 24 percent, followed by services, 10 percent; manufacturing, 9 percent; oil and chemical, 6 percent; and financial, 5 percent.

AIC was founded in 1966 by Frederick Lang and Victor Benda, who still serve as CEO and president, respectively. The firm has about 3,800 employees, including 3,200 systems analysts, computer programmers and other technical personnel. AIC has 27 branches in 19 states, plus field offices in 13 other cities.

Late developments

The company recently acquired DPI, Inc., a San Jose operation that provides programming and consultation services to companies in the San Francisco area.

Performance

Stock growth (past two years through 12/31/96): 176% (from $10.25 to $28.25).
Revenue growth (past two years through 9/30/96): 94% (from $182.6 million to $354.5 million).
Earnings per share growth (past two years through 9/30/96): 56% (from $0.59 to $0.92).

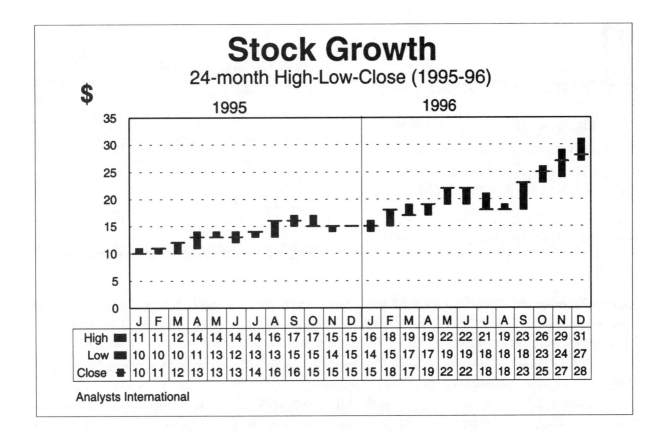

Stock Growth
24-month High-Low-Close (1995-96)

$	J	F	M	A	M	J	J	A	S	O	N	D	J	F	M	A	M	J	J	A	S	O	N	D
High	11	11	12	14	14	14	14	16	17	17	15	15	16	18	19	19	22	22	21	19	23	26	29	31
Low	10	10	10	11	13	12	13	13	15	15	14	15	14	15	17	17	19	19	18	18	18	23	24	27
Close	10	11	12	13	13	13	14	16	16	15	15	15	15	18	17	19	22	22	18	18	23	25	27	28

Analysts International

Quick Fix

P/E range (past two years):	13 - 30
Earnings past four quarters:	$0.92 (through 9/30/96)
Projected 1997 earnings (median):	$1.07
International sales:	none
Total current assets:	$70.1 million (1996); $60.1 million (1995)
Total current liabilities:	$24.3 million (1996); $18.9 million (1995)
Net Income:	$12.4 million (1996); $11.2 million (1995)

Financial history

Fiscal year ended: June 30
(Revenue in millions)

	1992	1993	1994	1995	1996
Revenue	$129.5	$159.7	$176.0	$218.4	$329.5
Earnings per share	0.38	0.58	0.55	0.77	0.84
*Stock price: High	8.67	11.92	10.38	16.50	30.50
Low	5.17	7.50	7.25	9.88	13.63
Close	8.42	9.00	10.25	15.00	28.25

***Stock prices (only) reflect calendar year.**

92

U.S. Office Products Company

1025 Thomas Jefferson Street NW
Suite 600 East
Washington, DC 20007
Phone: 202-339-6700; FAX: 202-339-6755

Chairman and CEO: Jonathan Ledecky
President: Timothy Flynn

This is no automotive enterprise, but in terms of corporate strategy, U.S. Office Products is pure *hub and spoke*. The firm has been growing rapidly through an aggressive acquisition program that involves two steps: first it acquires a "hub"—a large, established office products company located in one of the firm's targeted metropolitan areas—then it acquires the "spokes," which are smaller companies in secondary markets surrounding the hub.

Founded in 1994, U.S. Office acquired 65 companies in its first two years, and was in the process of buying about 50 more companies through the second half of 1996. In all the company has offices in about 35 states, New Zealand and Australia. Because of its size and purchasing power, the company can offer customers discounted prices on many items.

U.S. Office sells more than 28,000 office and educational products to corporate, commercial, educational and industrial customers. Most of its sales are to medium and large corporate customers, although it is quickly expanding its customer base in the school supply and furniture markets.

The company also sells coffee, food, beverages and related supplies through its "Coffee Butler" division. And it sells and leases new and remanufactured furniture to businesses and retail customers.

The company operates with a decentralized management strategy that gives local management a greater role in decisions relating to day-to-day operations. Local managers are also responsible for the profitability and growth of their businesses.

U.S. Office, which went public with its initial stock offering in 1995, has about 6,000 employees.

Late developments

In February 1997, the company completed 13 acquisitions for $149.9 million, including office products and related operations in Philadelphia, New York, California, Louisiana, Colorado, Illinois, Virginia and Ontario.

Performance

Stock growth (past one year through 12/31/96): 50% (from $22.75 to $34.13).
Revenue growth (past two years through 10/31/96): 548% (from $194.5 million to $1.3 billion).
Earnings per share growth (past two years through 10/31/96): 123% (from $0.39 to $0.87).

Stock Growth
24-month High-Low-Close (1995-96)

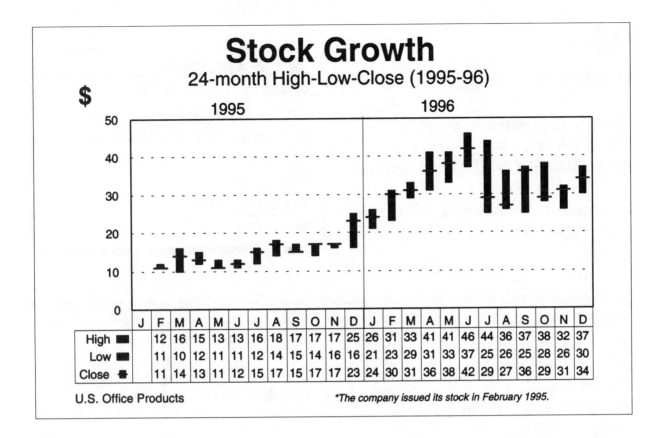

	J	F	M	A	M	J	J	A	S	O	N	D	J	F	M	A	M	J	J	A	S	O	N	D
High ■		12	16	15	13	13	16	18	17	17	17	25	26	31	33	41	41	46	44	36	37	38	32	37
Low ■		11	10	12	11	11	12	14	15	14	16	16	21	23	29	31	33	37	25	26	25	28	26	30
Close ◆		11	14	13	11	12	15	17	15	17	17	23	24	30	31	36	38	42	29	27	36	29	31	34

U.S. Office Products   *The company issued its stock in February 1995.

Quick Fix

P/E range (past two years):	27 - 66
Earnings past four quarters:	$0.87 (through 10/31/96)
Projected 1997 earnings (median):	$1.09
International sales:	New Zealand and Australia, less than 10% of total sales
Total current assets:	$639.8 million (1996); $509.2 million (1995)
Total current liabilities:	$519.0 million (1996); $261.3 million (1995)
Net Income:	$22.7 million (10/26/96); $8.74 million (4/30/96)

Financial history

Fiscal year ended: April 30
(Revenue in millions)

	1993	1994	1995	1996	*1997
Revenue	$234.3	$267.8	$355.8	$701.9	$996.4*
Earnings per share	0.17	0.75	0.95	0.37	0.53*
Stock price: High	NA	NA	24.88	45.50	NA
Low	NA	NA	10.00	20.63	NA
Close	NA	NA	22.75	34.13	NA

1997 revenue and earnings through Oct. 31, 1997 (six months).
**Stock prices (only) reflect calendar year.*

93

Oakley, Inc.

10 Holland Street
Irvine, CA 92718
Phone: 714-951-0991; FAX: 714-951-8326

Chairman and President: Jim Jannard
CEO: Mike Parnell

Some of the world's finest athletes wear Oakley shades. The company makes a broad line of sunglasses and goggles for skiers, cyclists, runners, surfers, golfers, tennis and baseball players and even motocross riders. The company has also expanded into the fashion sunglasses arena, and currently markets its shades in 65 countries.

The Irvine, California, operation manufactures sunglasses under the names *M Frames*, *Zeros*, *Wires*, *Trenchcoats*, *Frogskins* and *Eye Jackets*. It also has three goggle lines, including *Motocross*, *Ski* and *H20*. It recently introduced three more lines of glasses, including *X Metal*, *Straight Jacket* and *Square Wires*.

At Oakley, the company's designers use the latest state-of-the-art technology to set their glasses apart from the competition. Designers use a three-dimensional CAD-CAM system and liquid laser prototyping to shorten the time-to-market for each new model. It takes about four months from design to introduction.

One of Oakley's most significant developments has been the iridium coating on its Plutonite lens. The coating increases contrast and color saturation, enabling skiers, cyclists and other users to perceive details in shadows or low or bright light conditions.

Another popular feature of Oakley glasses are their detachable and interchangeable components, such as lenses, frames, temples and nosepieces—all offered in different shapes and colors. The interchangeable pieces allow users to customize their sunglasses to their personal tastes, and to modify them for specific conditions such as low and bright light.

The firm markets its glasses through optical stores, specialty retailers and specialty sports stores. They are not sold through department stores, drug stores or discount stores.

Founded in 1977, Oakley sold its first sunglasses in 1984. The company went public with its initial stock offering in 1995. Oakley has about 700 employees.

Late developments

Oakley recently won a court case in Paris, France, in which the court ruled that Bausch & Lomb's "Northside" sunglasses infringe on the registered design for Oakley's Eye Jacket model. The court awarded damages to Oakley, and ordered Bausch to discontinue selling Northside glasses.

Performance

Stock growth (past one year through 12/31/96): -35 % (from $17.00 to $11.00).
Revenue growth (past two years through 9/30/96): 100% (from $111.1 million to $222 million).
Earnings per share growth (past two years through 9/30/96): 300% (from $0.18 to $0.72).

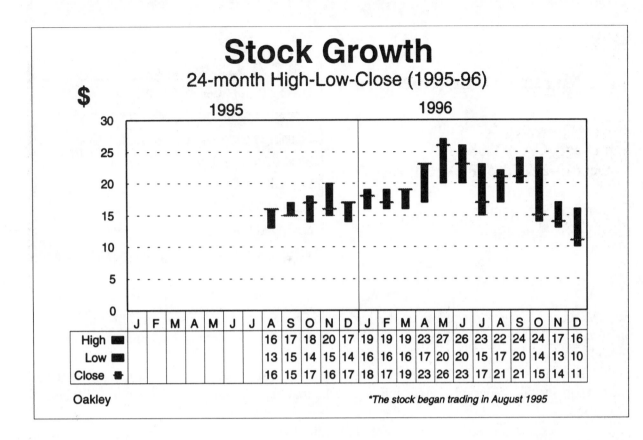

Stock Growth
24-month High-Low-Close (1995-96)

	J	F	M	A	M	J	J	A	S	O	N	D	J	F	M	A	M	J	J	A	S	O	N	D
High ■								16	17	18	20	17	19	19	19	23	27	26	23	22	24	24	17	16
Low ■								13	15	14	15	14	16	16	16	17	20	20	15	17	20	14	13	10
Close ●								16	15	17	16	17	18	17	19	23	26	23	17	21	21	15	14	11

Oakley

The stock began trading in August 1995

Quick Fix

P/E range (past two years):	12 - 55
Earnings past four quarters:	$0.72 (through 9/30/96)
Projected 1997 earnings (median):	$0.94
International sales:	33% of total sales
Total current assets:	$77.7 million (1996); $55.9 million (1995)
Total current liabilities:	$19.3 million (1996); $20.7 million (1995)
Net Income:	$26.7 million (6/30/96); $20.2 million (6/30/95)

Financial history

Fiscal year ended: Dec. 31
(Revenue in millions)

	1992	1993	1994	1995	*1996
Revenue	$76.4	$92.7	$123.9	$172.7	$179.2*
Earnings per share	0.13	0.12	0.12	0.48	0.59*
Stock price: High	NA	NA	NA	19.63	27.19
Low	NA	NA	NA	13.06	9.50
Close	NA	NA	NA	17.00	11.00

1996 revenue and earnings through Sept. 30 (nine months).

94

FPA Medical Management, Inc.

2878 Camino del Rio South, Suite 301
San Diego, CA 92108
Phone: 619-295-7005; FAX: 619-299-0708

Chairman: Sol Lizerbram
President : Seth Flam

FPA Medical Management serves as the middleman between physicians and health maintenance organizations (HMOs). FPA manages networks of primary care physicians that contract with HMOs and other payers.

Known as a "management service organization" (MSO), FPA organizes small primary care practices in specific geographic areas into networks that can contract more efficiently with HMOs as a group.

For doctors, the arrangement makes life easier because they can turn over time-consuming tasks such as claims administration, payer contact negotiations and the management of information systems to FPA. Doctors can either contract with FPA for those administrative services, or sell out the practices (and business assets) to FPA.

HMOs also like the arrangement because it lowers their medical-loss ratio—the percentage of premiums spent on direct medical care—and it efficiently delivers entire networks of doctors into their organization.

FPA, which was founded in 1986, organized its first physician's network in its home city of San Diego. The firm went public with its initial stock offering in 1994, and has expanded rapidly since then by buying out existing physician management organizations around the country.

In 1994, FPA's organization included only 95 physicians, primarily in the southern California area. But by 1997, it operated physician management networks in 24 states and was affiliated with about 4,000 physicians serving well over a million customers.

Late developments

FPA acquired Sterling Healthcare Group in late 1996 in a stock swap valued at about $159 million. Sterling is physician practice management company that specializes in hospital emergency room physicians. It has more than 1,000 affiliated physicians in 20 states. FPA also acquired two physician networks and 30 healthcare clinics from Foundation Health. The acquisition added about 245 physicians and 265,000 HMO enrollees to FPA's existing base.

Performance

Stock growth (past two years through 12/31/96): 258% (from $ 6.25 to $22.38).
Revenue growth (past two years through 9/30/96): 1186% (from $16.4 million to $211.1 million).
Earnings per share growth (past two years through 9/30/96): 95% (from $0.21 to $0.41).

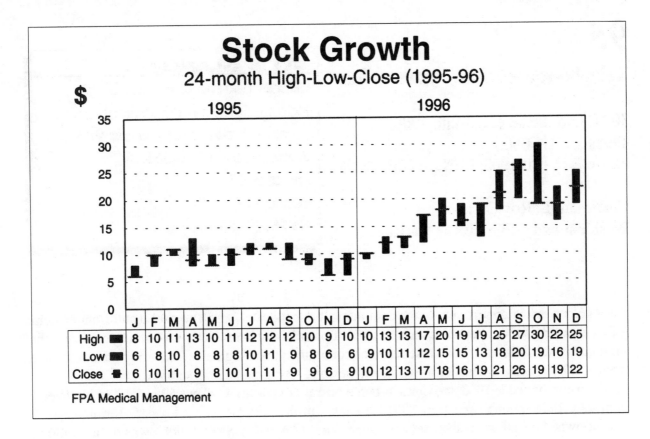

Stock Growth
24-month High-Low-Close (1995-96)

$

	J	F	M	A	M	J	J	A	S	O	N	D	J	F	M	A	M	J	J	A	S	O	N	D
High	8	10	11	13	10	11	12	12	12	10	9	10	10	13	13	17	20	19	19	25	27	30	22	25
Low	6	8	10	8	8	8	10	11	9	8	6	6	9	10	11	12	15	15	13	18	20	19	16	19
Close	6	10	11	9	8	10	11	11	9	9	6	9	10	12	13	17	18	16	19	21	26	19	19	22

FPA Medical Management

Quick Fix

P/E range (past two years):	45 -100+
Earnings past four quarters:	$0.41 (through 9/30/96)
Projected 1997 earnings (median):	$0.75
International sales:	none
Total current assets:	$47.9 million (1996); $10.9 million (1995)
Total current liabilities:	$74.8 million (1996); $5.8 million (1995)
Net Income:	$1 million (1995); $389,000 (1994)

Financial history

Fiscal year ended: Dec. 31
(Revenue in millions)

	1992	1993	1994	1995	*1996
Revenue	$8.3	$14.0	$18.4	$52.7	$188.5*
Earnings per share	-0.01	0.27	0.07	0.13	0.34*
Stock price: High	NA	NA	6.75	12.50	29.50
Low	NA	NA	5.13	5.88	8.63
Close	NA	NA	6.25	9.38	22.38

*1996 revenue and earnings through Sept. 30 (nine months).

95

Telephone and Data Systems, Inc.

30 N. LaSalle Street, Suite 4000
Chicago, IL 60602
Phone: 312-630-1900; FAX: 312-630-1908

Chairman: LeRoy Carlson
President and CEO: LeRoy Carlson, Jr.

AT A GLANCE
Held by number of funds: 2
Industry: Telecommunications
Earnings growth past 2 years: 94%
Stock price 1/1/97: $36.25
P/E ratio: 17
Year ago P/E: 22
NYSE: TDS

It is a golden era of opportunity in the communications industry, and Telephone and Data Systems (TDS) is battling for market share on a number of promising fronts. TDS is a holding company that ties together subsidiaries in a diverse range of communications segments, including local telephone service, cellular telephones, radio paging and personal communications services.

Incorporated in 1968, the Chicago-based operation now draws about 50 percent of its revenue from its cellular phone operations. TDS operates in the cellular phone industry through its 81-percent-owned subsidiary, United States Cellular Corp. (AMEX: USM), which owns or has the right to acquire 200 markets with a population of 24 million. USM's consolidated markets have about 800,000 cellular telephones in service. The firm's other leading subsidiaries include:

• *TDS Telecommunications Corp.*, a wholly-owned subsidiary that operates 102 local telephone companies in 28 states. The firm has 454,000 access lines in service. Telephone service accounts for about 37 percent of the company's annual revenue.

• *American Paging* (AMEX: APP), which provides radio paging and related services through 38 sales and service operating centers. It has about 800,000 pagers in service. TDS owns an 82 percent share of APP.

• *American Portable Telecom* (NASDAQ: APTI), which provides personal communications services in six major markets with a total population of 27 million. TDS owns an 83 percent share of APTI.

• *Associated services companies.* TDS owns several service subsidiaries which provide data processing, custom printing, telephone answering and other related products and services.

In all, TDS serves about 2 million customers in 37 states. It has about 6,400 employees.

Late developments
The company's American Portable Telecom subsidiary is proceeding with a planned microwave relocation and cell site acquisition program in each of its six markets. By late 1996, the company had secured more than 500 cell cites, and commercial service was expected to begin in 1997.

Performance
Stock growth (past two years through 12/31/96): -21 % (from $46.13 to $36.25).
Revenue growth (past two years through 12/31/96): 60% (from $730.8 million to $1.21 billion).
Earnings per share growth (past two years through12/31/96): 94% (from $1.08 to $2.09).

Stock Growth
24-month High-Low-Close (1995-96)

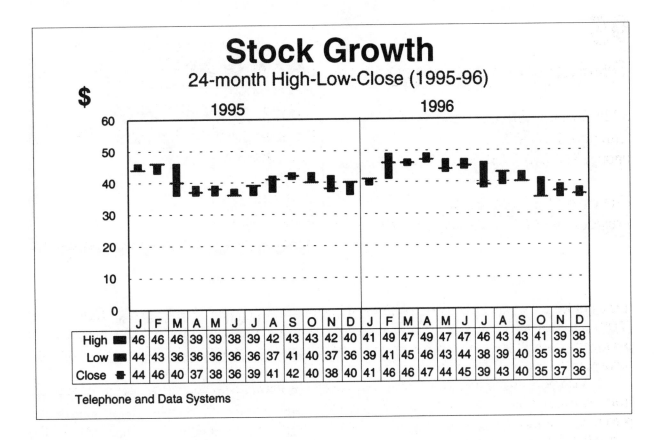

		J	F	M	A	M	J	J	A	S	O	N	D	J	F	M	A	M	J	J	A	S	O	N	D
High		46	46	46	39	39	38	39	42	43	43	42	40	41	49	47	49	47	47	46	43	43	41	39	38
Low		44	43	36	36	36	36	36	37	41	40	37	36	39	41	45	46	43	44	38	39	40	35	35	35
Close		44	46	40	37	38	36	39	41	42	40	38	40	41	46	46	47	44	45	39	43	40	35	37	36

Telephone and Data Systems

Quick Fix

P/E range (past two years):	17 - 27
Earnings past four quarters:	$2.09 (through 12/31/96)
Projected 1997 earnings (median):	$1.40
International sales:	None
Total current assets:	$362 million (1996); $261.2 million (1995)
Total current liabilities:	$370.5 million (1996); $427.7 million (1995)
Net Income:	$128.1 million (1996); $104 million (1995)

Financial history

Fiscal year ended: Dec. 31
(Revenue in millions)

	1992	1993	1994	1995	1996
Revenue	$432.7	$557.8	$730.8	$954.4	$1,215
Earnings per share	0.92	0.67	1.08	1.74	2.09
Stock price: High	41.25	57.00	51.50	46.38	48.88
Low	30.13	33.25	35.50	35.63	34.75
Close	40.63	52.13	46.13	39.50	36.25

96
CalEnergy Company, Inc.

10831 Old Mill Road
Omaha, NE 68154
Phone: 402-330-8900; FAX: 402-330-9888

Chairman and CEO: David Sokol
President: Thomas R. Mason

As energy companies go, there aren't many like this one. Based in Omaha, Nebraska (which is a story in itself), CalEnergy generates more than 700 megawatts of electricity each year without burning a drop of oil or a cubic centimeter of natural gas. Nor does it use nuclear reactors or solar power. No windmills either.

CalEnergy is the world's leading producer of geothermal energy. It drives its electric generators from steam drawn from deep beneath the earth's surface. Geothermal steam is produced naturally when water from underground reservoirs comes into contact with hot molten rock known as *magma*. CalEnergy taps into this natural steam source, piping it to the surface where it is used to drive specially built turbine generators.

Originally known as California Energy, the firm moved its headquarters from San Francisco to Omaha in 1991 as part of a comprehensive cost cutting initiative. Founded in 1971, CalEnergy has always drawn most of its steam from reservoirs in southern California. But recently the firm set its sites abroad, opening new generating plants in the Philippines, with several more under development both in the Philippines and Indonesia.

Geothermal energy is most readily available in areas of high seismic activity, which is one reason most of CalEnergy's plants are parked in earthquake-riddled regions, such as southern California and the Philippines. That's one of the few hazards of geothermal business. Reservoirs can also run dry, but CalEnergy has found a way to sustain the flow of steam by returning most of the water to the geothermal reservoir via injection wells.

CalEnergy's largest reservoir is at Coso, California in the Mojave Desert about 150 miles northwest of Los Angeles.

Late developments
CalEnergy recently acquired Falcon Seaboard Resources, which operates three cogeneration plants and related natural gas pipelines in Texas, Pennsylvania and New York. Cost of the acquisition was $226 million.

Performance
Stock growth (past two years through 12/31/96): 115% (from $15.63 to $33.63).
Revenue growth (past two years through 12/31/96): 210% (from $186 million to $576 million).
Earnings per share growth (past two years through 12/31/96): 69% (from $0.95 to $1.61).

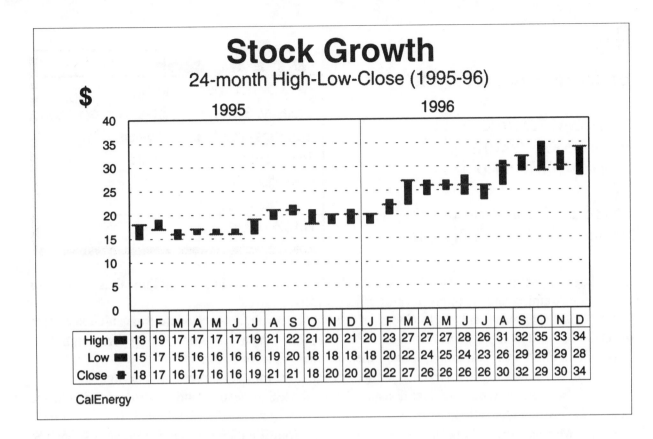

Stock Growth
24-month High-Low-Close (1995-96)

	J	F	M	A	M	J	J	A	S	O	N	D	J	F	M	A	M	J	J	A	S	O	N	D
High	18	19	17	17	17	17	19	21	22	21	20	21	20	23	27	27	27	28	26	31	32	35	33	34
Low	15	17	15	16	16	16	16	19	20	18	18	18	18	20	22	24	25	24	23	26	29	29	29	28
Close	18	17	16	17	16	16	19	21	21	18	20	20	20	22	27	26	26	26	26	30	32	29	30	34

CalEnergy

Quick Fix

P/E range (past two years):	12 - 22
Earnings past four quarters:	$1.61 (through 12/31/96)
Projected 1997 earnings (median):	$1.89
International sales:	Foreign operations not yet generating revenue
Total assets:	$3.55 billion (1996); $2.65 billion (1995)
Total current liabilities:	$2.83 billion (1996); $2.11 billion (1995)
Net Income:	$92.5 million (1996); $66.4 million (1995)

Financial history

Fiscal year ended: Dec. 31
(Revenue in millions)

	1992	1993	1994	1995	1996
Revenue	$127.5	$149.2	$185.8	$398.7	$576.2
Earnings per share	0.92	1.00	0.95	1.25	1.61
Stock price: High	17.38	21.75	19.50	21.50	35.00
Low	11.38	15.75	15.25	15.38	18.38
Close	16.75	18.50	15.63	19.50	33.63

97

BDM International, Inc.

1501 BDM Way
McLean, VA   22102
Phone: 703-848-5000

Chairman: Frank Carlucci
President and CEO: Philip Odeen

AT A GLANCE

Held by number of funds: 2
Industry: Systems & software integration
Earnings growth past 2 years: 1%
Stock price 1/1/97: $54.25
P/E ratio: 45
Year ago P/E: 19
NASDAQ: BDMI

BDM International works hand in glove with the U.S. military, providing technological assistance for a variety of training and weapons development projects.

BDM chairman Frank Carlucci formerly served under President Ronald Reagan as Secretary of Defense; and company president and CEO, Philip Odeen has served in several high-level government positions, including a spot on the National Security Council.

BDM is currently involved in a number of sensitive military projects, including:

• Engineering and technical assistance for the design, testing and control of the Ballistic Missile Defense Organization;

• Management and operation of elements of the Joint Readiness Training Center of the U.S. Army Training and Doctrine Command, where 50,000 soldiers per year are trained on integrated battlefields with near-real-time performance feedback.

• Consolidation of defense logistics computer systems for the U.S. Air Force;

• Development and implementation of the Terminal Radar Approach Air Traffic Control (TRACON) system for the Department of Defense and the Federal Aviation Administration.

BDM also provides logistic support services to the Royal Saudi Air Force, and it assists the German Ministry of Defense in a broad range of strategic military-related projects.

The company is also involved in a number of non-military projects. One of its largest on-going projects is the creation of the Securities and Exchange Commission's on-line corporate document filing system known as the Electronic Data Gathering Analysis and Retrieval (EDGAR) program. As of 1996, all public companies were required to use EDGAR to file their financial documents electronically.

Founded in 1959, BDM went public with its initial stock offering in 1995. The McClean, Virginia, operation has about 8,000 employees.

Late developments

The company recently received a five-year contract worth about $150 million to provide information technology support to the Air Force Material Command at Wright-Paterson Air Force Base in Dayton, Ohio.

Performance

Stock growth (past one year through 12/31/96): 87% (from $29.00 to $54.25).
Revenue growth (past two years through 9/30/96): 28% (from $774.2 million to $993.7 million).
Earnings per share growth (past two years through 12/31/96): 1% (from $1.20 to $1.21).

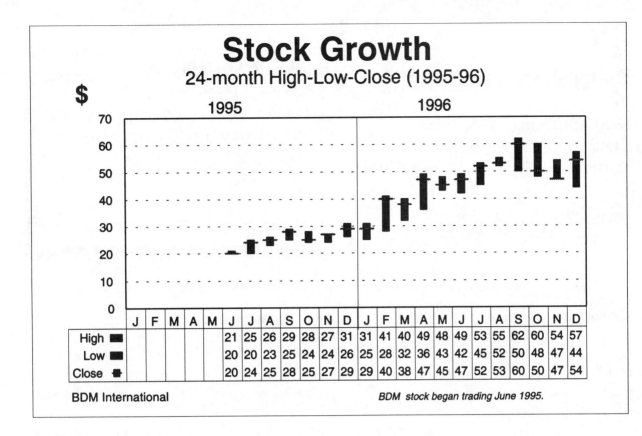

Stock Growth
24-month High-Low-Close (1995-96)

	J	F	M	A	M	J	J	A	S	O	N	D	J	F	M	A	M	J	J	A	S	O	N	D
High						21	25	26	29	28	27	31	31	41	40	49	48	49	53	55	62	60	54	57
Low						20	20	23	25	24	24	26	25	28	32	36	43	42	45	52	50	48	47	44
Close						20	24	25	28	25	27	29	29	40	38	47	45	47	52	53	60	50	47	54

BDM International   *BDM stock began trading June 1995.*

Quick Fix

P/E range (past two years):	13 - 51
Earnings past four quarters:	$1.21 (through 12/31/96)
Projected 1997 earnings (median):	$2.21
International sales:	41% of total sales (Europe, 27%; Middle East, 14%)
Total current assets:	$287.3 million (1996); $294.6 million (1995)
Total current liabilities:	$150.2 million (1996); $178.5 million (1995)
Net Income:	$17.7 million (1996); $18.4 million (1995)

Financial history

Fiscal year ended: Dec. 31
(Revenue in millions)

	1992	1993	1994	1995	1996
Revenue	$424.4	$558.3	$774.2	$890.0	$1,002
Earnings per share	0.81	0.92	1.20	1.56	1.21
Stock price: High	NA	NA	NA	30.50	61.50
Low	NA	NA	NA	19.88	28.75
Close	NA	NA	NA	29.00	54.25

205

98

Rational Software Corp.

2800 San Tomas Expressway
Santa Clara, CA 95051
Phone: 408-469-3600; FAX: 408-970-0715

Chairman & CEO: Paul Levy
President: Michael Devlin

Rational Software develops software that helps other companies develop software.

The Santa Clara, California, operation produces a broad line of products designed to help companies create software programs tailored specifically to their needs. Rational's integrated family of software tools spans the major phases of the software development process from the initial graphical object modeling of business processes (such as order processing) through detailed design, coding, compilation, delivery and maintenance.

In addition to its software development products, Rational also provides a broad range of technical consulting, training and support services for its corporate customers.

Rational has sold more than 70,000 licenses of its software tools to more than 10,000 customers worldwide. Traditionally its strongest markets have been aerospace-defense and transportation-related companies, but it is aggressively moving into other growing markets such as telecommunications, banking and financial services and manufacturing.

The company's product line, which covers all of the critical phases of the software development cycle, include:

- *Rational Rose graphical object modeling products*;
- *Rational Apex products,* used to enforce the software architecture and manage development teams;
- *VADS products*, used to develop, debug and deliver high-performance embedded and workstation-based applications.

Rational generates about 36 percent of its revenues in foreign markets. The company, which went public with its initial stock offering in 1994, has about 700 employees.

Late developments

Rational acquired SQA , Inc. in November 1996. SQA is the leader in automated testing of Windows client/server applications. Rational also recently acquired Microsoft Visual Test, a leading software quality automation tool, from Microsoft Corp. for a single cash payment of $23 million.

Performance

Stock growth (past two years through 12/31/96): 1030% (from $3.50 to $39.56).
Revenue growth (past two years through 12/31/96): 60% (from $71.1 million to $114 million).
Earnings per share growth (past two years through 12/31/96): NA (from -$0.46 to -$0.02).

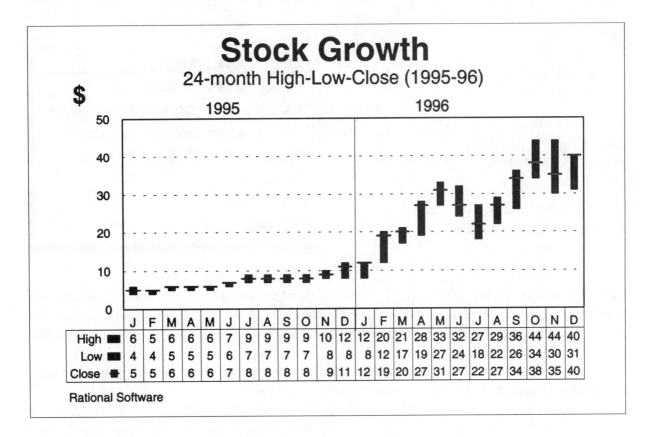

Stock Growth
24-month High-Low-Close (1995-96)

		J	F	M	A	M	J	J	A	S	O	N	D	J	F	M	A	M	J	J	A	S	O	N	D
High	■	6	5	6	6	6	7	9	9	9	9	10	12	12	20	21	28	33	32	27	29	36	44	44	40
Low	■	4	4	5	5	5	6	7	7	7	7	8	8	8	12	17	19	27	24	18	22	26	34	30	31
Close	●	5	5	6	6	6	7	8	8	8	8	9	11	12	19	20	27	31	27	22	27	34	38	35	40

Rational Software

Quick Fix

P/E range (past two years):	19 - 45
Earnings past four quarters:	$0.01 (through 9/30/96)
Projected 1997 earnings (median):	$0.46
International sales:	36% or total sales
Total current assets:	$83 million (1996); $30 million (1995)
Total current liabilities:	$26 million (1996); $22.2 million (1995)
Net Income:	$4.8 million (9/30/96); $4.7 million (1995)

Financial history

Fiscal year ended: March 31
(Revenue in millions)

	1993	1994	1995	1996	*1997
Revenue	$71.0	$70.3	$72.9	$91.1	$88.3*
Earnings per share	- 0.09	- 0.57	0.19	- 0.13	0.02*
**Stock price: High	NA	4.69	12.00	44.25	NA
Low	NA	2.06	3.57	7.94	NA
Close	NA	3.47	11.19	39.56	NA

1997 revenue and earnings through 12/31/96 (9 months).
***Stock prices (only) reflect calendar year.**

99
Aspen Technology, Inc.

10 Canal Park
Cambridge, MA 02141
Phone: 617-577-0100; FAX: 617-577-0722

Chairman and CEO: Lawrence Evans
President: Joseph F. Boston

Aspen Technology creates software intended to help manufacturers design, manage and operate their manufacturing process more profitably and efficiently. Aspen works primarily with companies in process industries, such as chemicals, petroleum, pharmaceuticals, electric power, and pulp and paper producers.

Aspen's software is programmed to handle such factory floor functions as monitoring temperature ranges, fuel rates and compression control.

Aspen is the world's largest process modeling supplier, dealing with more than 500 commercial customers and 350 universities. Among its more prominent customers are BASF, Dow Chemical, du Pont, Eastman Chemical, General Electric, Merck, Mitsubishi Chemical, Procter & Gamble and Unilever Research. In all, Aspen's customer base includes 44 of the 50 largest chemical companies in the world, and 19 of the 20 largest petroleum refineries.

The Cambridge, Massachusetts, operation offers an integrated family of off-the-shelf software products for use across the entire process manufacturing life-cycle, from off-line applications used primarily in research and development and engineering to online applications used in product production. The off-line software is used to simulate and predict manufacturing processes in connection with the design of new facilities or processes and the analysis of existing operations.

Its online software, which is connected directly to plant instrumentation, adjusts production variables in response to constantly changing operating conditions in order to improve process efficiency.

The company was founded in 1984 by Lawrence B. Evans, who continues to serve as chairman and CEO. Aspen, which went public with its initial stock offering in 1994, has about 1,100 employees.

Late developments
The company made two acquisitions in late 1996. It acquired the process control division of England-based Cambridge Control, Ltd., and it acquired B-JAC International, a Virginia-based supplier of detailed heat exchanger modeling software.

Performance
Stock growth (past two years through 12/31/96): 309% (from $19.63 to $80.25).
Revenue growth (past two years through 12/31/96): 226% (from $46.5 million to $152 million).
Earnings per share growth (past two years through 12/31/96): 0% (from $0.71 to $0.71).

Stock Growth
24-month High-Low-Close (1995-96)

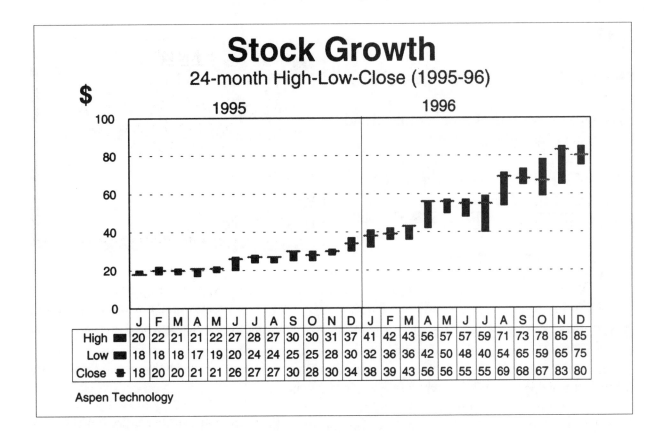

	J	F	M	A	M	J	J	A	S	O	N	D	J	F	M	A	M	J	J	A	S	O	N	D
High	20	22	21	21	22	27	28	27	30	30	31	37	41	42	43	56	57	57	59	71	73	78	85	85
Low	18	18	18	17	19	20	24	24	25	25	28	30	32	36	36	42	50	48	40	54	65	59	65	75
Close	18	20	20	21	21	26	27	27	30	28	30	34	38	39	43	56	56	55	55	69	68	67	83	80

Aspen Technology

Quick Fix

P/E range (past two years):	24 - 53
Earnings past four quarters:	$0.71 (through 12/31/96)
Projected 1997 earnings (median):	$1.84
International sales:	52% of total sales (Europe, 31%; Japan 12%; other 9%)
Total current assets:	$112.1 million (1996); $46.1 million (1995)
Total current liabilities:	$43.2 million (1996); $18.5 million (1995)
Net Income:	$6.0 million (1995); $3.7 million (1994)

Financial history

Fiscal year ended: June 30
(Revenue in millions)

	1992	1993	1994	1995	1996
Revenue	$29.7	$33.9	$45	$57.5	$103.6
Earnings per share	0.17	0.31	0.58	0.70	1.10**
*Stock price: High	NA	NA	20.25	37.00	85.00
Low	NA	NA	15.75	17.00	31.50
Close	NA	NA	19.63	33.75	80.25

*Stock prices (only) reflect calendar year.
**1996 earnings per share does not factor in a non-recurring acquisition charge of $3.02 per share.

100

Danka Business Systems, PLC

Masters House, 107 Hammersmith Road
London, W14 0QH, England

(U.S. office) 11202 Danka Circle North
St. Petersburg, FL 33716
Phone: 813-576-6003; FAX: 813-577-4802

Chairman: Mark Vaughan-Lee
CEO: Daniel Doyle

AT A GLANCE

Held by number of funds: 2
Industry: Copiers and office equipment
Earnings growth past 2 years: -1%
Stock price 1/1/97: $35.38
P/E ratio: 42
Year ago P/E: 41
NASDAQ: DANKY

Danka doesn't make copiers, but it sells them worldwide. It is one of the fastest growing independent suppliers of Canon, Konica, Minolta, Sharp and Toshiba photocopiers, facsimiles and other automated office equipment in North America and Europe. As a result of its recent acquisition of Infotec, a European retail and wholesale equipment supplier, Danka has also become one of the largest suppliers of Ricoh products in Europe.

Based in London, England, Danka does most of its business in the U.S. About 75 percent of its sales revenue is generated in the U.S., while less than 10 percent comes from its home market in the United Kingdom. In the U.S., Danka has its headquarters in St. Petersburg, Florida. Its stock trades on the NASDAQ over-the-counter exchange. In all, Danka has offices in 40 states, nine Canadian provinces and seven European countries.

The firm has been expanding at a rapid rate primarily through acquisitions. Over the past three years, it has acquired more than 100 smaller companies. New acquisitions are integrated into the company's sales and service network, capitalizing on the efficiencies of scale. The firm plans to continue an aggressive acquisition strategy, buying up small independent copier dealers in the highly-fragmented U.S. and European markets.

Copier sales account for only about half of the company's total revenue. The other half comes from retail service, supplies and rentals. Leasing is a key element of Danka's business, and an option its sales force aggressively pushes because of the continuing stream of income.

With its recent acquisition of two Eastman Kodak divisions (see section below), Danka now has about 22,000 employees.

Late developments

In late 1996, Danka acquired the sales, marketing and equipment service operations of Eastman Kodak's Office Imaging business, as well as Kodak's facilities management business known as Kodak Imaging Services. The business will serve more than 700 offices in 35 countries. Cost to Danka was about $684 million.

Performance

Stock growth (past two years through 12/31/96): 64% (from $21.63 to $35.38).
Revenue growth (past two years through 12/31/96): 125% (from $733 million to $1.65 billion).
Earnings per share growth (past two years through 12/31/96): -1% (from $0.65 to $0.64).

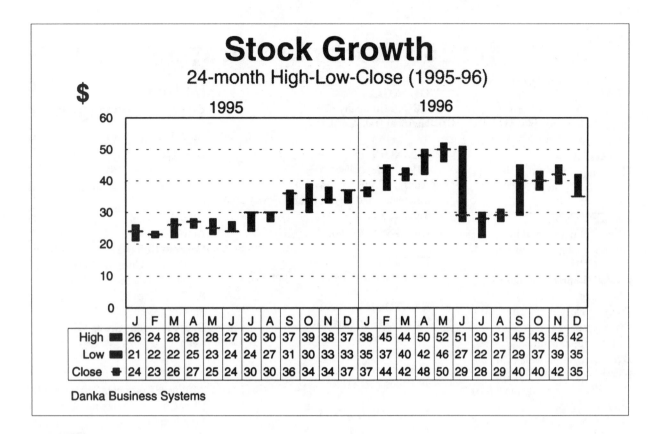

Stock Growth
24-month High-Low-Close (1995-96)

	1995												1996											
	J	F	M	A	M	J	J	A	S	O	N	D	J	F	M	A	M	J	J	A	S	O	N	D
High	26	24	28	28	28	27	30	30	37	39	38	37	38	45	44	50	52	51	30	31	45	43	45	42
Low	21	22	22	25	23	24	24	27	31	30	33	33	35	37	40	42	46	27	22	27	29	37	39	35
Close	24	23	26	27	25	24	30	30	36	34	34	37	37	44	42	48	50	29	28	29	40	40	42	35

Danka Business Systems

Quick Fix

P/E range (past two years):	24 - 50
Earnings past four quarters:	$0.64 (through 12/31/96)
Projected 1997 earnings (median):	$1.14
International sales:	24% of total sales (UK, 8%; Netherlands, 5%; other, 11%)
Total current assets:	$569.2 million (9/30/96); $509.7 million (3/31/96)
Total current liabilities:	$304.8 million (9/30/96); $292.1 million (3/31/96)
Net Income:	$28.7 million (9/30/96); $46.3 million (3/31/96)

Financial history

Fiscal year ended: March 31
(Revenue in millions)

	1992	1993	1994	1995	1996	*1997
Revenue	$236.0	$352.7	$531.4	$802.2	$1,240	$1,264*
Earnings per share	-0.33	0.02	0.09	0.28	0.90	0.40*
**Stock price: High	5.09	20.00	23.38	38.5	51.88	NA
Low	4.53	5.09	16.75	21.38	22.38	NA
Close	5.06	20.00	21.63	37.00	35.38	NA

*1996 revenue and earnings through 12/31/96 (nine months).
**Stock price (only) reflects calendar year.

Hot 100 Stocks by Location

ALABAMA
HEALTHSOUTH Corp. (21)
Just For Feet, Inc. (46)

ARIZONA
Microchip Technology, Inc. (52)
PETsMART, Inc. (22)

CALIFORNIA
Adaptec, Inc. (61)
AirTouch Communications (34)
Altera Corp. (48)
Ascend Communications (5)
Atmel Corp. (72)
Cadence Design Systems (68)
Cisco Systems (1)
DSP Communications (71)
Dura Pharmaceuticals (25)
Electronics for Imaging (30)
FPA Medical Management (94)
Informix Corp. (28)
Maxim Integrated Products (19)
McAfee Associates (15)
Money Store (75)
Oakley, Inc. (93)
PairGain Technologies (13)
PeopleSoft (16)
Rational Software Corp. (98)
Solectron Corp. (50)
Synopsys, Inc. (27)
3Com Corp. (10)
Total Renal Care Holdings (45)
Viking Office Products (17)
Xilinix, Inc. (11)

COLORADO
Boston Chicken (73)
Corporate Express (8)

CONNECTICUT
Air Express International (83)
CUC International (26)
Oxford Health Plans (32)
United Waste Systems (14)

DISTRICT of COLUMBIA
U.S. Office Products (92)

FLORIDA
Catalina Marketing (81)
Health Management Associates (51)
Lincare Holdings (80)
Republic Industries (49)
Wackenhut Corrections Corp. (74)

GEORGIA
HBO & Company (2)
National Data Corp. (54)

ILLINOIS
APAC Teleservices (63)
Andrew Corp. (44)
Telephone and Data Systems (95)
Tellabs, Inc. (18)
U.S. Robotics Corp.(3)

KANSAS
Lone Star Steakhouse & Saloon (37)

KENTUCKY
Papa John's International (20)
Vencor, Inc. (60)

MARYLAND
JP Foodservice (84)

MASSACHUSETTS
Analog Devices (39)
Aspen Technology (99)
Cambridge Technology Partners (31)
Cascade Communications (7)
Parametric Technology (9)
Security Dynamics Technologies (59)
Shiva Corp. (6)
SystemSoft (88)

MINNESOTA
Analysts International (91)

NEBRASKA
CalEnergy Company (96)
Transaction Systems Architects (70)

NEVADA
Mirage Resorts (53)

NEW JERSEY
Bed Bath & Beyond (47)
HFS, Inc. (4)

NEW YORK
Paychex, Inc. (41)

NORTH CAROLINA
Culp, Inc. (89)
Oakwood Homes Corp. (79)

OHIO
Omnicare, Inc. (12)
Steris Corp. (38)

OKLAHOMA
Chesapeake Energy Corp. (69)

PENNSYLVANIA
Fore Systems (24)
JLG Industries (66)
SunGard Data Systems (87)

TENNESSEE
AutoZone (86)
Concord EFS (43)
Corrections Corp. of America (42)
Logan's Roadhouse (78)
PMT Services (56)
PhyCor (33)
Quorum Health Group (90)
Regal Cinemas (55)

TEXAS
Affiliated Computer Services (82)
Clear Channel Communications (23)
Input/Output (58)
Kent Electronics Corp. (76)
Service Corp. International (35)
Sterling Commerce (77)
USA Waste Services (57)

VIRGINIA
America Online (29)
BDM International (97)
LCI International (67)

FOREIGN

The BAHAMAS
Sun International Hotels (85)

CANADA
BioChem Pharma (36)
Cognos (65)
Newbridge Networks (62)

ENGLAND
Danka Business Systems (100)

HONG KONG
Tommy Hilfiger (40)

IRELAND
CBT Group (64)

Hot 100 Stocks by Industry

Apparel and Accessories
Tommy Hilfiger (40)
Oakley (93)

Business Services
APAC Teleservices (63)
BDM International (97)
Catalina Marketing Corp. (81)
National Data Corp. (54)

Computer-related Products
Adaptec (61)
Altera Corp. (48)
Analog Devices (39)
Ascend Communications (5)
Aspen Technology (99)
Atmel Corp. (72)
CBT Group (64)
Cadence Design Systems (68)
Cisco Systems (1)
Cognos (65)
Electronics for Imaging (30)
Fore Systems (24)
Informix (28)
Maxim Integrated Products (19)
McAfee Associates (15)
Microchip Technology (52)
Newbridge Networks Corp. (62)
Parametric Technology (9)
PeopleSoft (6)
Rational Software (98)
Security Dynamics Technologies (59)
Shiva Corp.(6)
SunGard Data Systems (87)
Synopsys (27)
SystemSoft, Corp. (88)
3Com (10)
Transaction Systems Architects (70)
U.S. Robotics (3)
Xilinx (11)

Computer Services
Affiliated Computer Services (82)
America Online (29)
Analysts Intl. (91)
Cambridge Technology (31)
HBO & Company (2)
Sterling Commerce (77)

Communications
AirTouch Communications (34)
Andrew Corp. (44)
Cascade Communications (7)
Clear Channel Communications (23)
DSP Communications (71)
LCI International (67)
PairGain Technologies (13)
Telephone and Data Systems (95)
Tellabs (18)

Consumer Services
CUC International (26)
Service Corp. Intl. (35)

Corrections
Corrections Corp. of America (42)
Wackenhut Corrections Corp. (74)

Distributors
JP Foodservice (84)
Kent Electronics (76)

Electronics
Input/Output (58)
Solectron Corp. (50)

Energy
CalEnergy Co. (96)
Chesapeake Energy (69)

Financial
Concord EFS (43)
The Money Store (75)
Paychex (41)
PMT Services (56)

Healthcare Organizations
FPA Medical Management (94)
Oxford Health Plans (32)
PhyCor (33)

Industrial Manufacturing
Culp, Inc. (89)
JLG Industries (66)
Oakwood Homes Corp. (79)

Lodging and Entertainment
HFS (4)
Mirage Resorts (53)
Regal Cinemas (55)
Sun International Hotels (85)

Medical Care Providers
Health Management Services
HEALTHSOUTH (21)
Lincare Holdings (80)
Omnicare (12)
Quorum Health Group (90)
Total Renal Care (45)
Vencor (60)

Medical Products
BioChem Pharma (38)
Dura Pharmaceuticals (25)
Steris Corp.(38)

Office Products
Corporate Express (8)
Danka Business Systems PLC, (100)
U.S. Office Products Co. (92)
Viking Office Products (17)

Restaurants
Boston Chicken (73)
Logan's Roadhouse (78)
Lone Star Steakhouse (37)
Papa John's International (20)

Retail
AutoZone (86)
Bed Bath & Beyond (47)
Just For Feet (46)
PETsMART (22)

Transportation
Air Express Intl. (83)

Waste Management
Republic Industries (49)
United Waste Systems (14)
USA Waste Services (57)

INDEX